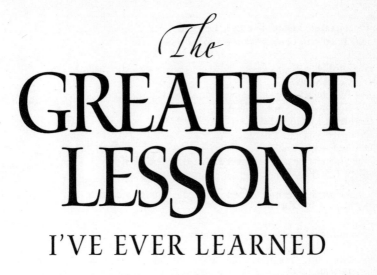

The GREATEST LESSON

I'VE EVER LEARNED

BILL BRIGHT &
VONETTE BRIGHT

Editors

*Life*CONNEXIONS
The Publishing Group of Campus Crusade for Christ

The Greatest Lesson I've Ever Learned
Sixty Prominent Leaders Share Wisdom For Your Life

Published by
Life ConneXions
The Publishing Group of Campus Crusade for Christ
375 Highway 74 South, Suite A
Peachtree City, GA 30269

Previously released as
The Greatest Lesson I've Ever Learned - Men's Edition
ISBN 1-56399-084-9

The Greatest Lesson I've Ever Learned - Women's Edition
ISBN 1-56399-085-7

Previously published by New *Life* Resources

Cover by Kocchel-Peterson Design

Printed in the United States of America

ISBN 1-56399-084-9

Scripture quotations are from:

The *New International Version,* © 1973, 1978, 1984 by the International Bible Society. Published by Zondervan Bible Publishers, Grand Rapids, Michigan.

The Living Bible, © 1971 by Tyndale House Publishers, Wheaton, Illinois.

The New American Standard Bible, © 1960, 1962, 1963, 1968, 1971, 1972, 1973, 1975, 1977 by the Lockman Foundation, La Habra, California.

The *New King James Version*, © 1982 by Thomas Nelson, Inc., Nashville, Tennessee.

The *King James Version.*

*To my dear friends who have been open
and honest in sharing their challenging and
heartwarming "greatest lessons" to make
this remarkable book possible;
and to my beloved wife, Vonette,
who is a constant encouragement to me*

Contents

BOOK 1

Contents

BOOK 2

Contents

BOOK 1

*To my dear friends who have been open
and honest in sharing their challenging and
heartwarming "greatest lessons" to make
this remarkable book possible;
and to my beloved wife, Vonette,
who is a constant encouragement to me*

To the Reader

While reading the women's version of *The Greatest Lesson I've Ever Learned*, edited by my wife, Vonette, I was genuinely moved. These heartwarming stories, in which many well-known women shared their "greatest lessons" of how God had become a reality in their lives, ministered to me deeply.

Suddenly it occurred to me that I should edit a similar book for men. So I invited a number of dear friends whom I greatly admire and whom God is using in special ways to join me in this project. Although not all of them could participate for good and valid reasons, I am deeply grateful to those who did. My heart has sung praises to God again and again as I have read the testimonies of these men whose stories you are about to read. In the process, I also have shed tears and laughed a lot.

As I was writing and editing the introductions of each author, I found myself expressing my love and appreciation for each one in such phrases as "he has a special place in my heart" or "he is a beloved friend" or "he is very dear to me." Finally, it occurred to me that after reading a few chapters you would, no doubt, have good reason to question my sincerity. Therefore, I have chosen to express my deep love and profound appreciation for each one in this introduction.

I am confident that you will enjoy and greatly benefit from reading each contribution as I have. To benefit the most from your reading, ask God to help you respond to the lessons these men have learned. Open your heart to the joy and the pain they have so generously shared.

Thousands of Christians have found the women's version of *The Greatest Lesson* to be an ideal gift for every occasion. You may want to send copies of both books to your friends and acquaintances.

This book can be a tool to share meaningful and heartwarming stories with those who need encouragement. *The Greatest Lesson* can be a powerful witness to the men in your life and can draw them closer to our Savior.

Bill Bright,
Editor

Bill Armstrong

PEOPLE REALLY
WANT TO KNOW

For many years, Senator William Armstrong was one
of the most articulate legislators in Washington. During
his distinguished political career, Bill was admired by both
friend and foe for his integrity and knowledge of the issues.
He served in the Colorado House of Representatives, the Colorado Senate, and the U.S. House of Representatives before
his election to the U.S. Senate in 1978.

I met Bill and Ellen at a small dinner party which
another congressman hosted to share the gospel with his colleagues. Few men in secular employment have had such a
powerful witness for our Lord, as many thousands have come
into the kingdom through Bill's anointed communication of
the gospel.

Retired from office since 1991, Bill devotes even more
time to evangelism. In his stirring account, he shares with us

his deep desire to introduce his neighbors and friends to the love of Christ.

"I have done something so terrible, I do not see how God could ever forgive me," the young woman told me.

It was a startling disclosure and all the more so because of the circumstances. She had come to visit me in my office in the U.S. Senate. And her admission took me totally by surprise because this was a woman with a sunny disposition and a winning smile. She had a good job and many friends. In short, she was someone with few cares as far as I could see.

But her manner was unusually serious as she told me of her concern, and then she asked me one of the most significant questions I have ever encountered. "I have heard that you have a personal relationship with God. Could you tell me how I could have such a relationship?"

I didn't have to think twice. Referring to a little pamphlet called the *Four Spiritual Laws*,[1] I quickly explained God's plan of salvation.

"Law One: God loves you and offers a wonderful plan for your life.

"Law Two: Man is sinful and separated from God. Therefore, he cannot know and experience God's love and plan for his life.

"Law Three: Jesus Christ is God's only provision for man's sin. Through Him you can know and experience God's love and plan for your life.

"Law Four: We must individually receive Jesus Christ as Savior and Lord; then we can know and experience God's love and plan for our lives."

I briefly elaborated on each of these points and explained that each is drawn directly from the Bible. Then after a few minutes of discussion, I assured my young friend that, if she wished to do so, she could receive Jesus Christ as her personal Savior. According to the Bible, several things would instantly happen: Her sins would be forgiven; she would be assured of eternal life in heaven with God, the Father, and with His Son, Jesus; and in this life, she could aspire to peace, joy, gentleness, self-control, and much, much more.

She prayed the brief prayer suggested in the booklet: "Lord Jesus, I need You. I open the door of my life and receive You as my Savior and Lord. Thank You for forgiving my sins. Take control of the throne of my life. Make me the kind of person You want me to be."

She departed realizing that her life was changed forever and that God had wonderful plans for her. As you can imagine, I considered it a high privilege to be able to share the Good News in this way. How great God is to have made it possible!

However, it wasn't until some time later that I recognized the unusual aspect of our meeting. We had talked about Christ and prayed together, but I had often done so previously. What was remarkable was this young lady's presence of mind and poise to ask such an intelligent and direct question: "How can I have a personal relationship with God?"

It finally occurred to me that perhaps many people have the same question but are too embarrassed to ask. Or don't know whom to ask. Or feel that they have to purify themselves before approaching God. Or think that extensive study is required. Or have some other opinion that obscures the simplicity and love of Jesus Christ.

As I thought it over and began to look around me more carefully, it became obvious that there are many people, some of them hoping desperately for significance and meaning in their lives, who simply do not have the clarity of thought to ask directly, "How can I have a personal relationship with God?"

I have tried to become more sensitive to people around me. As I have done so, it has become clear that most people will rarely ask directly for spiritual help unless someone else begins the conversation or, in some way, gives them an opening to do so.

I DO NOT HAVE TO GO TO A THIRD-WORLD COUNTRY TO BE A MISSIONARY.

I have discovered that there are people all around us—in our offices, at our schools, on airplanes, in service clubs, possibly even in our own churches or among our own families—who would love to know God but do not know how to ask or are too timid to ask. Many are tormented by guilt or distracted by the false notion that God wants them to suffer.

Even those who are in dire circumstances—facing severe illness, financial problems, addiction, divorce, or contemplating suicide—usually do not know how to ask for help in the intelligent and direct manner of the young woman in my office. Hindered by lack of experience, embarrassment, or misunderstanding, they silently try to cope alone.

Interestingly, however, the vast majority of people I have come in contact with are willing, often eager, to discuss spiritual issues if someone else will break the ice. And, if given an opportunity to do so, a high percentage of those hearing the gospel will respond.

In the last twenty-five years or so, I have had the privilege of speaking personally with many people about Jesus Christ, often using the *Four Spiritual Laws* as the basis for discussion. A few have responded indifferently; a tiny number have been hostile; but thousands have listened with an open mind to what Jesus promises and have received Him as their personal Savior.

Even those who were not ready to personally accept Christ have often expressed appreciation that someone cared enough about them to explain how to have a personal relationship with God. I can only assume that in many cases they wished to reflect further and subsequently made a life-changing decision.

One young couple in Washington comes to mind. A member of the U.S. House of Representatives and his wife attended a dinner party in a fashionable Capital neighborhood. Dr. Bill Bright spoke informally about how to become a Christian. This young congressman and his wife listened courteously but without visible reaction. I learned later what happened. After hearing the brief explanation of how to become Christians, this rising young political couple went to their own home, knelt down in their bedroom, and prayed to receive Christ. In the years since, they have become role models of Christian family life and have led thousands to Christ.

So I have learned a great lesson. I do not have to go to a third-world country to be a missionary or to the inner city or to some other place I instinctively think of as a mission field. One of the greatest missionary opportunities in the world is in my own neighborhood, my own home, and my own place of work.

People we encounter every day are longing to find answers to life's major questions: Who am I? Where did I come from? What's life all about? Is there a God? Is there life after death? People are eager, often desperate, for someone to explain how their lives can be significant and meaningful. And while most will not initiate a conversation about Jesus, they almost always are open to discussing Him if someone else gets the conversation started.

What a noble opportunity—to introduce our friends, our business and professional colleagues, people in our neighborhood, even our own family, to the One who promises forgiveness of sin, eternal life, the right to become a child of God, and so much more.

I have also learned that the best opportunities often arise in completely secular settings. Frankly, most of those who need to hear the gospel will never come to church. But we meet them daily in our offices, clubs, and schools, in airports and restaurants. Jesus lived among everyday people, just as we do. He spoke to them of life-and-death issues in mundane settings—over meals, while traveling, in the country, in cities. He did not wait for people to come to Him. He went to them. And we have the extraordinary privilege of following His example.

Pat Boone

WHAT DO YOU SAY TO A JEWISH PORNOGRAPHER?

Pat Boone has been in the entertainment business since his teenage years in Tennessee, when he won a spot on the Ted Mack Amateur Hour. Since that time, he has sold more than 45 million records.

Not only is Pat an accomplished singer, but he is also an author, actor, and television performer. He is the author of The Miracle of Prayer, *and coauthor of two books with his wife, Shirley.*

I have observed Pat closely through the years and know him to be a true ambassador for our Savior. He has championed many wonderful causes on behalf of our Lord and country. He has co-chaired the National Day of Prayer, and has served the Easter Seal Society as spokesman, national chairman, and telethon host.

Pat relates an intriguing story of his encounter with a pornographer in Las Vegas in which Pat learned how much God personally loves each of us.

"Hey, Boone, I read your book!"

I cringed.

Normally, I'm delighted to know the Lord has provided another opportunity for me to share my story.

But—*a Jewish pornographer?*

In the steam room at the Sands Hotel?

In Las Vegas?

I sensed a punch line coming and braced myself for it. But none came. The squat, curly-haired man whose current business was selling pornographic material and grotesque sex machines was looking at me earnestly.

"You're serious about this, aren't you?"

I nodded, still apprehensive. "Sure I am. Where in the world did you get hold of my book?"

"From Frankie Avalon." (I had given several copies to entertainer friends, including Frankie, Dean Martin, Bob Goulet, and Johnnie Ray—but *not* to anybody I thought might find it "weird" or just joke material, like Ace here. I guess he'd be the *last* guy in Las Vegas I'd have shared my story with—and now we stood dripping and steaming together, with several friends looking on in disbelief.)

"I'd like you to pray for me," Ace said softly.

I guess everybody's jaws dropped, including mine. Was

this guy joking? Was he setting me up for something?

"I mean it. I always thought this religion stuff of yours was some kind of phony trip, just part of your 'image'— you know. But the book really got to me.

"Look, I know why my life is so messed up. I'm my own worst enemy. I've been married four times, bankrupt twice, and if I knew some other way to make a living, I wouldn't be selling this junk. I sure ain't proud of it.

"I'm fat, flabby, and over forty, and now the doc tells me I've got to go in for a gall bladder operation—and I'm scared to death. I'd really like you to pray for me."

I could swear I felt goose bumps in that 170-degree heat!

"Look, Ace," I said, not daring to glance at the other guys, "I'll be happy to pray for you. I will. But you know, God wants to hear from *you* about your problems. That's really the whole idea. Will you pray, too?"

The look on his face seemed a mixture of sadness and hilarity, if you can imagine such a thing. The twin forces rushed together and erupted into a loud laugh, "Me? *Pray?* Oh, come on! God would strike me dead, tell me to get lost or go to hell, or something! You gotta be kidding!"

I sensed a real loneliness, a vacuum in this man, and suddenly saw the hard, gruff exterior for what it was—a disguise.

"Ace," I said, obeying an inner impulse before I realized how rash it was, "so many people have the wrong idea about prayer and about God Himself. He's not interested in just hearing religious words from so-called religious people. Jesus Himself said there was only one really *good* person— and that was God! So God wants to hear from each one of us, not because we're good, but because He just plain ol' *loves* us!

27

"Look, I didn't arrange for you to read my book. I would have tried to keep it *away* from you, figuring you wouldn't dig it at all. So God must have wanted you to read it and made it possible. He knows your heart a whole lot better than I do, and I know now He'll hear and answer your prayer.

"Tell you what—I've never suggested this to anybody, but I'm going to pray that *God will be real to you in some way that you'll recognize!* I don't know what He'll do, but I believe He'll show you in some way that He hears you, and that you're getting through. Will you pray for the same thing?"

"I don't know how to pray, Boone—I really don't." Ace looked a little uneasy, suddenly aware of the unbelieving stares of the others.

"I don't mean right here, now," I said, "but later, when you're alone. You don't have any trouble talking to me, do you?"

Ace grinned, a little relieved maybe. "No—but you're not God!"

"That's right, I'm not! But you can talk to Him just like you're talking to me. The words don't matter because He's listening to your heart anyway. It's important, though, that you speak to Him. Will you do it?"

"Okay. I'll try it, but—I don't know." He shook his head, and we walked out of the steam room.

On the way down to the hotel where I was working, I talked to the Lord out loud, "Dear Jesus, I don't know what I've gotten us into, but I really do pray for Ace. And I do pray right now that You'll show him—*in some way he'll recognize*—that You're listening to his prayer. Will You do it—please? Thank You, Lord."

It sounds good now when I tell it, but I confess that my faith was pretty shaky. A Jew? A pornographer? A wild Las Vegas character—what had I gotten the Lord and me into? Or was it just me?

I prayed a lot for Ace the next two days.

I didn't see him, and I wasn't sure I wanted to.

But my engagement had come down to its final night, and for one last time, I went back to the Sands Health Club for a good steam and massage. I imagined I'd see Ace —and was sort of nervous about it.

He wasn't there. But while I was sitting in the steam room, the attendant pushed open the door to tell me I was wanted on the phone—a guy named Ace. As I went to pick up the receiver, I couldn't help wondering if I'd been set up for an elaborate joke, and this was the punch line.

The excitement on the other end of the line quickly erased the thought. "Your prayers are answered! *Your prayers are answered!*" The voice was so loud I had to hold the phone away from my ear.

"Hold on, Ace," I squeezed the words in edgewise. "What happened? What do you mean?"

"Boone! You know you said to just talk to God like I was talking to you? And to ask Him to show me something? Well, I thought you were probably crazy, but I did it. I mean, I talked right out loud, like you said. I really felt like I was talking to the lamp or the air, and I didn't think my words were gettin' outta the room—but I did it."

"And you must have been praying too—right?"

I chuckled. "I sure was!"

"Well, *lemme tell you what happened!*

"I went in today for my last examination before the gall

bladder operation. I was scared to death. The doc gave me this chalky stuff to drink and then X-rayed me. In a little while he came in with the X-rays just shaking his head—he said he couldn't find the stones! *The gallstones are gone!* The doc says he can't operate on me when he can't find the stones!"

I was numb. "That's fantastic, Ace!"

"Yeah—but what do I do now?"

Again, I was practically speechless. I said the first thing that came to my mind. "Well, Ace, the main thing is—don't look at this as the end of anything, just the beginning!"

THE GOD OF MIRACLES CARES ABOUT EACH OF US PERSONALLY!

"Yeah…?" He was eager. He wanted more.

"Why don't you get yourself a Bible and start reading about the One who's done this for you? It's obvious that He loves you, Ace. I'm amazed myself—but you know now that He's listening to you, don't you?"

Ace interrupted, "Yeah. Yeah! I can dig it!" And he hung up!

He was running somewhere to get a Bible!

And there I sat, my mouth full of "Buts" and "Waits," my brain full of directions for him, my heart wanting to urge him into a good church fellowship—and my hand full of dead phone.

Slowly, as I sat there, I began to see how much God loved this "former" pornographer—and I realized Ace was in good hands.

God loves every last one of us—*equally.* And He knows

which ones are ready to respond to His miraculous touch. We don't. If all the people in Las Vegas had lined up for me to talk and pray with, I'd have asked Ace to stand at the end of the line.

God put him at the very front.

The God of miracles cares about each of us personally! And because He's supernatural and miraculous in His very nature, a personal relationship with Him will invariably produce miracles in anyone's life.

What is a "miracle"? *The touch of God in your life.* I purposely chose this simple, all-encompassing definition because I have discovered that God uses many means to change things for us. It may *seem* natural, but if it has God's fingerprints on it, it's a miracle! And life becomes very exciting.

Does this God touch your life through the chaos and uncertainty of our crumbling world? Then respond! It's a miracle! God Himself, in His gentle, loving concern for you, is cutting across the laws of nature and science—for you!

I've never seen Ace again. He ran to get a Bible, and I didn't get to tell him anything more. Lord, You sure love him, don't You? Well please don't let him get away.

And Ace, wherever you are—God loves you.

Charles Colson

MY CANCER AND THE GOOD-HEALTH GOSPEL

Having served seven months in federal prison for a Watergate-related offense, former presidential aide Chuck Colson saw firsthand the tremendous obstacles facing prisoners, ex-prisoners, and their families. In 1976 following his release from prison, Chuck founded Prison Fellowship, a Christian outreach to inmates behind and beyond prison walls.

As chairman of the board of Prison Fellowship, he ministers regularly in prisons across the country and around the world. Recognizing that America's overcrowded prisons are failing to rehabilitate offenders, Chuck often speaks out for reform of existing criminal justice practices.

He is a sought-after speaker, has a daily radio commentary heard by three million, and contributes regularly to

numerous newspapers and magazines. Chuck is the author or coauthor of several books, including Born Again, Kingdoms in Conflict, The Body, *and* How Now Shall We Live? *He was the 1993 recipient of the Templeton Prize for Progress in Religion.*

Chuck has become a friend whose intellect and warm heart yielded to our Lord has made him one of the most popular speakers and writers of our generation. He is always an inspiration and a blessing to me.

Through his bout with cancer, Chuck found new purpose for the trials Christians suffer. His experience will inspire you to view your suffering in a new light, too.

Coming out of the anesthesia, I first saw the smiling faces of my wife, Patty, and daughter, Emily. "Did they get it all?" I asked. Patty gripped my hand. "Yes."

"Was it malignant?"

Emily nodded. "Yes, Daddy—it was cancer. But they got it all, and you're going to be okay."

Cancer.

I had always wondered, in secret fear, what it would be like to be told I had cancer. I thought I would be shattered. But I had prayed for the grace to withstand whatever the doctors found. And, as many have discovered before me, I saw in the confrontation with fear and suffering that there is nothing for which God does not pour out His grace abundantly. I felt total peace—and great thankfulness that a merciful God had brought me to that recovery room.

My stomach problems began in November 1986 during

a ministry trip to the Philippines. I flew home. My doctor told me that I was badly run-down, that I had a bleeding ulcer, and to stay away from airports for a while. With rest and proper diet, the problem was soon cured.

Just when my stomach seemed fine, I talked with a dear Christian brother, Dr. Joe Bailey of Austin, Texas. Joe urged me, as my own internist had already done, to have a gastroscopy. The idea of inhaling a tube so doctors could view the scenery in my stomach was not particularly inviting. Besides, the ulcer had already healed. But Joe kept insisting.

So I submitted to the horrors of the gastroscope. The doctor told me, as I had expected, that the ulcer was gone. Then came the unexpected: he had discovered a tumor in my stomach lining.

After weeks of additional tests, experts concluded the growth was benign. There was no reason to hurry to have it removed. Once again Joe Bailey called. "Chuck," he said in his Texas drawl, "get that thing out, and get it out as quick as you can."

"I can't! I'm writing a new book. I have ministry commitments, speaking obligations."

But Joe would not be moved. And since by then I suspected that God was speaking through him, I scheduled the operation for early January.

To everyone's surprise, the tumor was a low-grade malignancy. Because it was caught early, however, doctors have assured me that my prognosis is excellent. If it had gone undetected, the outcome could have been far different. The previous fall's nagging ulcer served as a warning by which God got my attention—and then he used Joe Bailey's stubborn concern to get me into the hospital.

God's grace provided not only peace and protection, but

new purpose. I had, as some friends know, begun to burn out from too many writing, speaking, and ministry commitments.

But as I lay in my hospital bed, I thought through my real priorities. Had I unconsciously boarded the evangelical treadmill? Trying to do all those worthy things that everybody wanted me to do, had I become beholden to a tyrannical schedule rather than to God's will? Several weeks tied to hospital tubes is a good time to reflect on the larger perspective of God's design in our lives.

My suffering provided some fresh insights as well into the health-and-wealth gospel. If God really delivers His people from all pain and illness, as is so often claimed, why was I so sick? Had my faith become weak? Had I fallen from favor?

No. I had always recognized such teaching as false theology. But after four weeks in a maximum-care unit, I came to see the good-health gospel as something else: a presumptuous stumbling block to real evangelism.

During my nightly walks through the hospital corridors dragging an I.V. pole behind me, I often met an Indian man whose two-year-old son had endured failed kidney transplants, a brain aneurysm, and was now blind for life.

When the father, a Hindu, discovered I was a Christian, he asked if God would heal his son if he, too, was born again. He said he had heard things like that on television.

As I listened, I realized how arrogant health-and-wealth religion sounds to suffering families: Christians can all be spared suffering, but little Hindu children go blind. One couldn't blame a Hindu or Muslim or agnostic for resenting, even hating, such a God.

I told my Hindu friend about Jesus. Yes, He may mirac-

Paul Crouch

PARTING THE SEA OF IMPOSSIBILITY

Paul Crouch began his career in radio and television in 1954 on the campus of Central Bible Institute and Seminary. Since that time, he has moved through a variety of broadcast experiences.

He founded the Trinity Broadcasting Network (TBN) in 1973, and the following year purchased its first television station KLXA-TV, which later became KTBN Channel 40. Under Paul's direction, TBN has become the world's largest Christian television network with over 500 broadcast stations.

I am especially drawn to Paul because of his deep love for our Lord and his vision to use his expertise in electronic media to help take the gospel of our Savior to the entire world.

Paul and his wife, Jan, appear together regularly on TBN. The account of how Paul and Jan and their coworkers struggled to begin a television ministry and how he learned to let

37

God "part the sea of impossibility" will inspire you to greater faith in our Lord.

❧

When we began our Christian television ministry, the initial stages were like scaling a cliff with only a thin rope between life and death. If the rope didn't hold or our hands lost their grip, all would be lost!

Everything we owned was at stake. We had agreed to pay Bill Myers, the station owner, $10,000 a month for air time. And Jan and I had invested $20,000, which was our life savings, into the new ministry to build the sets, pay the utility deposits, install the phones, rent some TV equipment, and buy the TV time. But after only the third day on the air, our funds were nearly exhausted.

Mr. Myers did not believe in credit, so he demanded an additional $3,000 before he would sign the station back on the air that night. I remember turning to a co-worker and saying, "Now what do we do?" We prayed for God's direction, and in just a few minutes our pastor, Syvelle Phillips, a vital partner in ministry, walked in the door. We explained our predicament to him and asked if he would speak to Mr. Myers. He did and after a lengthy discussion and the payment of our very last $1,000, Mr. Myers agreed to sign the station on that night.

My emotions were so drained after that meeting, I knew it would be impossible for me to face the TV cameras that night. Pastor Phillips said, "Paul, it is time to tell the people our need." He agreed to host the program in my place, and I went home to pray. As I drove toward home, I again began to cry out my complaint to the Lord. "Why does it have to be so hard, Lord? Why do we have to suffer so much? Lord, You have provided everything we have needed up to now—what does this all mean?"

As I wept before the Lord, a still small voice spoke sweetly to me—so clearly that it startled me. The Lord said, "Paul, it is difficult because you have not *given* Me anything."

The message startled me even more. "What do you mean, Lord? I have given you everything—my job at KHOF, my life, my talents, *even* our $20,000 savings!"

The Lord spoke again: "You did not *give* Me your savings, you *loaned* them to Me."

Yes, it was true! The Lord knows everything—even our thoughts. I had taken a note back for the money Jan and I had placed in the ministry. We had only loaned God the money.

God was saying, "I want you to *give* Me your savings." For me this was an awesome request. Didn't God know how Jan and I had sacrificed for sixteen years to save this money? Didn't He know we had gone without to put this money away for our future? But money had become a hindrance to my spiritual growth—perhaps even a god, of sorts, and the Lord was asking me to give it up—all of it!

I struggled with the decision all the way home, and finally as I fell across the bed, I conceded, "All right, God, I will make a bargain with You. If You will cause Your people to give an equal amount tonight on television, I promise I will give it *all* to you!"

I picked up the phone and called the station. By now a full-fledged telethon was underway. Pastor Phillips was pouring out his heart to the people, telling of our need at TBN. It seemed that an unusual anointing of the Holy Spirit was upon him as he and his co-host spoke of our vision to reach fourteen million people in Southern California with the gospel.

Somehow I reached Jan, who was helping on the telephones. I said, "Honey, God has spoken again." I told her what I had promised the Lord. Then I said, "Tell Pastor Phillips that a pledge for $20,000 has come in from a man who loves the Lord and believes in Christian television very much—if God's people will match it with an equal amount tonight."

There was a long pause on the other end of the phone as Jan began to weep softly. She knew better than anyone the struggle raging within my soul. My mind was in such turmoil by then, I don't remember all that was said between us, but I do remember Jan's last words over the phone: "I love you…" and she was gone.

In a moment I watched as Jan, tears streaming down her face, slipped onto the TV set beside Pastor Phillips and gave him the message. The challenge was given and the phones began to ring and ring and ring…

In less than one hour, God's people had not only matched the challenge, but had given a $10,000 surplus!

After only three nights on the air—on a station that had been silent for six months—God spoke to His people to give $30,000. And since the need was so urgent, dozens of God's beautiful people drove to the studio and personally delivered the gifts to "their" TV station. All praise to His wonderful name! The "Red Sea" of impossibility had parted, and we were walking across on dry ground!

One of the pledges from that first telethon came from a most unusual source. A missionary couple, Robin and Marva Farnsworth, had just returned from New Guinea on furlough. They had been working for eight years in the most primitive, disease- and mosquito-infested jungles of the world as Bible translators with Wycliffe. The privation and physical pain they and their three children had endured would fill a book, and the evidence was clearly written on their drawn faces.

Brother Farnsworth met me at the door of TBN the next day. "Paul, God has spoken to me, and I am giving you the balance of our travel fund for your new TV ministry." He held out a check with trembling hand. "God will supply our needs, I know. Please take it with our love."

My heart nearly burst within me as I saw this thin little man with the scars of spiritual and physical battle upon him standing before me, asking to minister and give to my need. Tears welled up in my eyes as I opened the check—it was for $1,480. "Oh, Brother Farnsworth, no! I cannot take your travel funds!"

A look of intense physical pain rushed over his face. His voice was almost stern as he pressed the check into my hand. "Paul, God told me to do this; I have to obey the Lord! You *have* to take it!"

Through experiences like these, I have learned one of my greatest lessons in life: God will part the sea of impossibility if we are willing to give our all for Him.

If you ever wonder why God is blessing TBN, look back at the precious seed that has been planted by faithful servants of God who gave sacrificially like the Farnsworths. They beautifully exemplify the principle in Psalm 126:6: "He that goeth forth and weepeth, bearing precious seed, shall doubtless come again with rejoicing, bringing his sheaves with him" (KJV).

God is worthy of all that we are and have and is faithful

to complete His plan in and through our lives. This missionary family has already proven this. Though they are back in the jungles of New Guinea, they are rejoicing and sharing in the reward of thousands of souls who have accepted Jesus as Savior since TBN began!

Ted DeMoss

SITTING ON THE SIDELINES WHILE GOD WORKS

Ted DeMoss was an outstanding businessman who worked in the insurance business for many years. At one time, he had nineteen offices in five states with more than a hundred salesmen.

One of the most popular speakers for the Christian Business Men's Committee of USA, Ted averaged more than 100,000 miles of travel a year for more than thirty years. He was president of CBMC for more than fourteen years and served on their national board.

Ted went to be with our gracious Lord in 1997. I knew, loved, and respected Ted for many years. He was a layman who inspired tens of thousands of other laymen to seek first the kingdom of God and to be faithful witnesses for our Savior. He was the author of The Gospel and the Briefcase.

THE GREATEST LESSON I'VE EVER LEARNED

Ted describes a humorous and tender experience as a young insurance salesman that changed his life dramatically and started him on an adventure of bringing Christ's message of love and forgiveness to many others.

❦

In the course of my job selling insurance, I walked into an apartment building one day to call on a man whose name had been sent to my office in response to a direct mail program. I went to the door of his third-floor apartment and knocked.

The man inside spoke through the door without opening it, "Who's out there?"

I had learned that in selling insurance you never say, "The insurance man," because people might not open the door. So I just replied cheerfully, "I'm Ted DeMoss…"

I'm one of those fellows who received Jesus Christ and soon afterward became convinced of the greatest lie ever perpetrated on Christians by Satan: There are two kinds of Christians in the world, the full-time worker and the rest of us. I thought my job was to make money and put it in the offering plate, thus allowing the preacher, missionary, and evangelist to win the world to Christ. No one ever told me that they were supposed to be the coaches and we the players in this great contest for the souls of men.

When I was in my mid-twenties, I became involved with a local Christian Business Men's Committee (CBMC). There, for the first time, I met men who were committed to sharing their faith in Jesus Christ. They believed their responsibility was to help fulfill the Great Commission of our Lord in which He said, "Go into all the world and preach the Good News to everyone, everywhere" (Mark 16:15, TLB).

At first I was skeptical. I thought of my college professor who had taken his life some years before and recalled the anger I felt because no preacher had reached him with the gospel message. Yet, as a Christian, I had actually taught under this scholar for a year and had never sensed any responsibility to share Christ with him. As I became more involved with CBMC, I was encouraged to start praying for men who did not know Jesus Christ and, as the Holy Spirit directed, to share the Good News with them as a way of life. This meant talking to them about Christ one on one, bringing them to a CBMC luncheon or dinner where a lay speaker would give his testimony, or inviting them to my home for dinner to tell them about Jesus Christ.

Through CBMC I learned that as long as I was usable and available, the Holy Spirit would show me when I was supposed to speak to someone. I started to pray that, sometime before I died, the Lord would let me see just one person commit his life to Christ as a result of my sharing the Good News with him.

So as I stood outside the door of that third-floor apartment and answered, "I'm Ted DeMoss," I was ready for such an opportunity.

The man inside bristled defensively. "If I open this door, I'll throw you down those stairs. Now get away from my door!"

Since I sincerely thought that he had inquired about insurance, I persisted. "Mister, I'm not going to hurt you. Please open the door. I've got to talk to you."

I fully intended to talk with the man about insurance, but when he opened the door, I realized there was no point in that. Before me stood a man with a white beard who looked like a thin Santa Claus. I hadn't been in the business long, but I knew he was too old to buy any insurance I might sell him. Looking directly at me, he demanded, "I opened the door. Now, what do you want to talk about?"

"I want to come in and talk to you."

"What do you want to talk about?" he snapped.

I persisted. "May I come in?"

As I spoke, the Spirit of God impressed me to talk with this man, a complete stranger, about Jesus Christ. At age twenty-five, I had never done that before.

Finally, he stepped aside and said, "Come in, then."

I entered, and we both sat down on the couch in the living room. Looking straight at me, the elderly man asked curiously, "What do you want to talk about?"

I paused just for a moment, then said the only thing that came to mind. "I want to read the Bible to you."

Talk about no training in witnessing for Christ! I had absolutely no preparation apart from what my CBMC friends had told me about reading the third chapter of John.

"Go ahead," he consented.

"I don't have a Bible," I said weakly. "Do you have one?"

He looked puzzled for a moment. "I don't know whether I have a Bible or not. I've been blind for many years."

I asked if I could look around the apartment for one, and he agreed. After a brief search, I found a Bible covered with dust on top of a stack of books.

Walking back to the couch, I opened the Bible to the third chapter of John and began to read slowly. The further I read, the more scared I felt. My friends at CBMC had never told me what to do next. So I read slower and more deliberately until I got to verse 18:

> He that believeth on Him is not condemned: but he that believeth not is condemned already, because he hath not believed in the name of the only begotten Son of God (KJV).

I finished that verse, praying silently for the Lord to give me wisdom as to what I should do. I looked over at the old man, and what I saw shocked me—his beard was wet with tears! God had indeed spoken to this man through His Word.

GOD HAD INDEED SPOKEN TO THIS MAN THROUGH HIS WORD.

"Sir, would you like to invite Jesus Christ into your life right now, right here?" I asked softly.

The man nodded thoughtfully, "Well...I would like to do it right now, but not here."

"Where do you want to do it?"

"I want to do it with my mother."

Mentally, I was scratching my head. The man had told me he was eighty-one, and I thought, *What do I say now?*

I decided to ask, "Where is your mother?"

"In the kitchen," he pointed.

Thinking he had a picture of her hanging in the kitchen, I supposed he wanted to go there for sentimental reasons. We made our way back to the kitchen, and to my surprise, there was his mother sitting in a canvas-backed chair. She was ninety-eight years old and an invalid.

I can still hear the man's words as if he were speaking them today: "Mother, God has sent a man to our home."

I had gone on this call thinking the insurance company had sent me, but I quickly realized that what he was saying was true.

"He's been reading the Bible to me, and I'm going to accept Jesus Christ."

I have never in my life heard anyone scream like she did! When she regained control of her emotions, the aged woman said an amazing thing: "Mister, I don't know who you are, but I have prayed for my boy every day for over eighty years."

Her son and I got on our knees, and I had the joy of praying with him and seeing him come to Christ. God had answered two prayers: hers of eighty years, and mine of just a few weeks.

In the Bible, I had read that some people plant, some water, and God gives the increase (1 Corinthians 3:6). I had been there to participate in the increase. The man's faithful mother and a Christian man on the first floor of the building had done the planting and watering. The neighbor, I learned, had been taking care of their physical needs for several years. He would come up every day and get their grocery order, find out what other needs they had, and take care of them. He had often shared Christ with the blind man.

I was so excited that I didn't work the rest of the day. My wife, Edith, was a registered nurse at the hospital on the 11 P.M. to 7 A.M. shift. I had to tell her what had happened, so I drove home and woke her up. I spoke enthusiastically of how God had answered my prayer and had given me the joy of seeing a person find Christ even though I didn't know much about sharing my faith. "Honey, I've found a reason for living as a Christian—something I can give my life to, and that is *people!*"

ulously intervene in our lives. But we come to God not because of what He may do to spare us suffering, but because Christ is Truth. What He does promise us is much more—the forgiveness of sin and eternal life. I left the hospital with my friend studying Christian literature, the Bible, and my own account in *Born Again*. If he becomes a Christian, it won't be on false pretenses.

I thought often in the hospital of the words of Florida pastor Steve Brown. Steve says that every time a nonbeliever gets cancer, God allows a Christian to get cancer as well—so the world can see the difference. I prayed I might be so filled with God's grace that the world might see the difference.

Steve's words represent a powerful truth. God does not witness to the world by taking His people out of suffering, but rather by demonstrating His grace through them in the midst of pain.

He allows such weakness to reveal His strength in adversity. His own Son experienced brokenness—and died—that we might be freed from the power of death. But we are promised no freedom from suffering until we are beyond the grave.

Thus, I can only believe that God allowed my cancer for a purpose—just as He allows far more horrific and deadly cancers in fellow Christians every day. We don't begin to know all the reasons why. But we do know that our suffering and weakness can be an opportunity to witness to the world of the amazing grace of God at work through us.

Editor's note: Colson's surgery was successful, and he has had no recurrence of cancer.

I went back to visit the man once before Edith and I moved to Chattanooga, Tennessee, later that year. It is amazing—when I try to think of other events that happened in 1951, I can't remember anything more significant than this experience! It changed the course of my life.

Can you imagine a person coming to Christ the first time you ever tried to witness? I guess our Lord knew I might never try again had I been rebuffed. The Holy Spirit prepared the old man's heart and convinced him to accept Jesus. He just let me sit on the sidelines and watch as He worked. And I've been doing it ever since!

James Dobson

SURRENDERING MY-EXPECTATIONS AND AMBITIONS

The founder and president of Focus on the Family, Dr. James Dobson is a leading authority on the family.

Jim is one of the most respected and honored leaders in the Christian world. His commitment to building strong families has brought blessing to millions of people. And because of his expertise on family matters, he was invited regularly to the White House to consult with Presidents Ronald Reagan and George Bush and has served on numerous commissions on family-related matters.

Jim is the distinguished author of fourteen best-selling books, including Dare to Discipline, *which has sold more than three million copies and was selected as one of fifty books to be rebound and placed in the White House Library. He also can be heard daily on an internationally syndicated* radio program.

Jim's dramatic account of his struggle to let God control and bless his work and ministry can help each of us learn how to turn our ambitions over to Him.

I've spent most of my professional life writing and speaking about person-to-person relationships of one kind or another. So it may be surprising to hear that one of the most important lessons I've had to learn had to do with the way I relate to people—specifically, the way I respond to them on paper.

Let me explain.

I am a writer. I've always expressed my thoughts best in written language. Even when I was ten years old, I would write letters to my parents if I thought they had disciplined me unfairly. I much preferred to make my case on paper than face to face.

Through the years, therefore, my first reaction when I was irritated was to express that sentiment in writing. It was not until about 1981 that I began to see the disadvantages of that approach. There are many.

First, *when words are put on paper, their intensity does not diminish with the passage of time.* There in the files, or at home in a spouse's possession, is a fiery message that carries its original impact even years after everyone has forgotten the issue that motivated it. When angry thoughts are expressed in black and white, they remain alive and dangerous—like an armed pipe bomb!

Second, *there is something powerful about the written lan-*

guage. Remember that Jesus identified Himself entirely with the Scriptures: "In the beginning was the Word, and the Word was with God, and the Word was God" (John 1:1, NKJ). Even the words of man can be a two-edged sword that cuts the soul to the quick. Harsh, spoken words can also be destructive, of course, but they can't compare to those that are carefully arranged on paper and served piping hot.

Third, *I found that my tendency to put my reprimands in writing set the stage for other members of my staff to do the same.* They began criticizing one another in memo-form, which brought immediate retaliation and counter charges. I quickly realized this was wrong.

Fourth, *I discovered that my face-to-face encounters with those who needed correcting were not nearly so severe or painful.* Sometimes the person was able to give me a logical explanation that I hadn't considered. On other occasions, I saw vulnerability in his or her eyes that softened my own irritation.

What I'm trying to say is that the Lord began talking to me about this entire area, and I have mellowed significantly in recent years. But the criticism of harshness some have leveled at me has certainly been valid in times past. I was never capricious or vicious to people as a matter of course. Most of my strong memos went to those who deliberately or slovenly failed to meet a need or follow a well-known policy. I have never been a tyrant to work for. Still, I needed to make some significant changes in the way I related to my colleagues—and I've attempted to do that.

As you might expect, this tendency to be tough, especially in writing, has applied to my relationship with business associates outside Focus on the Family, too. As a matter of fact, it was in this area that the Lord hit me between the eyes with one of the strongest, most direct warnings I've ever received from Him on this subject.

As I've grown older and a bit wiser, I have actually felt constrained to go back to the publishers of some of my early books and ask forgiveness for the things I demanded of them. I'll never forget the time when my second book, *Hide or Seek*, came out. It arrived on the heels of *Dare to Discipline*, which had been enormously successful. I did not want to be a flash in the pan—a one-book author—who had nothing else of importance to say. As a result, I felt a great deal of pressure to produce another best-seller. It was carnal pride, pure and simple.

For some reason, I found *Hide or Seek* difficult to write, and I bogged down for two years in the process. It is probably my favorite book now, but I went through a tough time giving birth to it. When the book finally came off the press, I was one uptight young author. I was determined to make it go, or else. I went to New York City in 1974 and participated in seventeen radio, television, and newspaper interviews within a span of only three days. No price was too great to let the world know the book was available.

Shortly thereafter, Ernie Owen, my publisher from Fleming H. Revell in New Jersey, came to see me at Children's Hospital. We went to eat together, and I gave him fits during lunch.

"How come I can't find copies of *Hide or Seek* in the Christian bookstores?" I demanded. "Where are you advertising the book, and why are you not keeping me informed of your plans?"

On and on I went. Suddenly, the man who is now my good friend fired his own shots at me.

"I want to know something about *you*," Ernie said firmly.

"How come this book is so important to you? Why are you acting like this? Why are you so uptight about the job we are doing?"

Ernie probably didn't know it at the time, but his responses made me furious. Instead of doing his job as my representative, I believed he was being rude to me and making me feel foolish for insisting on quality work from my publishers.

I quickly finished eating, shook hands with Ernie, and headed across the street to the hospital. I got about fifty yards from the restaurant when the Lord spoke to me. It was not an audible voice, but it was unmistakably His!

He said, "Son, those questions that Ernie was asking you a few minutes ago did not originate with him. They came from Me. I also want to know why you are pushing and shoving everyone so hard. Tell Me why you're trying to force this book to be a success. Don't you know that you have nothing but what I have given you and that *Hide or Seek* will be successful only if I choose to bless it? So why are you trying to promote it on your own?"

IF YOU HAVE EVER BEEN "SPANKED" BY THE LORD, YOU KNOW IT IS AN UNPLEASANT EXPERIENCE.

If you have ever been "spanked" by the Lord, you know it is an unpleasant experience. I felt about three feet high.

"I understand, Lord," I said humbly and released *Hide or Seek* into His hands. "It is Yours. If You can use it, that's fine, and if not, I surrender my personal ambitions."

Hide or Seek took off like a rocket that month and is still selling well over two decades later.

My point is that I am an intense person with strong opinions about how things ought to be done. I was especially that way when I was younger. I also had a pretty powerful temper in those days. But the Lord is beating those characteristics out of me. If I can live another hundred years, I may turn out to be a pretty nice guy!

Steve Douglass

REDEEMING THOSE DRIFTING MOMENTS

Since 1967, it has been my privilege and delight to work closely with Dr. Steve Douglass as a fellow staff member of Campus Crusade for Christ where he now serves as our executive vice president.

Steve is a man of God with a brilliant mind and a vision for helping to change the world for the glory of God. He is in great demand as a speaker on leadership, management, and various biblical topics, and has been used to introduce many thousands of students and executives to Christ through his speaking and personal ministry.

Steve graduated with highest honors from Massachusetts Institute of Technology and Harvard Graduate School of Business Administration. He is the author or coauthor of several books including Managing Yourself, How to Get

Better Grades and Have More Fun, *and* Enjoying Your Walk With God.

Here Steve reveals his secret to walking supernaturally with God even when circumstances don't go his way.

The elderly lady stepped off the small commuter plane and started walking in my direction. She was angry. She was greeted by a woman standing near me—her daughter—who hadn't seen her for some time. The mother continued to grumble and fume, so I couldn't help but hear.

It seems she was led to believe that her commuter flight gate in Los Angeles International Airport was just a hundred yards away when, in fact, it proved to be nearly two hundred yards.

Yes, that was it. She had to walk another hundred yards and apparently hated every step of it. By now she had meditated on that for two hours and had worked herself into quite a stew.

That incident led me to learn a crucial spiritual lesson. Like this lady's mind, my mind also has almost a life of its own. Something goes wrong and it's off to the races. Before long, I can be concerned and even upset at a level far beyond what the original circumstance warranted.

How does that work? Well, over time, my mind adds fuel to the fire. It brings to memory other things the offending person has done. It projects future conversations I might have with that person and guesses that he might say further unkind things in such a dialog. It supplies other reasons why I shouldn't like him.

Before long, I have mentally "tried and convicted" that person of "crimes" he has never and likely will never commit. What is as bad is that I am experiencing real and present anxiety over my fabricated storyline.

So what did I discover was the cure to this persistent mental malady? *Displacement*—pushing the fabrication out of my mind with a reality even more true than the original bad event.

What is displacement? It occurs when one thing pushes another out of place. For example, when two automobiles try to occupy the same spot in an intersection at the same time, we witness physical displacement—an accident in which one of the cars often ends up pushed out of the way.

I HAVE DIS-COVERED THAT I CAN BECOME "PREOCCUPIED" WITH GOD.

So it is with our minds and hearts. Two different sets of thoughts cannot easily occupy our mind at the same time. Like the elderly lady on the commuter plane, a single concern can enlarge and totally occupy a mind until it becomes unaware and insensitive to the needs of people around it. In her case, she wasn't even civil to her daughter who, I imagine, was expecting a warm and loving reunion.

That is the bad side of our human tendency to be preoccupied. But there is a good side, a way to harness the tendency: I have discovered that I can become "preoccupied" with God. And when I do, my thoughts of Him displace my usual concerns.

King David discovered this truth long before I did: "I have set the Lord continually before me; because He is at my right hand, I will not be shaken. Therefore my heart is glad, and my glory rejoices; my flesh also will dwell securely" (Psalm 16:8,9, NASB).

David learned to keep a consciousness of the Lord *continually* in his mind. The word "continually" in Hebrew is *tamid*, which means "without interruption." In other words, David had a constant sense of the presence of God and probably had a fairly continuous conversation with Him.

What was the impact of his conscious closeness to God? Peace and joy.

And it wasn't that David had no problems. Look at Psalm 16:1: "Preserve me, O God, for I take refuge in Thee" (NASB).

His mind was filled with the reality of the presence of the all-powerful Creator-God. From that perspective, David's problems must have seemed very manageable—apparently not even worth worrying about.

I have found the same thing to be true. When I focus my mind on God, pray to Him, cast my cares on Him, even just stay in touch with Him, my normal concerns are pushed right out of my mind. They seem puny compared to God.

So how does this work in practice? The secret is in the implementation. The displacement seems to occur only when I keep the Lord *continually* before me.

The average person thinks on one specific thing for only about eleven seconds at a time. My mind frequently illustrates this statistic. I drift from one thought to another. Oh, I may come back fairly quickly to the main subject on my mind, but even when I am fairly focused, I will drift momentarily to listen to or look at something around me or to pursue a spurious thought.

Redeeming those drifting moments has been the key to

setting the Lord before me. When I drift, I try to "let my first stop be God." Most everything I think about can easily be related to and discussed with God in some way. I can thank Him, cast a concern on Him, pray for His provision or solution, or in some other way talk to Him about it.

So my momentary departure from my train of thought can become a wonderful stimulus to talk to God, as opposed to a launching pad for preoccupation with a distracting concern.

Sometimes I find it helpful to be reminded to keep up this habit. When I look down at my wedding ring, I can be reminded not only of my relationship with Judy, my wife, but also of my relationship with God. I ask, "How many minutes has it been since I last talked to God?" If it has been very long, I may well pause right then, sit back, and restart my dialog with the Lord.

Does this really work? Let me close with an illustration of how powerfully a continuous walk with God can affect my attitude.

A number of years ago I was having lunch with a friend. When his wife came to the table with her tray of food, the only available seat was to my left. She sat there.

As I talked with my friend, I practiced "letting my first stop be God." Whenever my mind drifted, I talked to God. It was brief. I didn't bow my head, close my eyes, or fold my hands. I just directed my thoughts to God for a moment and then returned mentally to the conversation with my friend.

I hardly noticed when his wife got up and returned with a Styrofoam cup of hot water for tea. She set it on my side of her tray. She suddenly turned to say something to me, and she tipped over the cup of hot water, dumping it

entirely onto my leg. Not a drop splashed on her. (Life isn't always fair.)

What did I do? You would think that I'd have cried out in pain and jumped up, right? Wrong! I laughed.

"That's weird," you say.

True, that's weird.

"That's not natural," you add.

True—it's supernatural.

You see, it was a long distance from the presence of God to my leg. My mind was elsewhere. My peace and joy were being supplied supernaturally. So it took a while for the pain from my leg to penetrate into my conscious thoughts.

In the words of the song, "The things of earth will grow strangely dim in the light of His glory and grace."

Ted W. Engstrom

SOUND ADVICE, WELL TAKEN

The former president and chief executive officer of World Vision (now president emeritus), Dr. Ted Engstrom is one of the most influential leaders in American religion and social service.

A prolific editor and author, Ted has written hundreds of articles and more than forty books, including the best-sellers The Making of a Christian Leader, The Fine Art of Mentoring, *and* Managing Your Time.

Ted is a giant among men, with whom I have had the joyful privilege of being associated for many years. Among his many other responsibilities, he also serves as chairman of the International Committee of Reference for our worldwide evangelistic effort called New Life 2000.[1] The committee consists of Christian leaders who serve as centers of influence for this comprehensive global strategy to help reach the world for Christ.

Ted W. Engstrom

I have admired and respected Ted for his management and writing skills, his sensitivity to the needs and hurts of men, and his warm, loving heart for God.

Ted tells how he learned the value of good advice and how listening to counsel from others has affected his life and ministry.

<hr/>

After more than fifty years of serving the Lord, I am constantly amazed at the results of heeding the bits of sound advice given to me as a boy and as a young man just starting on a career path.

The first good advice that significantly influenced my life came to me from my mother when I was only eight or nine years of age. Although she had completed only eight years of schooling, she was a wise woman.

One day she said, "Ted, I want to introduce you to some of the greatest friends you can ever know. Come with me."

Taking me by the hand, she led me to the East Cleveland, Ohio, Public Library where she helped me get my first library card. That day we picked out the first two books—apart from my school books—that I had the joy of reading: *Heidi* and *Black Beauty.* At that moment I was introduced to "friends" who have stood me in marvelous stead over the years.

That incident started me out on a career path I have followed for these many years. I fell in love with books; they have fascinated me. For more than five decades of ministry, I have read an average of at least one book per week and written more than two score.

The second piece of sound advice came years later when, as a nineteen-year-old college freshman, I received the Lord Jesus Christ as my Savior and Lord. Shortly after that dramatic and dynamic experience, a young college friend suggested that I select a "life verse." Some days later, while reading avidly from God's Word, Psalm 32:8 popped off the page into my heart. God said to me, "I will instruct you and teach you in the way you should go; I will guide you with My eye" (NKJ).

Immediately, I felt that this was the verse God wanted me to claim for my life. I have clung to its assurance of guidance and direction over the years as a drowning sailor might cling to a raft. I have written this verse after my autograph in Bibles and books an untold number of times. And as a constant reminder of God's faithfulness, I have a calligraphy of this beautiful promise hanging on the wall in my study. I am convinced that every Christian ought to have a life verse!

> PUT YOUR BODY,
>
> MIND, WILL, TIME,
>
> ENERGY, AND ALL
>
> THAT YOU HAVE
>
> INTO THE HANDS
>
> OF THE LORD.

Not long after, another marvelous suggestion came to me from a young Christian friend. He said, "Ted, begin your day with the emphasis of Romans 12:1,2." Here the apostle Paul reminds us, "Present your bodies a living sacrifice, holy, acceptable to God, which is your reasonable service. And do not be conformed to this world, but be transformed by the renewing of your mind, that you may prove what is that good and acceptable and perfect will of God" (NKJ).

This friend explained, "Begin every day by offering your life, walk, and ways to the Lord as a living sacrifice. Put your body, mind, will, time, energy, and all that you have into the hands of the Lord. Make it a daily experience."

What a wonderful bit of advice this has been. I have found that God is faithful to tie the promise to guide me in my life verse into this injunction to offer my life to God for His direction.

The final bit of cherished advice came from a man who was to be my beloved father-in-law. My wife, Dorothy, and I were college sweethearts. A year or so after graduation, I asked her father for her hand. Shortly afterward, he offered me a share in his successful watchmaking and jewelry business. Since Dorothy was his only child, he would train me in the business and turn it over to me in due time.

Reflecting upon this generous offer, I realized that my heart could not be in that kind of business and, though I deeply appreciated his generosity, I explained that my fingers were thumbs and I would not be a good watchmaker nor a capable storekeeper!

Breathing a sigh of relief, he gave me marvelously sound advice. He said, "Son, I'm glad you feel that the Lord is leading you in a specific direction, not necessarily into business with me. As you move on into your career, whatever you do, make yourself as close to indispensable as possible. Strive for this level of performance and excellence in your service for God."

I've never forgotten his wisdom. And I have learned over the years that, when we accept such advice, often unsought, we are greatly benefited. I have fallen in love with books; the Lord has given me the assurance of His guidance; I have learned the lesson of daily submission to the will of

God; and I have sought excellence in my performance. All of this is a result of good advice given and heeded, and I have found these helpful gems to be among "the greatest lessons I have ever learned."

Paul Eshleman

HE WILL PROVIDE

Paul and Kathy Eshleman have been a vital part of my life and the ministry of Campus Crusade for Christ for almost thirty-five years. Since joining staff, Paul has assumed major responsibilities and has completed each with remarkable success.

He directed Explo '72 in Dallas, Texas, which brought 85,000 students and laymen to the city for training in how to share their faith in Jesus Christ. Paul also directed the "I Found It" campaign in 1976, which spread to 245 major cities and thousands of smaller communities.

In 1945, God impressed me to produce a film on the life of Jesus to help accelerate the spread of the gospel to the world. Paul has played a major role in helping to make that dream a reality. In 1978 he was named executive vice president of the Genesis Project, which produced the JESUS film for Campus Crusade. Under his exceptional leadership, the film has been translated into more than 520 languages and, at this writing, has been viewed by over two billion people worldwide—one-third of the world's population. No doubt, tens

of millions of these have already received Christ.

In 1983 Paul served as program director for the International Conference for Itinerant Evangelists in Amsterdam, an event sponsored by the Billy Graham Evangelistic Association. Currently, Paul continues to direct the JESUS Film Project.

In his story, Paul describes how the plans for the huge Explo '72 conference in Dallas almost collapsed, and shows how God led him to the right contacts at the right time to pull all the details together.

The starting date for the Explo '72 conference I was directing was less than thirty days away. Every hotel, motel, school, and campground within sixty miles of Dallas was filled to capacity. We had already assigned housing to 50,000 people, but still the registrations poured in at more than 1,000 a day.

"We now have over 20,000 people registered who don't have rooms," the registration coordinator told me. "What are we going to do?"

"How about the students who are going door-to-door asking for places for the delegates to stay? How are they doing?" I inquired.

"They're finding about one hundred places a day. But each day we get further behind."

Concerned about the problem, I decided to call Bill Bright. As president of Campus Crusade for Christ, he had assigned to me the task of preparing for this giant congress. At that time, his office was in Arrowhead Springs, California.

"Bill," I began frankly, "you sent me down here to Dallas to get things ready. You should know that right now I'm not doing a very good job."

"I'll catch the next plane to Dallas," he said after I explained the situation to him.

When he arrived from the airport, I gave him my desk, and we studied the problem.

"Has the Lord given you any ideas of what to do?" he asked.

"Our best idea at this point is to rent empty warehouses and equip them with cots and portable toilets," I suggested. "If you could help us find about 40,000 cots, we could hopefully give everyone a place to sleep."

Immediately, Bill went to work. He called the office of the Secretary of Defense. He talked to the officials in Civil Defense. He even spoke to the President's personal assistant in Washington. Although nothing was confirmed, there seemed to be some hope of a few cots. "Let me know if there is anything else I can do and how this all goes. I'll be praying." And he flew back to California.

Two days later all the government agencies turned us down because of various policy issues. We didn't get one cot. Even Bill Bright—the president of the organization—hadn't been able to solve the problem. It was time to get on our knees again.

A few of us gathered in my office to pray. In the quiet of my heart, I remembered the words of a speaker I had heard early in my Christian ministry: "If God calls you to a task, He will supply all your needs." Many of this man's talks were based on the example of Nehemiah, whom God told to return to Jerusalem and rebuild the wall of the city. And God provided all that Nehemiah needed by touching the heart of the king who gave him the materials necessary to complete the task.

I had great confidence that God had led us to hold this conference. Already we had seen wonderful answers to prayer in other areas of the project. But this problem was so big—and serious.

I knew that lack of housing could cause everything to come to a halt. If that happened, we would have to notify people and tell them not to come. I felt so discouraged.

But as we prayed, I remembered again that I was in God's service. This was not my conference. Whatever He wanted would be fine with me.

"Lord, we don't know what to do," I prayed earnestly, "but You do. Show us what to do. You have always supplied our needs. We ask You to do it once again—for Your glory."

As we prayed, I felt impressed again that we should try to rent empty apartments. I had mentioned this to a board member some time earlier.

At the time, he thought it was a terrible idea. "I own apartments myself. I would never let you put ten high school students in one of my apartments for a week. You couldn't pay me enough to make it worthwhile. I'd have to repaint the apartments after they left."

So I had abandoned the idea.

But now, as we finished praying, I felt impressed to explore this possibility again. I called the vice president of Lincoln Properties, the largest apartment owner in Dallas.

"Is there any way you would rent us your empty units?" I asked.

"We might be willing to help you, but on two conditions," he said firmly. "First, we want a guaranteed contract.

Second, we want insurance on each apartment against damage of any kind."

"Thank you so much. We'll get to work." And I hung up.

Writing the contract was not difficult. Obtaining the insurance at a price we could afford was almost impossible.

Explo '72 was held at the height of the anti-Vietnam War movement in the United States. The FBI had informed us that a radical group was making plans to explode a bomb in our main meeting place—the Cotton Bowl. It had taken seven insurance companies to underwrite a fifty-million-dollar liability and personal injury policy.

GOD PROVIDED ALL THAT NEHEMIAH NEEDED BY TOUCHING THE HEART OF THE KING.

When we went back to these companies and asked them to insure five to ten thousand apartments, they were unwilling. So we talked with an expert in Chicago. He knew of only one company in America that might help us, and they happened to be headquartered in Dallas. He gave us the name of a man in the company we had to see. He doubted anyone else would even be willing to discuss it.

Jerry Franks, one of our staff members, went to the company's office and asked for this man.

"He's never here at the office," the receptionist said. "He's always out on the road."

Then she looked up, surprised. "I don't believe it. There he is now, standing in the hall."

Jerry rushed to see him. "You're the person I have been told to see."

The man frowned. "I'm expecting a very important call. As soon as it comes, I'm leaving. But I'll talk to you until the call comes."

Jerry explained what we needed.

The man nodded, "I'm going to help you."

He led Jerry into the office of an underwriter. "Write this man an insurance policy for damage on apartments in the amount of $20,000 per apartment for as many apartments as he wants to cover. And charge him, oh, fifty cents a night per apartment."

The underwriter exclaimed, "We can't write a policy like that."

But this man said firmly, "I'm telling you to write this policy. Now write it."

Later, we found out why he had given us the insurance. This man had four daughters. The youngest, his pride and joy, had become a Christian six months earlier. During that time, she had been asking her dad if she could have a trip to Explo '72 as a high school graduation present.

That morning during her high school chemistry class, acid had accidently been thrown into her eyes. He was waiting for the call from the hospital to tell him whether his daughter would ever see again.

Did he help because he thought God might save his daughter's eyes? Were his daughter's eyes spared because he helped? I don't know.

I do know that with the insurance we got the apartments. I know that 30,000 high school students had housing. I know that during the week more than 20,000 people received Christ and 1,000 were called into full-time Christian service.

And I also know that I had nothing to do with it. God did it!

Had Bill Bright been able to solve my problems and find the cots, I would have missed one of the greatest lessons of my life.

As God's Word says, "He who calls you is faithful, who also will do it" (1 Thessalonians 5:24, NKJ).

Leighton Ford

BEGINNING THE REAL RACE

Dr. Leighton Ford is president of Leighton Ford Ministries, which focuses on encouraging younger leaders to spread the message of Christ worldwide. He has spoken to millions of people in thirty-seven countries on every continent of the world.

Dr. Ford served as associate evangelist and later vice president of the Billy Graham Evangelistic Association. For many years, he was featured as the alternate speaker to Billy Graham on the Hour of Decision broadcast and had his own daily TV and radio spots in the United States, Canada, and Australia.

Heralded by Time *magazine as being "among the most influential preachers of an active gospel," Dr. Ford also serves as chairman of the Lausanne Committee for World Evangelization.*

He and his wife, Jean, have become close friends to

Vonette and me as we have served our Lord together in many different projects. I am sure you will be touched, as we were, by their warm witness to the faithfulness and sufficiency of our dear Lord as you read their story of the loss of their oldest son, Sandy, in 1981.

Time, they say, heals. Time also sets ambushes. On a cold, clear Carolina afternoon, driving by Myers Park High School, memories suddenly come flooding back.

I stop...park...walk around the track where he ran so many races. It has been nearly seven years since Sandy ran his last race, more than three years since he left us...

It had been a quiet, undistinguished day after weeks of hectic travel. Jeanie, my wife, and I were enjoying an evening at home together.

Shortly after nine o'clock, the phone rang. A woman's voice asked, "Is this the Ford residence?"

I identified myself. She continued.

"This is Dr. Brazeal from Memorial Hospital in Chapel Hill. Your son Sandy has had a heart problem. He's here at Memorial."

In the dead calm after the phone call, we were numb with disbelief. We were still dazed when Kevin, our youngest son, charged in from his Young Life meeting. We told him about Sandy. Then I called our daughter, Deb; she burst into tears.

Jeanie and I talked briefly about driving up immediately or the possibility of me driving up alone. But there was no point in that. We would leave in the morning. I pulled the file on Sandy's first heart operation, laid away and forgotten for six years. The old nightmare was back.

The day after Thanksgiving, Sandy went in for surgery. The doctors told us it would be a difficult operation with only a slight possibility of death. He was rolled away about 7:15 A.M. We waited all morning and all afternoon. His surgery had lasted much longer than expected.

At 6:50 P.M. the door opened. A doctor I had never seen before came in. His face was solemn; so was his manner. He spoke quietly and deliberately. They had finished the surgery, and the problem had been corrected. But they could not get Sandy off the heart-lung machine. Suddenly, the terrible truth hit me: *His heart won't start!*

Everyone prepared for the worst: *Sandy has a problem; he may die.* We gathered and prayed. More quickly than I could believe, people began to arrive. We were whirling about in a maelstrom of calling, praying, crying, and holding each other.

I went into the room next door and prayed, not for Sandy's healing this time, but just to pray. Suddenly, an upsurging sense of peace and strength came over me. Calmly, I went back to the others, and I touched Deb and Jeanie. The terrible anxiety that had built up all afternoon, though still there, was under control, for a time, as we continued to wait.

Sometime after 8 P.M. the door opened and the doctors came in. We read the worst in their faces before they spoke. "We never got him off the table."

Groping for control and understanding, Jeanie asked, "Has this ever happened before?"

"Yes, ma'am." The doctor offered no more; there was nothing more to say…

Just as I pass the starting line on the track, I wish Sandy could start his whole life again. But would we want him back if it meant going through all the pain and hurt?

Suppose God had come to us and said, "You can have Sandy. Here is what he is going to be like, but you can have him for only twenty-one years!" What would we have chosen? No question. We would take him again—and again.

Nobody could have told me three years ago how much we would miss him or for how long. There is nothing quite like the death of a child. I guess most folks think that in a few weeks or in a few months the pain is over. Maybe for some people. But not for me. Not for Jeanie.

I want so much to see him again. Watch his flying feet going around the track. See him duck his head in a moment of embarrassment. Watch him touch the corner between his eyes and his nose when he is thinking. See him pray, long fingers pressing together—moving them up and down or pulling them apart when he can't get the right word. But the pain of death is its finality. Things are never the same again.

And yet they have gotten better. We can talk more freely about Sandy now. As a family we can laugh at his foibles, remembering how spacey he could be. But still I find it hard to look at his picture. Deb can't read his journals. Jeanie's eyelids began having spasms three months after he died. They are better but still not perfect. And still the questions come.

I walk around the final curve on the track past the green wall with the "Go Mustangs" sign, past the scoreboard. I stop and look down at the spot twenty yards from the finish line where his legs began to wobble in that final race.

Why? What happened that day? Why did his heart run

away again? Why was his heart flawed in the first place? And why was he not healed?

"When a good man dies; what a waste, who can explain it?" That question headlined a newspaper story the Sunday after Sandy died. Many would say, "What a tragedy; his race was cut short." But that gives me pause. *Tragic* is a word from the ancient Greeks, not from the language of the Bible.

I have looked at a lot of Sandy's pictures since he died. And I have realized what a great difference it makes whether I look at them from the viewpoint of life or of death.

Here is what I mean. When Sandy was physically alive and with us, I would have looked at those pictures with more or less interest, regret or pride, with a sense of wonder at what he grew into.

Now, after his death, I look at each one with a little voice saying over my shoulder, "How tragic, that Sandy would live only until he was twenty-one."

It is the same way when I read his journal. A sense of tragedy keeps murmuring, "And he only had six months, or one month, or one week left to live."

How important then to decide what is Sandy's true end! If twenty-one years *was* the end, then it does seem tragic.

But if eternity is his end, then I can look from his infancy to his manhood and see each part fitting into an eternal whole which is beyond my understanding, but not my hope.

In one view, death leads to the trash heap.

In the other, death is swallowed up in glory.

So as I think of the infant who became our grown-up son, I can imagine him a man who has become a glorious creature of eternity.

Philosophizing, however, does not take away the pain that twists my insides when I achingly miss him. But as Jeanie has reminded me, "We have got to see things from Sandy's perspective."

Was twenty-one years enough time to make his life fruitful and meaningful? Or would it have taken seventy-three? Then why not seventy-four?

Isn't it what fills those years that matters? Is time just clock-time or opportunity-time—or God-time? Is it how long or how full? For Sandy, the cup of time was overflowing.

The year after Sandy died, Kevin and I were raking leaves and talking about how we missed him. Kevin said, "But, Dad, maybe Sandy's influence has been far greater than if he had lived. His life was like a very bright light—a spotlight—focused intensely. But his death has been a floodlight. It has covered a much wider area."

LIFE BLOSSOMING

FROM DEATH—

THAT IS-GOD'S WAY.

IT IS THE WAY OF

THE CROSS.

I have become convinced that John 12:24 is not just a metaphor but a literal truth. "Unless a grain of wheat falls into the earth and dies, it remains by itself alone; but if it dies, it bears much fruit" (NASB).

Life blossoming from death—that is God's way. It is the way of the cross. And we have seen how God has taken characteristics of Sandy, godly traits, and placed them into the friends who loved him. More compassion into one; more commitment into another.

Weeks after Sandy died, a letter came from the missionary under whose direction he worked one summer in France.

He wrote:

> We are so earthbound. We assume that the main part of God's will and work is here on earth. I believe that not only the best is yet to come, but the highest will also be there… *God never wastes anything*…Rather than being the end, this is the beginning!

So I stand here on the track. I want him. I want to see those pounding feet, the curly hair, the smile, the serious, thoughtful eyes. I want him to run not just here on the track, but all through his life.

With my toe, I draw a line where the finish line was, where Sandy finished his last race. But the finish line is also the starting line. And that is what makes the pain bearable. That is what undergirds the loss with hope. That is what makes the race worth running. Suppose that life is not the race. Suppose life is only the training season, and eternity is the real race.

Then Sandy's heart was beating, not just for a medley relay, not just for twenty-one years, but for eternity. The weight he carried—including a wounded heart—was preparing him for an eternal weight of glory.

Sometimes in my mind, I whisper, "What is it like, Son?"

And I hear him say, "I can think so deeply, and every thought is clear. I can speak and express exactly what I mean. I can run and never get tired. I am so surefooted in the paths of glory."

So a son leaves a legacy for a father. I have determined to run my race for Christ to the end. And when that time comes, maybe our Savior will let Sandy come running to meet me. Then with all the sons and daughters of the resurrection, our hearts will beat, and we will run for God forever.

Joe Foss

THE TEST OF TIME

A past president of the National Rifle Association, Joe Foss has had many titles during his life. He is a retired brigadier general, a former governor of South Dakota, past football commissioner and television host. But what impresses me most about Joe is his zeal for Christ and determination to help anyone on a spiritual quest find the One who transformed his life.

On numerous occasions, Joe has faithfully encouraged others to surrender their lives to Christ following one of the most powerful testimonies I have ever heard.

Joe has a distinguished military career. He served in the Korean War as a colonel in the U.S. Air Force. A hero in World War II, Joe shot down twenty-six enemy planes. He is the recipient of the Congressional Medal of Honor and the Distinguished Flying Cross.

Joe relates several lessons he has learned, but his greatest came after an experience that changed his life in the heart ward of a hospital.

There is only one way for me to relate the greatest lesson I've ever learned, and that is to mention some of the earlier lessons in my life that I thought were important.

Way back, I learned to stay within the guidelines my father set—or suffer the consequences. One such learning experience I remember well. I varied from my scheduled route in the drive to and from high school and had a slight accident. As a result, Dad made me walk a twelve-mile round trip to and from school for three months. That was my last variance while Dad was running the show.

When I went to college, the biggest lesson I learned was that studying was my responsibility. If I forgot to study the material, I flunked. I had to learn this fact the hard way.

Later, in the U.S. Marine Corps, I learned quickly that attention to duty was of number-one importance. In aerial combat my flight team and I had to work as a very close-knit unit. If we didn't, we were shot out of the sky by the enemy. The others and I were fortunate to become aces many times over.

Likewise, in politics I learned that you must be organized and have teamwork, or you lose the campaign. Learning this hard lesson the first time I ran for governor of South Dakota, I subsequently went on to win the gubernatorial elections for the next two terms.

And as commissioner of the American Football League, I soon learned that, in order for all the teams to operate strictly according to the constitution and bylaws, they had to be continually reminded. Some teams were always trying new ways to circumvent certain rules. This keeps the commissioner and his crew on the lookout for violations morning, noon, and night.

As an actor and television show host ("American Sportsman" and "Outdoorsman—Joe Foss"), I soon learned the importance of checking the words that the writers wanted to put in my mouth. An unfortunate comment could cause stacks of angry, critical letters. Once I forgot to wear my protective glasses while fly-fishing in a wind on the Big Hole River in Montana. Letters came in by the dozens letting me know I was setting a poor example because it was easy to lose an eye without them. In fact, a man who had previously worked for me wrote and indicated he had lost his right eye because he forgot his glasses while fly-fishing.

The years rolled on, and I figured that I had learned all the lessons I needed. Then the day came when it looked as though I was about to die. While filming a show, I got arsenic in my system from chewing corn stalks that had been sprayed for corn bores. The arsenic, being a cumulative poison, went to my nerve centers and caused me to lose the use of my arms and sense of taste.

While I was in this condition, I became interested in the spiritual side of life. My wife, Didi, and several of her friends had been praying for me. At this time Didi got me to attend a small, Bible-teaching church. It was here for the first time that I heard the message of how to become a born-again Christian. The minister said that one must have a personal relationship with Jesus Christ and must receive Him as Savior and Lord. The minister spoke about Nicodemus coming to Jesus in John 3 and inquiring about being born again.

This was all Greek to me, for I had never studied the Bible. I only knew a little about God and Jesus, His Son.

When the minister said, "I'm going to give those who don't know Jesus a chance to pray and receive Him," I was dumbfounded. He prayed, "Lord Jesus, I need You. Thank You for dying on the cross for my sins. I open the door of my life and ask You to come in and be my Savior and Lord. Thank You for forgiving my sins and giving me eternal life. Take control of the throne of my life and have me be the kind of person You want me to be."

As he prayed, I hesitated, thinking, *I can't do this.* Then it dawned on me: *Joe, you'd better get aboard now.* I prayed fast and caught up.

As time wore on, I still stayed in square one, but more people prayed for me. Some years later, I was flat on my back in a heart ward with pain in my chest. (It turned out to be pericarditis.) I came into the ward a bit nervous because I didn't know what was wrong. Five people were in there ahead of me. I noticed a TV set over each bed. I thought, *This will take up some of the time.* But as the nurse put me into the bunk, she explained to me that the show on that set would be my heart waves. This was Thursday night, so by Sunday I had been doing a lot of thinking. That Sunday morning I wished I could be in church. No one seemed to know or care that it was Sunday.

COMING TO KNOW JESUS CHRIST IS THE ULTIMATE PRIVILEGE OF LIFE.

All of a sudden, the man next to me got a straight line on the heart monitor. The nurses and the doctor came running. They pulled the curtain and hooked him up to the "battery charger." In a matter of minutes, the loudest cussing I'd heard in a long time came from behind the curtain.

Someone said, "He always does that."

That afternoon the curtain was pulled, and the man looked as though he wasn't long for this world. If only I knew enough, I could talk to him about Jesus. It was then, in answer to Didi's and others' prayers, that I made up my mind: *If I ever get out of here alive, I'm going to learn everything I can about the Lord and tell others about Him.*

Thanks to Didi, I did get highly involved in learning how to tell others about Him, eventually speaking to groups through Campus Crusade for Christ. Learning how to tell others about Jesus Christ, I've discovered, is the greatest lesson that I or anyone else can learn.

When folks ask me, "What, out of all the things you've done and all the honors you have received, do you rate as the highest?" I tell them, "When I asked Jesus Christ into my life as Savior and Lord. Nothing else compares with it." Coming to know Jesus Christ is the ultimate privilege of life. Without this one you are lost for all eternity. But my greatest lesson is learning how to tell others about Jesus.

Like a Tree Firmly Planted

How blessed is the man who does not
walk in the counsel of the wicked,
Nor stand in the path of sinners,
Nor sit in the seat of scoffers!
But his delight is in the law of the LORD,
And in His law he meditates day and night.
And he will be like a tree firmly
planted by streams of water,
Which yields its fruit in its season,
And its leaf does not wither;
And in whatever he does, he prospers.
(Psalm 1:1–3, NASB)

Daniel Fuller

FITTING INTO GOD'S PLAN

Dr. Daniel Fuller was a professor of hermeneutics at Fuller Theological Seminary in Pasadena, California, from 1953 until his retirement in 1993.

I first met Dan when we were students at Princeton Theological Seminary in 1946. The following year we transferred to Fuller Theological Seminary where we were both members of the first class. We became close friends, and I had the privilege of being best man in his wedding to his beloved Ruth. Dan was one of the first six to join the staff of Campus Crusade for Christ in 1952, and he led the ministry at the University of Southern California.

Dan tells of his longing as a young man to be an evangelist like his father and how the Lord led him into a teaching ministry instead. His love for God's Word and his desire to introduce others to our Savior continue to be an inspiration to me after more than fifty years.

At age thirty-seven, my father was a successful manager of a packing house for the orange growers around Placentia, California. But as he negotiated by telegraph with eastern buyers for the sale of his clients' fruit, he increasingly found himself asking, "Is this all there is to life—just trying to get two or three cents more for a box of oranges?"

Finally one day he went into a storage room in the packing house to talk to God about the possibility of becoming a minister. During his prayer, he felt called to resign from his position and to enroll in Bible classes at the Bible Institute of Los Angeles under Dr. R. A. Torrey and other godly professors.

As I heard him recount this story in subsequent years, one thought stuck in my mind: The only thing worth doing in life is preaching the gospel. So when I awakened spiritually at age 14, I decided to be a pastor. Therefore, at the conclusion of college and World War II, I prepared for the ministry at the newly founded Fuller Seminary.

By this time my father had about thirty years' experience —first as a pastor, then as a radio preacher with the "Old-Fashioned Revival Hour," a program aired on more than 1,000 stations in America and on several short-wave stations overseas.

My father was talking of having me take over his broadcast when he could no longer continue. So while at seminary, I sought to gain experience by teaching a high-school Sunday school class and occasionally by preaching. After I completed my studies, he gave me larger roles to play in his worldwide ministry. Then in May 1950, he asked me to take over the broadcast so he could have a Sunday off.

That day I performed passably in getting the audience in the Long Beach auditorium to stand and sing "Heavenly Sunshine" and in preaching the sermon. But during the last five minutes when I gave the "altar call," things went badly. My father, with his great gift of evangelism, always brought the broadcast to a triumphant climax by describing to the radio listeners the many hands going up throughout the audience. But at the end of my broadcast, I could report no decisions for Christ. Afterward, I drove back to Pasadena in tears because I had failed before so many people.

In the years from 1950 to 1955, I took over the entire broadcast six more times, but *never once was I able to report even one conversion while on the air!* Graciously, however, decisions for Christ from my preaching were made right after the broadcast ended. Letters reporting conversions also came in.

Bill and Vonette Bright had been my close friends since seminary days—first at Princeton, then at Fuller. At my wedding in October 1950, Bill was my best man and Vonette helped organize the ceremony. Soon after, he received a mighty vision from God to help reach the world for Christ starting with college students. God mightily blessed his new work at UCLA as he took gospel teams into sororities and fraternities, urging people to submit their lives to Christ.

The next fall I volunteered to do the same thing at USC, partly because I wanted to become an evangelist like Bill and my father. But as my team went from house to house along fraternity row having no results, I again felt frustrated and compared my ministry to that of Campus Crusade, which continued to grow at UCLA and several other campuses.

Then during that fall of '52, the Lord taught me an important lesson. It began when the dean at Fuller Seminary phoned to say that a faculty member had just suffered a heart attack. He wanted me to take over the professor's class on an inductive study of the Gospel of Mark the very next day. I had learned the inductive method under Dr. Howard T. Kuist at Princeton in '46–47 and had written a master's thesis on the study of this book the preceding year at Fuller. The dean argued that I was the only person he could turn to in this emergency.

Rebellion welled up in my heart. I didn't want to divert energy away from evangelism at USC to teach at seminary. My experience in explaining inductive Bible study was even less than my experience in preaching.

Many of those first classes in Mark were failures. But as I continued to teach, surprising things started to happen. Students began to remark that they were being blessed. And at the banquet given to honor the graduates that next spring, two of them publicly singled out my class in Mark as particularly beneficial. The next day a faculty member complained, "How come you get such outspoken praise when the rest of us are lucky if we hear a faint echo of approval for our teaching?"

> MY FAILURES EMPHASIZED THAT GOD DID NOT INTEND FOR ME TO BE AN EVANGELIST.

This confirmed the lesson that God had been trying to teach me since that first distressing broadcast in 1950. My failures on the radio and on fraternity row emphasized that He did not intend for me to be an evangelist. Rather, God's plan for me was to teach His Word.

So, except for years spent getting required degrees, I

have taught at Fuller Seminary. But I still try to evangelize when an opportunity arises, for this is what Paul urged Timothy to do even though he might not have had that special gift (2 Timothy 4:5). Also, in teaching the Bible inductively all these years, I have let the biblical texts themselves emphasize to students how they must make the furtherance of the gospel their first priority.

This method has borne fruit. For example, a couple who had ministered on the campus at UC Davis brought a young man to my class. "This is your great grandchild!" they proudly declared. One of my former students had influenced this couple, and this young man, in turn, was one of the fruits of their ministry—a third-generation follower of Jesus.

So the greatest lesson God has taught me is this: "[God] gives [gifts] to each one, just as he determines" (1 Corinthians 12:11, NIV). While fulfilling the Great Commission should always be our goal, we must leave it to the Lord to show each of us how we fit into His plan to make disciples of all nations.

Joe Gibbs

THERE'S ANOTHER SIDE OF LIFE

Few coaches in the National Football League have accomplished so much so quickly as Joe Gibbs, former head coach of the Washington Redskins. Under Joe's leadership from 1981 to 1992, the Redskins won three Super Bowls, played in three NFC Championships, won four division titles, and made six play-off appearances.

As I have come to know Joe personally, I have found that, in addition to being one of the great coaches of modern times, he is also a gifted, godly, dedicated man whose testimony for our Lord is a constant inspiration and challenge to me.

Joe is active in church and youth programs. He is the founder and chairman of the board of trustees of Youth For Tomorrow, a home for wayward teenage boys in Washington, D.C.

A few years ago, he was the guest speaker at a Super Bowl Prayer Breakfast sponsored by Athletes in Action and attended by 1,300 guests. On this occasion, God used him mightily, as He does so many times, to touch the lives of all of us who heard him speak.

Joe relates how his experiences as a football coach taught him to live by God's standards, not the world's.

When I graduated from San Diego State College in 1963 as a physical education major, my goal was to be successful and happy. I looked around and decided that the world was advising me of three things.

First, if you want to be happy, you need to make money, gain position and power, and become president of a company. Or in my case, win football games.

Second, the world loves you and will be your friend. I felt I could lean on people as I embarked on the adventure of my life. Third, since you have only one life, please yourself and do your own thing.

So I began to make decisions about my life and where I was going. Soon I found that even though I made more money and won more football games, there was still an emptiness inside of me. So I tried harder to accomplish more, thinking that at some point I would be happy.

I spent sixteen years striving for success and happiness. Then in 1972, I took a coaching position in Fayetteville at the University of Arkansas. My wife, Pat, and I had just had our first child, so I started to make some serious decisions about my life and family. At the same time, I met a group of people who had a different philosophy and set of goals than I did and who had a personal relationship with the Lord Jesus Christ and a commitment to His cause.

You know what I discovered? What the world had been telling me wasn't true at all. There was another side to life —God's. His view was that the most important thing I would leave on this earth was not money, position, or even winning football games, but the relationship I had with Him and with others who love Him. And He began to teach me a different way of life.

First, I learned that money, position, and power are not important compared to relationships. Let me illustrate.

In my second year with the Washington Redskins, we had the privilege of playing for the NFC championship against Dallas. We had just won a big game at home. I was really pumped up on myself.

I got up one morning thinking about how important I was. Pat reminded me, "Pick up your socks and your bathrobe." And she starting telling me about a problem one of our sons was struggling with.

I thought, *Why is she bothering me with this? After all, I'm an important guy on the verge of winning the NFC championship.* So I stormed out of the house, slammed the door, and huffed off.

I usually pray in the car on my way to work. As I talked to God that morning, the truth of what I had done grabbed me. *When I leave this earth*, I thought, *it will not be the football games or the fact that I am head coach of the Washington Redskins that will count. All of that will wind up in an ashtray some day. But the influence I have on my wife and two children, on those I've worked with or helped, and the investments I've made in someone else's life will last forever.*

So when I got to work, I called home. "Pat, taking care of our home is more important than what I am doing at work. I'm sorry for the way I acted."

Fame really is fleeting. Fifteen years from now, I'll be sitting on some corner someplace telling some older guy, "You know, I was the head coach of the Washington Redskins."

And this guy will probably turn to those around us and say, "This man is crazy. He thinks he was the head coach of the Washington Redskins."

And you know what I'll think about? How I wish I had spent more time with the ones I love than I did.

I LEARNED THAT THE WORLD LIES WHEN IT SAYS IT IS-MY FRIEND.

Second, I learned that the world lies when it says it is my friend.

We had a good football team in 1983. Our record was fourteen wins and two losses—and those two by only one point apiece. John Riggins, Joe Theismann, and all our guys had played great. We were headed for the Super Bowl, and we were the favorites.

The Washington, D.C., newspapers were actually saying that I was a pretty sharp football coach. The worst part was that I was beginning to believe their words. I thought, *Hey, the world really does love me.*

But at the Super Bowl, everything went wrong for us. We were getting killed. We even had a punt blocked.

Suddenly, with only twelve seconds to go in the first half, we were on our own twenty yard line. I had to make a decision. Either we could fall on the football right there and come back in the second half, or we could go for the score.

On the sidelines, Joe Theismann was talking a thousand miles a minute. I said, "Shut up, Joe. We are going to take a chance. We have a couple of time-outs left. We'll throw a screen pass and, if we happen to break out to midfield or something, call a time-out. Then we will take a shot at the end zone, and maybe we'll get pass interference or something."

I figured that when a team is on the twenty yard line, eighty yards from the opposing goal, the defense does not play man-to-man coverage. It just doesn't happen that way. That's why I called this particular play. Sounded like a good idea, didn't it?

I called a screen pass to Joe Washington. Joe Theismann went back and threw to Washington. But one linebacker covered Washington man-to-man. The linebacker picked off the ball and ran twenty yards for a score that sealed our loss.

Suddenly, I went from being a sharp guy to being, as *The Washington Post* described it the next day, a "buffoon." That's the world's reaction. When you live by the world's standards, if you win the game, you're smart; but if you lose, you're booed.

But God loves us in good times and bad. He cares when we win the games, when we get the rewards. But He is even more real in our lives when we are having tough times. And He uses the hard experiences to change us and to give us a greater appreciation for our friends and family.

I have experienced the truth of God's love during many hard times. A few years back, for example, I decided I needed financial security. I wasn't satisfied to let God work in my life and to coach football. I wanted to make some business deals. Pat didn't want me to do it, but I didn't listen to the mate God had given me and made the investments anyway.

The next three years were probably the worst we have ever lived through. Finally, I had to get on my knees and admit to God, "I am bankrupt. We have lost everything we have.

You are the only One who can straighten out this mess."

Over the next four years, I put the mess in God's hands. I went to all nine banks that were involved in my complicated financial deals and said, "Hey, I don't have this money, but if you are willing to help, I will work this out."

Miracle after miracle happened to untangle my financial problems. And God was with me through it all. Best of all, I discovered that He was more real to me during the tough times than the easy ones.

Third, I learned that the biggest lie the world tells us is that we have only one life to live, so we should do our own thing. God's side is this: He has created us with a soul for one reason—to have a personal relationship with Him. When we try to fill our lives with anything other than Him, we will always feel a void inside no matter what we accomplish.

Maybe you have been in business for twenty, thirty, or even forty years. You have been trying to accomplish something that will make you happy. But suddenly you stop and say, "What is the problem here? I am not happy."

I experience this as a football coach every day. If I live for the world's standards, I am not happy or successful. Only one thing fills my life with purpose: my personal relationship with God through Jesus Christ. That is a miracle.

God speaks supernaturally to us through His Word and changes our lives. He helps us influence others, and in the process, we find happiness and success. That, I have discovered, is the true reality.

Billy Graham

AN EXAMPLE OF-HUMILITY

Billy Graham is a statesman among statesmen, a leader among leaders, who endeared himself to me fifty years ago when he took a special interest in me and Campus Crusade for Christ while it was only a fledgling movement. In fact, the first one thousand dollars the ministry received was a gift from Billy.

In his worldwide ministry of more than five decades, Billy has preached the gospel in person to more people than anyone else in history. His love for the Lord, his integrity, and his genuine sense of humility have been a strong witness for Christ to the multitudes of the earth. Vonette and I are truly indebted to Billy and his wonderful wife, Ruth, for their friendship and encouragement through the years.

A popular author, he has written twenty best-selling books including Peace With God, How to Be Born Again, Storm Warning, *and his autobiography,* Just As I Am.

One of Billy's greatest lessons came through the example of a godly man whom he met during one of his crusades. Here is his story.

It was January 1950; the place was Boston.

Our evangelistic meetings in Los Angeles the previous summer had drawn unexpectedly large crowds and unprecedented media attention. When we finished in L.A., we began planning for our next crusade to be held in Boston. But everyone warned us that Boston—sophisticated, cultured, and steeped in tradition—would be far different from any other city in which we had preached. Many, in fact, doubted that we should even attempt any meetings there.

But Dr. Harold John Ockenga, the dignified and scholarly pastor of Boston's prestigious Park Street Church, believed otherwise. Risking his personal reputation, Dr. Ockenga urged us to accept a ten-day series of meetings in his church.

At once it became clear that God was at work in Boston in an unusual way. Thousands had to be turned away from the initial meetings, and we frantically found ourselves scrambling to find larger venues. The city's five newspapers competed in giving the crusade front-page coverage, and the national media picked up the story. Day after day, hundreds turned to Christ through the crusade.

Surely, I thought, *Dr. Ockenga must be taking great personal satisfaction and justifiable pride in what is happening and the important part he's played in bringing it about.*

One day in the midst of the campaign, I stopped by to see

him at the church. His secretary told me he was in his office and suggested I go on in. As I entered, however, I thought she must be mistaken, for Dr. Ockenga was not to be seen. Then a muffled sob caught my attention—and I discovered him prostrate on the floor, his head literally under the rug. He was praying as earnestly and fervently as anyone I have ever seen, humbly acknowledging his unworthiness and his total dependence on the Holy Spirit. He was beseeching God to pour out His blessings on the people of New England through the meetings. There was no hint of pride or self-satisfaction here.

For me, his example was a vivid and unforgettable illustration of one of the Bible's clearest commands: "Humble yourselves, therefore, under God's mighty hand, that He may lift you up in due time" (1 Peter 5:6, NIV). If Dr. Ockenga, with all of his education and prestige and success, needed to humble himself before God, how much more did I!

THE SCRIPTURES TEACH US THAT WE ARE TO HUMBLE OURSELVES.

God has taught me many valuable lessons throughout the years, but one of the greatest is that the Scriptures teach us we are to humble ourselves. Only then can He use us as He wills.

The Bible does not tell us to pray for humility, as if we should expect God suddenly to break through our pride and fill us with humble feelings. Instead, the Scripture teaches us to humble ourselves—to face pride and self-satisfaction honestly whenever they rear their heads—and then to repent of them and take whatever action is necessary to be humble before God. Time after time, when I have been tempted to take credit for something God has done, I have had to humble myself by turning to God and acknowledging my total dependence on Him.

Pride is deadly, and Satan will manipulate it every time to thwart God's work in us and through us—just as he did with Adam and Eve in the Garden of Eden. But God has said, "I am the Lord...I will not give My glory to another" (Isaiah 42:8, NIV). No matter how much God may use us, all the glory, praise, and honor must go to Him and Him alone.

Jack Hayford

THE MIRACLE
OF AIMEE

Dr. Jack Hayford is the senior pastor of The Church on the Way in Van Nuys, California. What began as a temporary assignment to pastor eighteen people in 1969 has continued fruitfully, and today the congregation numbers in the thousands.

Jack has long impressed and inspired me as a spiritual bridge-builder. He has a loving, gracious spirit that reaches out to embrace men and women of all denominations and movements that honor our Lord. He is a true ambassador of Christ's prayer, recorded in John 17, that His followers may be one even as He and the Father are one.

Jack is the author of almost three dozen books and is a gifted composer, having written more than five hundred songs, hymns, and other musical works, including the popular song "Majesty." He also ministers through his television and radio outreach, "The Living Way Ministries."

Jack has a special ministry teaching Christians how to worship and praise our wonderful Lord through song. Here he tells the heartwarming story of a little girl who taught him how personal and rewarding that worship can become.

She was the picture of shyness, standing at the door bashfully glancing my way, with one finger curled to her lower lip and her eyes eloquently inquiring, "Can I see you, Pastor Jack?"

I beckoned to her, and the eight-year-old walked across the prayer room to where I stood with some elders. I knelt to greet the child.

"Hi, Aimee," I smiled. "What do you want?"

She was so sweetly childlike. "Pastor Jack, I want you to hear a song the Lord gave to me."

Though the service was about to begin, right then she seemed a more precious and urgent matter than the multitude gathering for worship.

"Sing it for me."

She sang a tender little tune. The child's loving lyric voiced her worship and gave expression to her first discoveries in the Holy Spirit's creativity in song.

"That's beautiful, Aimee. You keep singing it to the Lord Jesus, will you?"

She nodded, and we hugged each other as I whispered, "Thank you for sharing your song with me. Tell Mama and Daddy hello for me, and...I love you."

Her smile would have melted a million hearts as she said, "I love you, too." She slipped out the door and hurried to find her mom and dad.

There's more to Aimee's story, but for the moment I pause to underscore one of the greatest lessons I have ever learned about worship and song: *God wants to give everyone their own song of praise to Him.*

The Creator, whose Word repeatedly says, "Sing unto the Lord a new song," wants to beget a new song on the lips and from the hearts of His own—a distinctly new song of your own!

My response to Aimee's song was more than a pastor's kindness to a child; it was my confirmation of a vital practice. She had never heard me encourage private song-making in worship, but at her tender age she was experiencing a creative possibility open to us all.[1]

Worship may be possible without song, but nothing contributes more to its beauty, majesty, tenderness, and intimacy. The breadth of style, the endless melodic possibilities, the delicate nuances of choral dynamics, the brilliant luster of instrumental arrangements, the soul-stirring anthems of anointed choirs, the rumbling magnificence of giant organs—all seem to be a God-given means for our endless expansion in worship.

What guidelines does God's Word offer us for expecting and cultivating music in corporate worship?

First, the fruitful implanting of the Word of God is linked to our singing and worshiping (Colossians 3:15,16). Most of us consider these separate functions—the Word as instructional and song as inspirational. However, I believe worshipful song is needed for the meat of the Word to be assimilated into our character and conduct. Just as our digestive system is necessary to process food and distribute nutrients throughout the body, so worshipful singing is essential for the integration of the Word into our life.

Second, Holy Spirit–filled worship is the means by which God's precepts are infused into the human personality. Worshipful singing quickens our minds to receive the Word and submits our souls to the Holy Spirit's implanting it within us. Spirit-filled worship allows us to receive power through the teaching from the Bible.

There is no mystery to the message here. If you want to walk in God's will and wisdom, avoid the world-spirit and remain filled with God's Spirit. Practicing song-filled worship is the way to do both!

One thing that did more to expand our own horizons in corporate worship came about through repeated frustration and failure: We couldn't get a choir to last.

> TO WALK IN GOD'S WILL AND WISDOM, REMAIN FILLED WITH GOD'S SPIRIT.

Each new try involved capable people. Each beginning seemed exciting for everyone. But after three tries in as many years, I concluded God was trying to tell me something. I surrendered to the Lord the idea that we needed a choir. God's declared moratorium on our efforts to form a choir was the key to unleashing the song of our congregation.

I began to treat the church the way I would a choir. I didn't believe choirs were an unholy tradition that should be demolished, but rather that we were all to be "the choir" for the present season in our body-life. (Incidentally, we still treat the body as a "choir," but we also have six vocal and two handbell choirs.)

The Book of Revelation unveils a massive angelic choir

of worshipers in heaven: "And the number of them was ten thousand times ten thousand, and thousands of thousands" (Revelation 5:11, KJV). But the Book of Hebrews goes further, and amazingly puts us *all* in that heavenly choir, there at God's throne, sounding our praises beside the angelic choir, joining in the timeless worship of the Most High—*right now...every believer!*

> You have come to Mount Zion and to the city of the living God, the heavenly Jerusalem, and to myriads of angels (Hebrews 12:22, NASB).

As these and other truths of God's Word began to register, something came unshackled. Suddenly the congregation perceived themselves in a new light—joined to the heavenly angel choir! Biblical truth had set them free to worship with a new sense of privilege and responsibility. Our absence of a formed choir became a pivotal point in releasing everyone to be "the choir."

Believers are learning to apply the power of song and worship to their everyday routine. It's not only contributing to the rise of homes filled with a holy happiness, but homes where the presence of God's kingdom crowds out the efforts of hell to erode the peace and unity of families.

It doubtless seemed "just another Sunday" as Aimee's parents, Mike and Cheri, were seated with the congregation that day more than a decade ago.

Mike and Cheri were unable to have children. Medical examination had indicated that it was very unlikely they would ever enjoy that parental privilege short of adopting a baby.

Of course, I knew nothing of these facts nor of their prayerful desire that, after eleven years of marriage, they might conceive a child.

That Sunday my subject was "The Conceiving and Bearing of Life." It wasn't really a message on having children, but on overcoming barrenness in the bleak spots of our life. Using "Sing, O barren" from Isaiah 54 as my text, I discussed God's call to worship and praise Him even when our lives seem hopelessly unfruitful. It was then that something very special took place. My understanding of at least one manifestation of the spiritual gift called "a word of knowledge" (1 Corinthians 12:8) is that the Holy Spirit will give someone *both* supernatural insight *and* a corresponding promise from God regarding the issue being revealed. While I was preaching, I paused, sensing the Holy Spirit's presence and prompting.

"Church," I said, "I need to interrupt myself for just a moment. The Holy Spirit is impressing me that there is a couple here this morning who long for a child and have been told they cannot have one. His word to you is this: "Fill your house with song, and as you do, the life-giving power of song will establish a new atmosphere and make way for the conception you desire."

I didn't ask anyone to indicate their personal situation or response to that word. Rather, I simply went on with the message, basically forgetting the incident until nearly a year later when Mike and Cheri came up to me with a baby in their arms. Mike reminded me of what I had said about the couple who had longed for a child.

"Pastor, we went home that day to do what the Holy Spirit instructed us—we filled our house with song. Cheri and I walked hand in hand into each room and sang praises and worship to the Lord. We just wanted you to know that this baby is the fruit of that song, that the Lord did fulfill

His word given that morning."

Can you imagine how I rejoiced with them?

That baby's birth was a holy phenomenon, not conjured up by man's efforts or enthusiasm. It was the precious fruit of one couple's natural union which, until the divinely appointed song of the Lord entered their situation, had not found the fruitfulness for which they longed.

I am especially touched as I remember the little eight-year-old girl who came to the prayer room door and sang "the song the Lord had given to her."

She was the fruit of a song—a song that now was finding a place in her young life.

Who knows what richness her song will bring as her years follow?

Who knows what a new song may bring to you?

Edward V. Hill

THE THIRD WORLD

More than thirty years ago, E. V. Hill spoke to about a thousand of our staff and students gathered at Arrowhead Springs for training. He boldly challenged us to come and witness for Christ in his Watts community, even though it was during the days of riots. He reminded us that his community had white insurance salesmen and white water-meter readers, but no white Christians witnessing in black South Los Angeles.

More than a thousand of us went to live that weekend in the homes of the Christians of Mount Zion Missionary Baptist Church where E. V. has faithfully served as pastor for more than forty years. Vonette and I stayed in the home of E.-V. and his late wife, Jane Edna. The weekend was an experience that had a dramatic impact on my own life as well as the lives of the staff and students who participated. More than a thousand blacks were introduced to Jesus Christ by our largely white staff and students.

Admired as one of today's great preachers and teachers of God's Word, E. V. is often asked to speak at conventions, conferences, and revival meetings. He reaches a wide television and radio audience around the world. Multitudes have received Christ through his evangelistic efforts.

E. V. illuminates for us the effects of growing up as a black man in the United States and honestly relates his journey from anger, pain, and hatred of white people to a love and compassion for them that is color blind.

There were two worlds in Guadalupe County, Texas: the white and the black. As children, we were encouraged to believe that if we went to school, remained in school, and made good grades, someday we might be a part of the small percentage of Negroes who were acceptable Americans.

There was never a feeling of hostility on our part. As a community, we never blamed the white man. We said it was somehow his good luck that he had the upper hand.

Until I was twelve or thirteen years old, I had no particular problem with this way of thinking. I believed that it was just this way; we had two worlds—and there wasn't really anything wrong with this system.

White people said this separation was not due to just the fact that we were black, but to the fact that Negroes were at a lower point in their development. They said there wasn't a great deal of prejudice against the fact that we were black, but rather they objected to us because we weren't educated, carried many diseases, had a different blood type, weren't cultured, didn't have money, and weren't socially mature.

Therefore, most—including many Negroes—accepted this situation. Some of the black community accepted it because we were told that if we prepared ourselves, educated ourselves, became clean and free of disease, and showed quality, then we would develop our own black society and, to some extent, become acceptable in the white community.

However, at about thirteen years of age, I learned, as did many Negroes throughout the United States, the hypocrisy of this "gospel."

We were always told that all whites were practically perfect. But we began to see that some whites were not clean, were not educated, and were filled with diseases. We learned there was nothing inherently different in our blood type as opposed to theirs.

We heard of Negroes who were educated, but who also received the same discrimination.

I was an active member of the 4-H Club at that time and raised livestock. I showed my stock in all of the Negro shows throughout the county, and I often won. I exhibited in major shows such as the Houston Livestock Show and the Dallas State Fair, but the limitations were always there.

For instance, Negroes could not show in the calf division; we could show only our hogs. We could win only the Grand Champion of the Negro section; our hogs were not judged against those of the whites.

I had an aspiration, a longing. I didn't hate, but I wanted to compete fairly.

I did not want to be white, but if I raised hogs better than the whites, why couldn't I receive the title?

Then suddenly I rebelled at the idea that there had to be separate black and white worlds based on the premise that blacks were at a lower level—dirty, diseased, and dumb. Clearly some of the whites were poor, uneducated, unclean, and much less earnest than many Negroes in their desire to excel; *we were thwarted because we were black.*

I could do nothing but hate such a system and hate the white people who were afraid to come out and compete fairly to earn their titles. We hated them for using the color of their skin as their only weapon of defense for the status quo.

This hatred boiled within me all through high school and on into college. It did not affect my relationship to the church, however. Somehow, I gained satisfaction from the Scriptures; for me, the white world and the white people who maintained that world were evil. Consequently, we just said, "The Lord will punish those evildoers."

I have often said that if the black militant movement had been alive in my era, it would not have been difficult for me to have led such a movement and to have called white people "blue-eyed devils."

Within my philosophy then, there existed no white Christian. The white church was established only to maintain white control. What about white people who had really experienced grace in their hearts and salvation through Jesus Christ? To me, there were none.

The real Christians were black people because they were like the Israelites who had been persecuted, held down, despised, and rejected. Therefore, the white people could be nothing but the devil.

I knew no whites who were Christian enough, or who believed in Jesus enough, to take a stand against discrimination. They all said, "Obey the law, for this is the law even though it is wrong."

I became a confirmed black man who believed in Jesus Christ, who knew of no whites who did, and who wanted nothing to do with them. The only connection I wanted with them was a chance, as a Negro, to become a greater man than they.

I hoped for a strong, materialistic, religious black race—not hostile to whites nor advocating the annihilation of them, but beating them, overcoming them, having more than they.

As a freshman at Prairie View College, the Negro auxiliary of the Texas A&M University system, I became involved in the Baptist Student Union and was selected to attend the National BSU Convention in Nashville, Tennessee. I had no money, but the BSUers at Texas A&M, through various projects, raised the money for two of us to attend. Both black and white students were going to this meeting.

I was happy to go, and I accepted the money the white students raised because I looked upon it as their attempt at pity toward a less fortunate person. I felt that they got a lot of glow and glee from knowing they sent a Negro somewhere.

Then my troubles began. This trip was to be by car, and in the car would be three whites and two Negroes. I was so filled with hatred and misgivings about the trip—traveling through the South—that I almost backed out. However, I finally agreed to go. We met at Texas A&M in College Station and began the trip with a very distinguished gentleman, Dr. W. F. Howard, then director of student work for the Baptist General Convention of Texas.

There I was, totally disliking the whole set-up, but anxious to show the whites that I was their superior. I didn't know where we would eat or where we would sleep. Dr. Howard informed us that we would travel together, stay together, and eat together, and if there were places that would not serve all, we would not eat at all. For the first time in my life, I had met a white man who acted like he was Christian enough to take a stand against injustice with a black, Christian brother. I couldn't believe it! I was sure the moment would come when he would buckle under, but he never did.

Up to this point, I had known two worlds: the white world with its social, religious, and economic systems and the black world with a separate church, economic, and social system. For the first time, I began to understand that there was another world—a third world, a world of Christians. I discovered that within this Christian world there were both blacks and whites who had been regenerated to believe that the color of a man's skin really made no difference.

I also discovered that there were whites working constantly in their local churches to rid themselves and their communities of prejudice and discrimination. There was no beating of drums; they were not seen in the headlines—but they were working, and they were sincere.

I saw myself in the same condition in which I had seen the white community—filled with churchianity and justification of the flesh and empty of the Spirit of God. I too was a hypocrite.

It was on this trip and at this meeting that I invited Christ to have complete control of my life.

I am still an advocate of strengthening the Negro as a people—but not for the purpose of beating or ruling over someone. I want to lead the Negro people to the many opportunities and the great fellowship of the third world—the Christian world.

I now look with prayerful compassion upon those white people who are fervent followers of Jesus Christ and who are sincerely witnessing and working daily to inform the white world that there is a Christian world.

I know the agony, the threats, and the danger they are experiencing daily. I, too, am in constant danger and under criticism and ridicule from those who feel that I am just another Negro who has gained acceptance in the white community and who is now simply saying to black people, "Be patient and quiet."

I now know that God did not create this world for the whites or the blacks, but He created it for Himself. It is very difficult to explain to black people that there is a third world. I live in a community where many are almost at the point of denouncing Christianity. Some consider it synonymous with racism.

For the most part, the majority of my people are those who have experienced the joy, inspiration, emotion, and fervor found in a Negro congregation of worship.

However, they have not yet experienced the reality of becoming a part of the third world because they have not received Jesus Christ. And so we labor daily, saying to men and women who are in the black world that there are many unfortunate and unjustifiable wrongs that have been committed toward us because we are black. There are many white churchgoers who use the Bible to protect their prejudice. But they do not truly represent Jesus Christ! They are not a part of His kingdom.

There is a third world where white and black men are planning, working, and praying together, sacrificing and accepting abuse together, so that the kingdoms of this world will become the kingdom of our Lord (Revelation 11:15). "It is He who has made us, and not we ourselves" (Psalm 100:3, NASB).

Bill Hybels

READING YOUR GAUGES

From 125 people in 1975 to an attendance of more than 22,000 today, Willow Creek Community Church in South Berrington, Illinois, continues to be one of the country's fastest growing churches under the leadership of senior pastor Bill Hybels.

I was very impressed with Bill when he spoke at our International School of Theology graduation ceremonies some years ago. His message was profound and his love for our Lord was communicated through his scintillating personality. It was obvious that God had great plans for Bill, and I am deeply grateful for his insightful, powerful contribution to this book.

Bill is the author of a number of books, including Honest to God, Too Busy Not to Pray, Becoming a Contagious Christian, *and* The God You're Looking For. *An internationally sought-after speaker, writer, and consultant,*

Bill was also the chaplain of the Chicago Bears for five years.
Despite a successful ministry and disciplined lifestyle,
Bill found himself drained of emotional resources. He shares
how he made an amazing discovery that the mundane and
ordinary things in his life provide a healthy balance to help
him serve God for a lifetime.

For almost all of the years I have served in ministry, I have monitored myself closely in two areas, continually checking two gauges on the dashboard of my life.

Until recently, I thought that was enough.

First, I kept my eye on the spiritual gauge, asking myself, *How am I doing spiritually?* Apart from Christ I can do nothing. I know that. I don't want my life's efforts to be burned up because they were done merely through human effort, clever tactics, or gimmickry. I am gripped by the fact that I must operate in the power of the Holy Spirit.

To keep my spiritual gauge where it needs to be, I have committed myself to the spiritual disciplines of journaling, fasting, solitude, sacrifice, and study, among others. These clarify spiritual issues and pump a high-octane fuel that provides intensity and strength for ministry.

Second, I have monitored the physical gauge: *How am I doing physically?* If I push my body too hard, over time I will experience a physical breakdown or psychosomatic complications associated with high stress. If I don't exercise, eat properly, and rest, I will offer the Lord only about two-thirds of the energy I have the potential of giving.

Since these spiritual and physical gauges—the only two

on my dashboard—have consistently signaled "go," I have pushed myself as hard and fast as possible. But recently a different part of my engine began to misfire.

While preparing for a particularly difficult series of sermons, I couldn't seem to get the message to come together. No matter how hard I tried, no ideas seemed worth saying. Suddenly I found myself sobbing with my head on my desk.

Individuals more aware of their feelings might have known what was wrong, but I didn't. So when I stopped crying, I said to myself, *I don't think that was natural.*

I forced my thoughts back to the sermon and managed to put something together for the service.

But the next morning as I wrote in my journal, I thought, *Am I falling apart in some area spiritually?* My gauges said no. *Physically, am I weak or tired?* No, I felt fit.

I concluded that maybe this was my midlife crisis, a phase I would simply have to endure. But four or five similar incidents in the next few weeks continued signaling that my anxiety and frustration could not be ignored.

After a Christmas vacation that didn't change my feelings, I began to seriously inspect my life. I talked with several respected people and learned that I had overlooked an important indicator: emotional strength. I needed a third gauge on the dashboard.

I slowly began to realize that certain activities drain my emotional reservoir. Because I am a minister, I now call these experiences IMAs—Intensive Ministry Activities.

An IMA may be a confrontation, an intense counseling session, an exhausting teaching session, or a board meeting about significant financial decisions. Preparing and delivering a message on a sensitive topic that requires extensive research and thought also wears me down.

The common denominator of these activities is that they sap me, even if only for a few hours. Not realizing this, I was oblivious to the intense drain I was experiencing.

Something was wrong. I needed that third gauge—an emotional monitor—to determine my ministry fitness.

I committed myself to installing an emotional gauge in the center of my dashboard and learning how to read it. Now I monitor my emotional resources so I don't reach that point of fatigue. What signals do I look for?

If I drive away from a ministry activity and say, "It would be fine if I never did that again," that's a warning signal. Something is wrong when I look at people as interruptions or see ministry as a chore.

Another indicator: *On the way home, do I consciously hope my wife, Lynne, isn't having a problem and my kids don't want anything from me?* That's a sign I don't have enough left to give. When I hope that the precious people in my life can exist without me, that's a sign of real trouble.

A third check for me is how I approach the spiritual disciplines of journaling and writing my prayers. For months I found myself saying, day after day, "I don't have the energy to do this." I journaled anyway, but more mechanically than authentically. I dislike myself when my Christianity is on autopilot.

Each person has to find the warning signals for his or her own life. But after an IMA, it helps to ask some questions of yourself: *Am I out of gas emotionally? Can I not stand the thought of relating to people right now? Do I feel the urge to take a long walk with no destination in mind? Am I feeling the need to go home, put on music, and let the Lord recharge my emotional batteries?*

My next discovery was humiliating. I found that when

my emotional fuel was low, I couldn't do an Indy pit stop and get a fast refill. Replenishing emotional strength takes time—usually more time than it took to drain.

The best analogy I can offer is a car battery. If you sit in a parking lot and run all of your car's accessories—radio, headlights, heater, horn, rear window defogger, power windows—you can probably sap that battery in about ten minutes. Suppose you then take the battery to a service station and say, "I'd like this battery charged. I'll be back to pick it up in ten minutes."

What would they tell you? "No, we're going to put the battery on our overnight charger. It's going to take seven or eight hours to bring it all the way back up." It has to be recharged slowly or else the battery will be damaged.

> THE USE OF YOUR MAJOR SPIRITUAL GIFT BREATHES LIFE BACK INTO YOU.

Likewise, properly recuperating from an emotionally draining activity takes time. When I see my emotional gauge is reading low, I take time to recharge. Some people recharge by running, others by taking a bath, others by reading or listening to music. Usually it means doing something totally unrelated to ministry. The important thing is to build a ministry schedule that allows adequate time for emotional recharging.

I've learned a second thing about maintaining emotional resources for ministry. The use of your major spiritual gift breathes life back into you. When you have identified your spiritual gifts and use them under the direction of Jesus Christ, you feel the affirmation of God, and many times you feel more energized *after* than before.

Conversely, serving outside your gift area tends to drain

you. If I were asked to sing or assist with accounting, it would be a long hike uphill. I wouldn't feel the affirmation of the Spirit because I wouldn't be serving as I have been gifted and called to serve. This is why many people bail out of various types of Christian service: They aren't in the right yoke.

Unwittingly I had allowed myself to be pulled away from using my strongest gifts. My top gift was leadership. My second gift was evangelism. Down the list was teaching and administration.

In order to adequately prepare my messages, I had slowly delegated away almost all leadership responsibilities. And too often, in elder or staff meetings, I was mentally preoccupied with my next message. My life became consumed by the use of my teaching gift, which wasn't my most fruitful or fulfilling ministry. Yet people kept saying, "Great message, Bill." And I wrongfully allowed their affirmation to thwart my better judgment.

Since realizing this, we have implemented a team-teaching approach at Willow Creek. It has been well received by the congregation and has allowed me to provide stronger leadership in several areas. It would be difficult for me to describe how much more fulfilled I'm feeling these days.

I have also found new opportunities for evangelism. Recently I met with three guys at an airport. One was a Christian, and the other two were his best friends whom he was trying to lead to Christ. As we talked, I could feel the Holy Spirit at work. After our conversation ended, I ran to my gate, and I almost started crying.

I love doing this, I thought. *This is such a big part of who I am. I used to lead people to Christ, but I've been preparing so many messages in the past five years that I've forgotten how thrilling it is to share Christ informally with lost people.*

God knew what He was doing when He distributed gifts for service. As we minister in a way that is consistent with the way God made us, we will find new passion for ministry.

Finally, becoming emotionally depleted re-taught me a lesson I had forgotten—that a Christian leader has to strike a delicate balance between involvement in the eternal and involvement in the mundane. The daily things of life provide needed counterweight to timeless truths.

When we started the church in 1975, I had discretionary time that I used to race motorcycles, fly a plane, golf, and ski. I had relationships outside the congregation and interests other than the church.

Since that time, the needs of the church inexorably squeezed out these earthly pursuits. I became consumed with the eternal. I'm an early riser, so from 5:30 in the morning until I crash at 10:30 at night, barely one moment of time is not related to something eternal. I don't exercise at the YMCA anymore; I work out on equipment in my basement. While I'm cycling, I read theological journals. When I pump weights, I listen to tapes or think of illustrations for a message. The eternal co-opted the daily routines.

Spiritually, I was fine—I had maintained my disciplines and was striving to obey Christ. Physically, I held up fine—it wasn't like running a marathon. But I was totally depleted emotionally.

I was filling my life chock full of eternal opportunities.

What's wrong with that? Besides the emotional drain, I realized two other hidden costs of such a ministry-centered lifestyle.

First, if you are concerned only with spiritual activities, you tend to lose sight of the hopelessness of people apart from Christ. You're never in the world.

Second, you lose your wonder of the church, of salvation, and of being part of the work of God. You can overload on eternal tasks to the point that you no longer appreciate their glories. Having enough of the mundane in my life makes me see the futility of the world and the wonder and delights of the Christian life.

I'm convinced God wants me to live in order to finish the race I've started. Knowing this, my goal is to monitor my spiritual, physical, and emotional resources so that I can minister, by God's grace, for a lifetime. That's the challenge of every Christian leader. And monitoring all three gauges —spiritual, physical, and emotional—plays an important part in our longevity.

Marvin Kehler

HOW MY COMMITMENT AND CONVICTION GREW

When Marvin Kehler came to a Campus Crusade for Christ seminar held at our international headquarters, he was a successful young businessman in British Columbia. During his stay, God began to give him a vision for investing his life in helping to fulfill the Great Commission. In 1974, he became the director of Campus Crusade for Christ in Canada, a position he holds today.

Marvin began his business career by taking over his father's egg-producing operation. Within a few years, it was the third largest in British Columbia. He expanded into many other businesses including contracting, industrial, electrical, mining, and land development.

Through Marvin's creative genius and dedicated life, he and his wife, Kathy, who leads the National Prayer Ministry for Canada, have touched the entire country for the glory of God. And he holds a deep vision for reaching men and women for Christ. His story tells how he first learned to share God's love and forgiveness with others and how this changed his life.

My wife, Kathy, and I have always wanted to live meaningful, dynamic lives—not just maintain the status quo. Together we worked hard to be successful in our egg-producing and wholesale operation while raising four active children. I was also president of the British Egg Producers Association and a construction company.

Our lives were packed with activity. We were motivated by material pursuits, but we also served in our church. I was an elder and the youth director; Kathy led the Sunday school choir and helped begin a Pioneer Girls club.

We also enjoyed family hobbies: snow skiing in the winter, water skiing and competing at various horse shows during the summer.

We loved the fast-paced, active lifestyle. But after a while, the challenge and novelty wore thin. I began to ask some serious questions. Where was I heading? I was supposedly happy, yet why did I feel so empty inside? Why did my successes seem so futile and meaningless?

Then someone encouraged us to attend a five-day seminar at the international headquarters of Campus Crusade for Christ. What we heard there changed our lives! We learned how to yield to God on a moment-by-moment basis and to be controlled and empowered by His Holy Spirit.

And God showed me through His Word that my self-reliance was keeping me from experiencing His supernatural power at work within me.

As part of the training, we were shown how to share our faith with people in the community. When I stood ready to press the first doorbell, I said to God, "You have to help me. I have nothing to say."

Suddenly, a voice inside me said, "Marvin, I am glad you realize that. I will give you the words to say."

That afternoon, for the first time in my life, I led someone to Jesus Christ. It was exciting to see God use me in this way.

Later that week, Dr. Bright challenged the conferees to "Come help change the world." Together, Kathy and I committed ourselves to go wherever God wanted us to go, do whatever He wanted us to do, say whatever He wanted us to say, and give whatever He wanted us to give.

I WAS SUPPOSEDLY HAPPY, YET WHY DID I FEEL SO EMPTY INSIDE?

When we returned to Canada, we reevaluated all of our priorities in light of helping to fulfill the Great Commission. Our conviction and commitment grew. We now shared our faith in a more effective way with our youth group and neighbors and soon experienced a spiritual awakening in our community.

What we were doing began to be multiplied into many people's lives. Many were carrying on with evangelism and discipleship—some full-time, others part-time. For example, Jack and Carol Klemke, an Alberta businessman and his wife, attended one of the seminars in Canada. They, too, accepted the challenge of helping to fulfill the Great Commission in this generation. Over the years, they have trained thousands of lay people in western Canada and hosted many, many evangelistic dinners for business and professional people. Later they were used by God to begin the Christian Embassy in Ottawa. Many members of Parliament and foreign diplomats have heard the message of God's love and forgiveness because of the Klemke family's availability and generosity.

Jack and Carol have also sponsored delegations of members of Parliament and businessmen to give their testimonies before presidents, heads of state, and political and business leaders in fourteen countries in Central America, Africa, and Europe, including the former Soviet Union and Poland.

Today, in leading the Canadian Campus Crusade for Christ ministry and in helping guide the Western European Crusade ministry, God has given me the privilege of working with a tremendous team of like-minded people. We have the satisfaction of sending between 200 and 650 people each year on *JESUS* film projects and Christian Embassy tours. God has also enabled our ministry to contribute millions of dollars to help fulfill the Great Commission in more than sixty countries. I can't help but thank the Lord for His faithfulness in allowing me the privilege of being a part of this great worldwide spiritual harvest.

D. James Kennedy

SHEDDING
MY BROAD
YELLOW STRIPE

Dr. D. James Kennedy is the senior minister of Coral Ridge Presbyterian Church in Fort Lauderdale, Florida, and founder and president of Evangelism Explosion International, which teaches laymen in over 200 nations how to share their faith in Christ. His weekly messages are televised to 35,000 cities in America and fifty-seven other nations and territories.

Jim has long been a favorite of mine since I met him when he was a young pastor many years ago. At that time his church had folding chairs and was located in a building next to a fire station, but he and members of his congregation demonstrated even then a great burden for introducing others to Christ. I have followed his great progress with prayerful interest and am always blessed when I hear him speak in person or on television.

Jim is the author of more than forty books and in 1984 was selected as Clergyman of the Year by Religious Heritage of America. He served as moderator of the General Assembly of the Presbyterian Church in America in 1988–1989.

You will enjoy his account of how he learned to tell others about Christ. His insights into the importance and necessity of training in evangelism are presented through humorous encounters with "the Hulk."

Whenever I heard of a minister who was noted for evangelism, I formed a stereotype of what he was like: a bold extrovert who grabbed people by the lapels and shouted, "Brother, are you saved?" That is about as foreign a description of myself as I can possibly imagine.

In fact, I have always considered myself shy, particularly when I tried to witness. Talking to others about Christ was extremely difficult for me. I could hardly say "Good morning" to a complete stranger, much less bring up something as personal as religion.

But I sensed God's call into the ministry and went to seminary, graduated, and came to Fort Lauderdale to start a new church. I was full of vim and vigor, a veritable Daniel come to judgment. I preached everything I had in every sermon. That wasn't a whole lot, but nevertheless I gave it what I could.

My team and I gathered about forty-five heterogeneous pagans into an un-air-conditioned cafetorium at 8:30 on Sunday morning. And I preached the greatest sermons in the history of the church…by Spurgeon and MacLaren and Luther and Calvin.

So powerful was my preaching that in ten months I had taken that struggling band of forty-five people and built it into a mighty army of seventeen. Any way I looked at it, I had about two-and-a-half months of ministry left until I would be preaching only to my wife, who was threatening to go to the Baptist church down the street.

So I decided to try something different. If the mountain wouldn't come to Muhammad, then Muhammad would go to the mountain. I would visit somebody and would proclaim the gospel to him right where he was.

I had a valid reason why I didn't usually do that sort of thing. You see, I have always suffered from a serious back ailment. This broad yellow stripe goes right down my back and somehow or another connects to my jawbone, which renders me absolutely silent in many circumstances when the less circumspect would have opened his mouth.

In spite of the back defect, I decided to visit anyway. I picked a visitor's card with shaky handwriting that looked like it had been signed by a little old lady. If I couldn't out-talk her, I could at least outrun her, even with my back problem.

So a layman and I knocked on the door of this home and waited for the little old lady with gray hair to open it. Instead, we found ourselves staring at the belly button of someone vastly different and very big—the Hulk. He wore an undershirt, held a can of beer, and clenched a cigar in his mouth. He was just my sort of person—the type I had been looking for to begin my witnessing career.

So I said to him, "Is Mrs. Jones home?"

"Nah."

"Thank you very much," I muttered politely and started to leave.

"Whatya want with her?" he demanded.

"Nothing. Nothing at all. Ah, the fact of the matter is, I'm the pastor of this little church down the street. Your mother visited us last Sunday, and I was just returning the compliment. Just tell her we dropped by."

Then this guy said one of the nastiest things I have ever heard come out of the mouth of any human being in a situation like this. Right out of the blue he said, "Come in."

Can you believe that?

I walked into that living room with my knees knocking. We sat and had an enlightening and edifying conversation about the weather. We progressed to sports. He was a Golden Glove fighter. I got off that subject in a hurry and moved to the news. Then back to the weather. It was getting warm.

The layman with me whispered, "Sic him!"

"Hush, man," I whispered back. "You'll get us both killed. I'm working up to it."

Fact is, I had been working up to it for years. I just wasn't up to it any way you looked at it.

Finally, with great chagrin, I told this man (God forgive me) how much I had enjoyed the visit. We excused ourselves and left. And you know, I couldn't even look at my layman friend all the way back. Not only would the mountain not come to Muhammad, but Muhammad couldn't even climb a molehill. It was a very embarrassing situation.

When I got back home, I prayed earnestly, "Lord, what am I doing here? Surely this is all a big mistake. You didn't call me into the ministry to miserably fail." I wondered if I should leave the ministry and take up something else.

About that time, I got a letter from a preacher in Atlanta who wanted me, believe or not, to conduct ten days of evangelistic services. That's right. Me. The one who had almost decimated one church. Now he wanted me to ship it across state lines. "Have plague, will travel."

I picked out some of "our" sermons and headed north, happy to get away from my Lauderdale fiasco. When I showed up, I told this fellow, "Well, here I am. I'm ready."

He said, "That's great! You'll be preaching every night."

"Wonderful."

"However, that's not the most important thing."

Suddenly a cold chill went right down my yellow stripe. I thought, *Oh, Lord, don't let this guy say what I think he's going to say next. He looks like "that type."*

Sure enough he was. He announced, "Every morning and afternoon, we are going to go out into the homes and sometimes at night after the services. You're going to have an opportunity to witness to these people eyeball to eyeball, toenail to toenail. I've saved all the tough nuts for you."

Thanks a lot, I thought.

"That's great," I said confidently. "Actually, we professional evangelists don't like to fool with anything but tough nuts. To be perfectly honest, in my whole ministry, I've never dealt with anything but tough nuts. There's just one problem, however. I came to Atlanta to tell you that I wasn't going to be able to come because of this funeral you are going to have in town if I don't get out quick."

No, I didn't say that. I was trapped, and I didn't know what to do. I went back to my hotel room that night and got down on my knees and prayed, "Oh, Lord, what am I going to do now? I don't know how to witness to anybody."

You know what happened? Nothing. So I got down on my face on the floor and prayed for hours. "Lord, you've got to help me! I can't do this. I am absolutely desperate. This fellow is coming to get me in the morning. You've got to do something!!"

The most amazing thing happened. Morning came. The preacher picked me up. We went to a home and knocked on the door.

The door opened. Remember that big hulk of a fellow in Fort Lauderdale? He had moved to Atlanta. Well, not really. It was his bigger cousin, I think. As we went in, my mind quickly went over the latest news, sports, and weather. Then this preacher blew the whole morning.

"Well, Hank," he said proudly, "I brought this professional evangelist out here to talk to you about your soul." And he pointed to me!

I gulped hard a couple of times and glanced at the preacher, then at the Hulk. I looked up to the Lord, trying desperately to grasp for something. All of a sudden I remembered a text, "Do the thing you fear." (I think that's 2 Ecclesiastes 3:2.) So I jumped right in, feet first.

In no more than twenty minutes I had that big fella… furious. He was getting redder, and I was getting whiter by the minute. Suddenly, a flash of illumination came right out of Systematic Theology 302B. The man was evidently "non-elect." I felt better immediately.

Meanwhile, my pastor friend had come to a very different conclusion—that I was a "non-evangelist." In fifteen minutes, he had this man on his knees accepting Christ. That was very traumatic for a budding theolog. The "non-elect" got converted right before my eyes.

During those ten days of meetings, fifty-four people came

forward. On any given evening, I could have told you who would respond because I had seen the pastor lead them to Christ during that week.

That was an amazing experience to me. I said to the pastor, "This is absolutely incredible. I saw a murderer accept Christ. I saw an adulteress accept Christ. And all sorts of people in between. How in the world did you ever learn to do this?'

"It was in this very same evangelistic crusade last year," he told me. "We really had an evangelist. He took me out with him, and I learned from watching him. A year ago, I didn't know how."

Well, I learned from watching this fellow. But there was one question buzzing around my mind as I was flying home: *This works in Atlanta, the heart of the Bible belt, but will it work in Fort Lauderdale?*

I found out that it does; it works anywhere that it's tried—in the inner city and the outlying rural regions.

IN NO MORE THAN TWENTY MINUTES I HAD THAT BIG FELLA...FURIOUS.

It works in America and Canada and England and Africa and Hong Kong and Singapore and Australia. It works because "it" is nothing other than believers carrying the gospel of Jesus Christ to others, just as He said we should.

I started witnessing to people everywhere, and people responded. After about a year, I stopped and panted breathlessly, "You know, there's only a certain number of people I can reach." Then I had an idea! Why don't I teach others to do the same thing? That's where Evangelism Explosion really began.

I took an elderly man who had been a Christian about

sixty years with me. He had always wanted to lead someone to the Lord and never knew how. He went with me for months and months; I thought I would never get rid of him. Finally I put both feet in the small of his back and pushed him out of the nest. And he began to lead a lot of people to Christ.

Then there was another man I took out for a month or so. He went on vacation and called me the next week. He had led somebody to Christ. I prayed, "Lord, this is it. This is the way."

It wasn't until somebody took my hand and led me out that I began to overcome the blinding fear that silences so many people in the church. This is what Jesus did. He called the disciples that they should be "with Him."

Dear friends, the greatest privilege and responsibility you will ever know is to lead another person to Jesus Christ. And to equip the saints to do the work of ministry as Christ instructed us. You will find, as I did, that that is the greatest lesson you could ever learn.

C. Everett Koop

GOD'S SOVEREIGNTY REMAINS MY GREATEST COMFORT

A pediatric surgeon with an international reputation, Dr. C. Everett Koop served as Surgeon General of the United States from 1981 to 1989. In 1995 he received the Presidential Medal of Freedom, the nation's highest civilian award. Today he continues to educate the public about health issues through the C. Everett Koop Institute of Health and Science and as chairman of the National Safe Kids Campaign.

Dr. Koop's reputation as a brilliant surgeon and dedicated Christian came to my attention long before he became Surgeon General. His love for Christ and his faithful, courageous witness for Him have been an inspiration to me since we met many years ago.

In his account, Dr. Koop relates the lesson he learned

through the death of his son. His story will give you a sense of security in knowing God's perfect plan for your life.

As I enter my seventy-fifth year, it seems I have learned many lessons; to label one of them the greatest causes me to look back at many situations, events, and dilemmas.

I can say without hesitation that my greatest lesson has been learning that I have a sovereign God. He has taken me through many trials that I certainly wouldn't have chosen for myself. He has taught me again and again that He has a plan for my life, and He will take me through the roughest and most painful of times with the tenderness and support that only a heavenly Father can give His earthly child.

The most clearly etched lesson that I learned about having a sovereign God who makes no mistakes occurred some years ago when our wonderful twenty-year-old son, David, was taken from us in a sudden, totally unexpected incident.

David was a junior at Dartmouth College in New Hampshire. He was climbing the granite face of Cannon Mountain, just above the Old Man of the Mountain in Franconia Notch. A large slab he was scaling loosened and carried him off the face of the cliff with it. David was roped to a companion, and when he came to the end of his tether, he was many feet below. Jerked to a halt, he then fell inward like a swinging pendulum, smashing his body into the face of the cliff. His companion lowered him to a narrow ledge, quickly secured the rope, then rappelled down to him. David had disrupted his right knee and bled to death on that ledge despite valiant efforts on the part of his companion to revive him with artificial respiration. It was an injury that anyone could have kept from proving fatal had it occurred on the ground and a tourniquet been applied.

Word of David's fall reached the college hours later. And then on that memorable Sunday evening, the dean called me at home to relay the unbelievable news that David was dead. Our grief was bone-crushing.

We were fortunate to have two of our children living at home and the remaining son and his wife only a mile away. We didn't know where or how to begin to cope, so I drew my family close and prayed a prayer that only the Holy Spirit could have inspired, asking God to be very close and give us the support we so desperately needed. I thanked Him for taking David to be with Him and then closed by asking Him to let us see blessing come from a tragedy that hurt us beyond description.

> I ASKED GOD TO LET US SEE BLESSING COME FROM A TRAGEDY THAT HURT US BEYOND DESCRIPTION.

I don't know what we expected of that prayer—I certainly know it didn't come naturally from a heartbroken father—but we all sensed a peace from knowing a sovereign God was in charge.

When a child is taken, the reality of one's faith either sustains and comforts or, if not rooted in a loving God, falls apart. In the weeks and months and even years that followed, we saw God's hand at work in the aftermath of our loss.

Just the absence of bitterness in our children was remarkable. They developed a greater closeness to the remaining family which continues to this day. And each child was locked onto his or her own faith in a loving, sovereign God. What greater blessing could we ask?

One of the greatest spin-offs was our ability to put behind us the "what ifs" and "if onlys" concerning David's accident—the common quagmire that can hold parents and siblings in the continuing inability to recover.

As a pediatric surgeon, I gained a new depth of empathy and understanding when I had to deal with the parents of dying children. They knew I meant it when I said, "I know what you're going through."

Learning a lesson usually implies going through a difficult process—with emotions varying from mild anxiety to devastation depending on the experience. It is certainly true that we grow and mature spiritually through adversity—not when everything is going smoothly. This, in a sense, is true for Christian and non-Christian alike. But in a time of adversity or trouble, the Christian has the opportunity to know God in a special and personal way. Indeed, it necessitates acknowledging our own inability to cope. It is then that we learn we must rely completely on the grace and mercy of a loving God. And how wonderful to know that we have a Lord who knows the end from the beginning! A God who has fashioned our lives according to His perfect will! We sometimes seem to forget that important fact.

God's sovereignty remains my greatest comfort in all things, but the outworking of His perfect plan for me and my family at the time of David's death—our greatest distress—was surely my greatest lesson.

Tim LaHaye

THE DECISION THAT SAVED MY LIFE

Tim LaHaye is an author, minister, television and radio commentator, and speaker. As founder and president of Family Life Seminars, Tim is being used by God to strengthen families throughout the United States and Canada by teaching them biblical principles.

Tim and his wife, Beverly, who founded Concerned Women for America, are being uniquely used by God as few other people to help awaken the Christians of America to our God-given responsibilities in government, media, and education.

Co-author with Jerry Jenkins of the phenomenally popular Left Behind *series on Bible prophecy, Tim is one of the world's best-selling authors, with over ten million copies in print. His nearly three dozen books include* The Act of Marriage *and* Spirit-Controlled Temperament.

Here Tim describes his struggle to control a bad temper.

The result will thrill you and give you hope for facing your worst habits in the power of the Holy Spirit.

❧

Listening to Dr. Henry Brandt present his last message at a Gospel Light Sunday School Conference at beautiful Forest Home Christian Camp was a highly combustible choleric/sanguine minister. Typical of his temperament, he was a workaholic, pastoring a dynamically growing church that was one month away from dedicating a new church auditorium. He didn't have ulcers—he was just spitting blood!

Brandt hadn't been speaking more than four minutes when the young pastor became blazing mad. He assumed his wife had invited him to come to the conference so that the Christian psychologist could preach to him, "Do not grieve the Holy Spirit of God…Let all bitterness, wrath, anger, clamor, and evil speaking be put away from you… And be kind to one another, tenderhearted, forgiving one another, just as God in Christ also forgave you" (Ephesians 4:30–32, NKJ).

Dr. Brandt told the unforgettable story of another young minister in the midst of a building program who was bleeding inside with ulcers. Three specialists told the bleeding minister, "We cannot find one thing wrong with you—you need an analyst." Being a Bible-believing minister, he didn't want to go to a secular "shrink," so he called Dr. Brandt, "a Christian psychologist" whose office was five hundred miles away, and made three appointments. When Dr. Brandt asked him who he was mad at, he blew up because Dr. Brandt had suggested he was angry. The pastor listening to this story at the conference got the message; he was just a few weeks behind the ulcerated minister of the story.

For the first time, this dedicated, hard-working, Bible-teaching pastor realized something about himself. He was not a godly man! He had tried to be. He loved God; he loved to serve Him and had led many to Christ and the church. He worked hard at maintaining a morally pure mind. But now for the first time, he realized he was a sinful pastor—he often grieved the Holy Spirit with his temper.

His anger had affected his marriage. Only a loving, godly wife could have put up with him during those years and that at great sacrifice. The entire family was afraid of him.

But now for the first time, he saw his sin and how he had limited God's use of his life. And that is the first giant step toward victory over anger—face it as sin. Don't justify it; confess it! When Dr. Brandt finished his message, the young pastor, under deep personal conviction over his angry spirit, went out to the prayer chapel to pray. Finding it occupied, he lay face down under a pine tree and poured out his heart to God.

This was the first time he was consciously filled with the Holy Spirit. Guess how God characterized Himself to this man? Peace! Incredible Peace! At last the war within was over.

How long do you think it lasted? Two-and-a-half hours! Just until the mindless driver of a red sports car cut him off on the freeway and almost caused him to wreck his car. Instantly, he blazed with anger. Then he recognized he had lost the peace, so he confessed his sin again and was restored to peace.

The first day, he had to repeat that process almost a hundred times. The next day it was only ninety times. And after many years, such outbursts almost never occurred. In fact, he has actually been known to laugh when someone cuts him off in traffic—particularly if they are driving a little red sports car. Today, he is a different man. If you don't believe it, ask his wife. Instead of a lifetime of marital conflict, they have a near perfect relationship—thanks to the ministry of the Holy Spirit.

Anyone who knows the pastor will tell you he is a different person today. I can certainly testify to this, for you see, I am that man!

Anger is a subtle sin—particularly for men because it appeals to their "macho" complex. Most men think it is an expression of manhood. It is not! It is an expression of selfish pride, the root sin, and should have no place in the life of a Christian. I have found twenty-seven verses in the Bible that condemn it, verses like Psalm 37:8: "Cease from anger, and forsake wrath."

ANGER IS AN EXPRESSION OF SELFISH PRIDE, THE ROOT SIN.

You may respond, "But the Bible approves anger," or as some people tell me, "Jesus Himself was angry." Yes, there is a justifiable anger at sin, but it is defined by Paul in Ephesians 4:26 as an anger in which you do not sin. You don't permit it to exist beyond sundown, and even then, you watch yourself, or you will be vulnerable to temptation from the devil. We call this kind of anger "righteous indignation." The Savior was righteously indignant at the way the Jews were defaming the temple, so He drove them out. This was objective anger for something or someone other than Himself. Later when He was reviled and persecuted, He did not get angry. Instead

He responded, "Father, forgive them, for they know not what they do." That kind of indignation does not make you bleed inside; it never prompts you to explode in wrath. It is "righteous" indignation.

The anger the Bible condemns is the one most of us are confronted with every day—anger based on selfishness. Someone offends us or violates our rights, and we respond in selfish-induced anger—a sin that grieves the Holy Spirit and sets us up for spiritual defeat.

Discovering the fact that anger "grieves the Holy Spirit" and that it can be overcome was the greatest discovery of my life. Facing anger as sin and then confessing it whenever it raises its ugly head has changed my life.

Erwin W. Lutzer

PROVIDENTIAL PARKING PLACE

As the senior pastor of Moody Church in Chicago, Dr. Erwin W. Lutzer is one of God's chosen men to continue a great ministry begun by its founder Dwight L. Moody, one of the great Christian leaders of the centuries. Whenever I meet leaders associated with Moody, I am immediately impressed.

A former assistant professor of Bible and Theology at the Moody Bible Institute, Dr. Lutzer is the featured speaker on Moody Church's three radio broadcasts.

Dr. Lutzer is the author of numerous books, including Failure: The Back Door to Success; Managing Your Emotions; Putting Your Past Behind You; All One Body: Why Don't We Agree?; *and* Hitler's Cross, *a 1996 Gold Medallion Book Award winner.*

Through Dr. Lutzer's story you will see how God works in even the smallest details of our lives to accomplish His will.

On April 3, 1977, my wife, Rebecca, and I were without a home church. The previous week had been my last as pastor of Edgewater Baptist Church in Chicago. I had resigned to devote time to my graduate studies and teaching at Moody Bible Institute. Since I had come to know Dr. Warren Wiersbe, the pastor of Moody Memorial Church, my wife and I, along with our children, drove from our suburban home to attend the church's morning worship service for the first time.

When we arrived, there were no parking spaces, so I left my wife and children at the church while I parked the car. To my delight, I saw a man walk across the street to his car and drive away. Immediately, I backed into the space.

As agreed, my wife and I met in the lobby. We were surrounded by crowds preparing to enter the auditorium. As we were deciding which door to enter, Dr. Wiersbe walked past wearing his topcoat. When he brushed by, I put my hand on his shoulder. "Warren, what are you doing in the lobby? It's only ten minutes before the morning service!"

"Erwin Lutzer!" he exclaimed. "I'm sick and on my way home. Would you preach for me this morning?"

Dr. Wiersbe introduced me to his staff, and I quickly recalled an outline of a message I had preached recently. As I stood on the platform and looked over the large congregation, I said in my heart, "Lord, if they ever call me to be pastor here, I'll say yes!" though I didn't seriously think that would ever happen.

But happen it did.

The first piece in the puzzle took shape a few months

later when Pastor Wiersbe began asking me to speak whenever he was on vacation or took a missionary trip. I was grateful for the opportunity to further develop my preaching ministry.

When Pastor Wiersbe resigned in June 1978, a committee was formed to seek his replacement. Since I was quite young and content teaching at Moody Bible Institute, I was not immediately considered as a candidate. The elders did ask me, however, to be interim pastor, so I spoke on the Sundays when there was no candidate in the pulpit. The second piece of the puzzle had fallen into place.

Even though I knew there were many men in America more qualified, I had the growing feeling that God was grooming me for this responsibility. Week by week that conviction strengthened.

But Rebecca was absolutely convinced that God did not want me to become pastor of Moody Church. During our successful five-and-a-half-year ministry at Edgewater Baptist Church, I had often expressed to her how weary I was with the many details expected of a pastor. Furthermore, she felt we were too young and unqualified. And she knew I thoroughly enjoyed teaching at the Institute. My schedule allowed me to write during the summer and speak in various churches on weekends. This, Rebecca believed, was best suited for my gifts and temperament.

Despite this disagreement, our marriage continued to be harmonious and fulfilling. We agreed on almost everything and enjoyed the three precious children God had given us. Only the subject of Moody Church caused tension.

I respected Rebecca's assessment, but God had planted Moody Church in my heart. God had led us there; we simply had to accept it. I would tell Rebecca, "Someday, I will be the pastor of Moody Church; it is as certain as the conclusion of a geometric theorem!"

Of course, I expected her to get used to the idea. But as the months progressed, she remained firm in her conviction. I had no idea how deeply she felt until I came home one evening to find her sitting on the couch, her right hand pressed against her bowed head. I assumed she had a migraine headache. But she kept repeating, "I can't believe it, I can't believe it. I thought I *knew* you!"

Suddenly I realized this was not simply a minor difference of opinion; it had become an unresolvable issue that threatened the unity of our marriage. I could not convince her that God was leading in this direction. When I reminded her of how He had providentially provided a parking space on our first visit to Moody Church, she dismissed it as a coincidence.

"God," she said, "wanted you to speak that Sunday and provide occasional pulpit supply, nothing more."

One day, the whole matter came into sharp focus. I faced an excruciating contradiction. On one hand, God's call to Moody Church was absolutely certain; indeed this was verified by the response of the leadership and the congregation at large. The pulpit committee had concluded that I was God's choice for the position.

On the other hand, I couldn't serve as long as Rebecca opposed my acceptance of this call. I walked over to the window, stared outside, and spoke audibly to God. "Lord, I know I have been called to Moody Church; I also know that I cannot accept as long as Rebecca is opposed." And in my anguish I added, "I have never knowingly disobeyed You before, but am I going to have to this time?"

That was one of the darkest days of our marriage. But

God began to use this conflict to teach us an important lesson about His providential guidance and faithfulness. I tried to understand why Rebecca, who loved the Lord so deeply, felt that Moody Church and its ministries were so formidable. As the days passed, God began to change her heart. By the time the committee extended a formal call for me to become the pastor, Rebecca had decided to trust my judgment and the Lord's leading through the congregation. But there was one more step in the process.

Though I began my duties on January 1, 1980, the installation service was on January 20. It was the most beautiful winter day in Chicago. The temperature was 42 degrees; the sun shone brightly. Even the sunshine seemed a further confirmation of God's leading. That evening I wrote these words in my diary:

> This day marks a highlight in my life. Dr. Walvoord and Dr. Sweeting each gave a good word. Even the weather was beautiful; the temperature is in the 40s with not one flake of snow on the ground. Lord, I am yours for whatever you desire! Grant me grace to minister with blessing!

In March of that year, Rebecca was asked to speak to a women's conference in Toronto. As she prepared, God healed her heart, dissipating the doubt and confusion by showing her that she could be free from the frustration she felt about my decision. She felt a sense of release and fulfillment as she shared about her own struggles and how God would help her be the pastor's wife she wanted to be.

Since then, she has been content with that decision. The reason I can serve with freedom and joy is because Rebecca stands at my side with her love and prayers.

Together we have learned that *God's providential guid-*

ance extends to all the details of our lives, even to a parking space! If we had not decided to come to Moody that Sunday back in 1977; if that man had not pulled out on LaSalle Street at exactly the right moment; if I had been standing somewhere else in the church lobby—if any one of these "ifs" had not happened, I would not be the pastor of Moody Church today. God gave me great liberty as I preached that morning, and He set the chain of events in motion that led to my call.

A corollary to the lesson of His providential guidance is that *when He calls, He enables.* God does not leave us without the resources to do His will. No matter how difficult obedience is, in the end, He will cause us to prevail.

Throughout the years, whenever I've been discouraged or faced inevitable disappointments in the ministry, I point to God's providential care as a reminder that the One who called me will be with me, no matter what. Frequently, I have had a great sense of release when I remind myself that the decision to become the senior pastor of Moody Church was His, not mine!

THE ONE WHO CALLED ME WILL BE WITH ME, NO MATTER WHAT.

Though God gives His enabling each day, some examples stand out in my memory. On January 15, 1986, an arsonist broke into the church and set the organ, piano, and pulpit furniture on fire, causing extensive damage. But the cleaning and refurbishing projects were so successful that it was hard to regret what had happened. Today our auditorium, instruments, and equipment are better than ever. What is more, God used this event to unify the congregation and renew our sense of mission.

On April 20, 1990, the press criticized Moody Church because of a temporary decision regarding a child with AIDS in our Sunday school. Though I woke up that morning unable to get out of bed because of severe dizziness, through prayer I was raised up to clarify the matter at a press conference at 2 o'clock that afternoon.

In these and a hundred other instances, I have learned that the God who chose a parking place for me is the God who chooses the challenges that come each day. "Faithful is He who calls you, and He also will bring it to pass" (1 Thessalonians 5:24, NASB).

Bailey Marks

LEARNING ABOUT FAITH FROM A HOSPITAL BED

Dr. Bailey Marks was president of a prestigious, success-
ful business when God led him and his wife, Elizabeth, to
join the staff of Campus Crusade for Christ in 1967. He
now serves as the international vice president of our minis-
try, and it gives me tremendous joy and delight to work side
by side with him in helping take the "most joyful news ever
announced" to the ends of the earth.

In 1985 Bailey gave leadership to Explo '85, the world's
largest satellite conference on evangelism and discipleship in
history. Through eighteen satellites, every square inch of the
earth was covered. More than 250,000 delegates from 164
countries participated in a week of training in discipleship
and evangelism. Few men have been so mightily used by
God to help reach so many millions for Christ as Bailey.

You will be inspired to hear how God used a serious illness to help Bailey learn to trust Him for the impossible—and how he applied this lesson to plan a worldwide conference that others thought could not be done.

"Look at all the things I gave up to serve you…and the way You treat me in return!"

These bitter thoughts tugged angrily at my heart as I lay on my hospital bed in San Bernardino, California. It was January 1969. As director of Asia and the South Pacific for Campus Crusade for Christ, I had recently returned from an extensive two-month trip into the area of my assignment. When I returned home just before Christmas, I felt very ill. Little did I know that I was dying a little bit each day; my liver was hardening and closing down.

Three years earlier my wife, Elizabeth, and I had left a lucrative position in business to take a more active part in helping to fulfill the Great Commission with Campus Crusade for Christ—a lot of responsibility for a relatively young Christian. Shortly after Elizabeth and I agreed that God wanted us to accept this opportunity, I became ill.

The doctors could not diagnose my problem, so I stayed in a hospital bed for a month, two-and-a-half weeks of that in isolation. Everyone I saw was suited in full surgical attire, including Elizabeth who was allowed to visit only thirty minutes each day.

As I lay in that bed, I acted spiritual. Day after day people would call me and close their conversations by saying how much of a blessing I was to them. But one day I could no longer keep up the facade.

Putting down the receiver, I began to cry. Lonely, fearful, and lying on that hospital bed far from my new field of service for my Lord—and dying—I couldn't understand why He had let me down. I felt like a fraud and a hypocrite for offering words of encouragement and blessing to others when inside I was angry and bitter at God. What I did not realize, of course, was that I was right where He wanted me, and I was about to learn one of the greatest lessons of my life.

I wanted to be a man of faith. I had not left my business to play games; I wanted to make an impact for God. Yet I had been play-acting with Him. Now that God had my attention, I began to ponder the whole matter of faith in the life of a believer.

I began to ask myself, "What is faith?" I recalled Hebrews 11:1: "Now faith is the assurance of things hoped for, the conviction of things not seen" (NASB). In other words, faith is confidence in God's holy Word and in His faithfulness.

Faith is not accidental, nor does it happen by osmosis. I must mentally decide that I am going to place my trust in God for something that I feel He desires me to do and even for my life. The decision is always mine, requiring an act of the will.

The synonym for faith is belief—to trust in something or someone to the extent that you know they will do what they say they will do. The antonym is unbelief. Somehow I thought that while faith required an action on my part, belief was passive and did not. So what about unbelief? It required, in my opinion, even less action. This was not correct.

Then while reading *God Unlimited* by Norman Grubb, I

saw a word I had never noticed before—"unfaith." I began to realize that, if faith required an act of my will, then "unfaith" did also. So, in reality, I had decided that I was not going to believe God for my situation.

Finally I understood that every aspect of my life—faith or unfaith, belief or unbelief—requires a mental decision on my part. The question is: Am I willing to place my confidence in God? Sometimes, I must admit, subconsciously I am not willing. Then I face a struggle that results in restlessness or lack of peace.

I WAS WILLING TO BE SICK AND FRAIL IF THAT WAS HIS WILL.

To exercise faith, however, I must come to grips with reality. First, I must get honest with myself and God and recognize my lack of faith for the situation I am facing. Second, I must say, "Lord, I am willing to believe You and Your promises."

That day in the hospital, I told the Lord that I knew He cared for me and knew what was best for me and that I was willing to be sick and frail if that was His will.

The moment I began to be honest with myself and with God, things started to happen. My spiritual condition changed immediately, and my physical condition also began to improve. The doctors finally performed surgery and corrected the situation. Rather than taking six months to a year to get back on my feet as the doctors had expected, I was traveling within three months. In less than a year, Elizabeth and I moved our family to the Orient. And I have lived the last twenty-plus years quite successfully with a crippled liver and dietary supplements.

But the illness is not what is important. It is merely what

God allowed me to go through so He could teach me one of the most important lessons I have ever learned: that faith takes an act of the will.

Since then, I cannot estimate the number of times I have had to apply this lesson. Subconsciously, it must be many times a day. And I have consciously had to work myself through countless difficult and faith-stretching situations— always with great blessing.

Over the next thirteen years, I saw God do many marvelous things, one of which was to see our full-time staff grow from 90 in nine countries to more than 2,700 in forty-four countries. I believe that and much more happened because I had decided to make active faith predominant in my life.

In 1983, after returning to the United States for two years, I took up my present position as executive vice president of our International Ministries. About that time, I was challenged by Bill Bright to plan for a worldwide training conference of about 30,000 students. Immediately, we realized that the cost was prohibitive.

But a worldwide conference could help accelerate our ministry throughout the world, so I continued to ask God for His direction. When it came, I was not prepared. In a rather unusual way, the Lord gave me the vision for a worldwide satellite conference that would take training to hundreds of thousands of conferees in many places around the world, rather than bring the 30,000 to one location.

To do something of this magnitude involved sophisticated technology that was totally foreign to me. Not only was I responsible for the conference and all the satellite aspects, but for the fund-raising as well. I felt apprehensive, frightened, and concerned about my personal reputation should the project fail. As a man of faith, I had been required to believe God for a lot of big things, but this was *really* big.

I could not say no to this challenge since that would have been "unfaith" to me. I had to get honest with myself and say to the Lord, "Help! I'm frightened and filled with doubts." I told Him I believed this was in accordance with His will and that I would exercise faith rather than unfaith.

Explo '85 became a reality in December 1985. More than 250,000 students and lay people—instead of the expected 30,000—attended in ninety-three locations around the world at a fraction of the original estimated cost! Each day, all were linked simultaneously by satellite. Miracle after miracle took place as God blessed in the lives of the conferees.

The benefits we experienced and continue to see in Campus Crusade are numerous. But the point is that I exercised my will to believe God in faith.

Trusting God in difficult situations is still not easy for me. But my prayer is that I will always be a strong, courageous, bold man—acting on my will to believe Him for the impossible.

Josh McDowell

LEARNING SERVANTHOOD THE-HARD WAY

As a member of the Campus Crusade for Christ family for more than thirty-five years, Josh McDowell is one of the most articulate and popular youth speakers today. He has endeared himself to me and to thousands of our staff and millions of students and laymen. He truly is one of God's anointed men for our times.

Josh has an ongoing television series and weekly radio program, and is the author or coauthor of fifty-two books. Two of his books, Evidence That Demands a Verdict *and* More Than a Carpenter, *have become modern classics in defending the Christian faith.*

His Why Wait? *campaign has been used by God to reach thousands of youth who want biblical answers to sexual questions.*

In his story, Josh shares how he grappled with resentment in learning the meaning of servanthood. Each of us can identify with the painful lessons he learned. You will enjoy reading about how he finally came to accept the role of a servant.

I felt so unappreciated. Once again I was put in charge of food at a student conference for a day of witnessing. Have you ever made 1,000 peanut butter and jelly sandwiches? The more I made, the madder I got. Out of frustration I stuck the *Four Spiritual Laws* booklet inside a number of sandwiches between the peanut butter and jelly.

I wanted to be used by God. It was my dream to be a traveling speaker. How I wanted to teach His Word!

I was a graduate of Talbot Theological Seminary, had been on staff with Campus Crusade for four years, and yet had not given a talk or taught a seminar at a conference. All I had ever done was administrate and take care of the book table. When the staff took students to the beach to witness, I was put in charge of transportation—and making all the sandwiches.

No one seemed to realize who I was—a seminary graduate and a speaker. They didn't understand what they had, so I thought. A sense of resentment developed in me toward Campus Crusade.

Then, suddenly, my hour of glory came. I got a call from Ted Martin of Campus Crusade's Institute of Biblical Studies to teach at the IBS meetings later that year! I couldn't believe it! I had gone from nothing to everything all at once.

I prepared thoroughly for almost six months. I planned

to teach a series from the Book of Romans and, when it was nearly time for the IBS meetings, had a wealth of notes and materials. I was looking forward to this teaching opportunity.

A week before IBS, I got a phone call from Bill Bright in California. "This is a special year for us at staff training at Arrowhead Springs," he said. "It's our international year, and we'll be having the largest number of staff ever. Josh…the administration at our hotel has fallen apart. I need you to help me. Please make arrangements right away. I'd like you to be back here in three days to take charge of the summer staff."

There was a pause on my end of the line. I had been looking forward to teaching at IBS. *What an abominable sense of timing,* I thought. *I don't want to go!*

"Josh, I need you," Bill Bright repeated.

"Okay…I'll be there."

Angrily, I threw my clothes and books together and packed them into the car. I fumed all the way to California, and my attitude hadn't improved when I arrived.

NO ONE SEEMED TO REALIZE WHO I WAS—A SEMINARY GRADUATE AND A SPEAKER.

My assignment was to supervise the thirty staff people and organize the facilities for the nearly 1,700 people from all parts of the world. I stayed up all night the first few days putting together procedures and organization, trying to establish a basic administrative plan to handle the logistics of the hundreds of internationals expected.

But my inexperienced staff of thirty was no match for 1,700 incoming people—many of whom had trouble with English. Some had customs regarding meals and housing that were at odds with the best laid plans. To make matters worse, the hotel's equipment broke down periodically—never when it was convenient and always when it caused even further disruption.

Finally, the proverbial straw: a terrible case of dysentery broke out. The sickness spread in a matter of two or three days to just about everyone. There were lines at every rest room, which were overworked to the point of breakdown as well.

I found myself—with bucket, mop, and toilet plunger in hand—making the rounds of the rest rooms. The rest of the staff were either sick or tied up with the needs of preparing meals and other chores.

I was sick, too, but had no time to think about it. Every toilet in the hotel and in the other buildings had to be scrubbed twice a day. I worked twenty to twenty-two hours a day, able to catch only catnaps of two or three hours a night.

Somehow it all got done. But I had not been able to attend a single meeting to hear any of the world-famous speakers brought in for the occasion. I did meet one of them, however.

One day after I had just finished with the toilets on the second floor and had filled my bucket with fresh water, I picked up a plunger and started down the stairs to the lobby. I ran into Bill Bright escorting Billy Graham on a tour of the facilities. "Oh, Dr. Graham," he paused, waving to me, "I'd like you to meet a member of our Canadian staff, Josh McDowell."

The tall evangelist smiled graciously and stuck out his hand. This was my dream come true, and I wasn't going to miss the opportunity to at least shake his hand.

I awkwardly stuck the plunger under my arm, took the

bucket in my left hand, wiped my right hand on my shirt, and sheepishly shook hands with Billy Graham.

As they walked away, Bill Bright remarked, "You know, our staff people are devoted. They're willing to do anything."

I wanted to shout after them, "I'm not willing!"

The next afternoon, I finally finished vacuuming the brand new red carpet in the lobby, which was my last chore before I could go to hear Dr. Graham speak. At long last I'd be able to participate in one of the meetings that had been so encouraging for others.

Then Bill Bright rushed up to me. "Come here—quickly!" He pointed to the cleaned carpet. Footprints were visible across the length of the lobby. The parking lot had just been tarred, and someone had obviously tracked in the thick, tacky tar. "Get something—some cleaner, some rags. Hurry and clean it up before it sets."

It took all afternoon and most of the night to clean up the tar. The more cleaning solvent I rubbed into each spot, the bigger it got. That in turn called for more scrubbing— hard scrubbing.

A staff person came by just as I was finishing and teased me. "Scrub harder, slave! I still see some spots."

He was joking, but I was obviously in no mood for humor. I was ready to throw in the towel—literally. Angrily, I stood, all set to heave the solvent can at the front desk and scream out my resignation. Somehow the urge was checked.

Sudden conviction came over me. No one was really out to get me. I had brought an attitude of bitterness with me from Canada.

I recalled the Scriptures I had read in devotions that morning describing how Jesus washed the feet of the disciples. The thought pierced me: *If Jesus can wash the disciples' feet, why can't I scrub the staff's floors and clean their toilets?* It was an immediate lesson in submission.

That night I prayed for grace to be a true servant for Christ. I realized that before I could ever become a leader, I needed to learn how to be a follower. And the next day, I began a new pattern of service. I went out of my way to find things that needed doing; I worked harder and later than anyone else. It was something I wanted to do as a service to Christ to make up for getting off on the wrong foot. For the next several weeks, I fervently scrubbed and cleaned.

GOD HONORS THE SERVANT AND PROMOTES THE ONE WHO DEFERS TO OTHERS.

This willing spirit was not lost to others. Bill Bright said sympathetically, "God can teach us many things in a servant's role. When we first started, there were so many valuable things I learned by washing dishes, planting flowers, mowing the lawns—and yes," he laughed, "even scrubbing latrines."

It was difficult to continue the backbreaking responsibility of the six-week international staff training. Because of the work, sleeplessness, and sickness, I lost more than twenty pounds.

I also found it difficult to measure the progress in my quest for submission and the attitude of a servant.

My first question was, *What can a person learn through servanthood?* Was Bill Bright merely trying to sound spiritual by indicating that God teaches through submission?

Second, I wondered, *Sure, the Lord said, "The greatest shall be the least," but wouldn't it be better to use your abilities for God in an aggressive, leadership capacity?* I thought the church lacked capable leaders and wondered if it was right to constantly put myself in the subservient role.

But everything I heard from Christian leaders, plus what I read about the subject in the Bible, all pointed to that earlier conviction—that God honors the servant and promotes the one who defers to others.

Not one easily learned, it is a lesson to consider again and again.

Patrick M. Morley

THE GOD WE WANT-VERSUS THE-GOD WHO IS

Pat Morley endeared himself to me many years ago when I spoke at a Thanksgiving Prayer Breakfast in Orlando, Florida, an annual event for which he served as chairman. He is an outstanding community leader who conducts a weekly Bible study with 150 key executives.

Pat founded Morley Properties Inc., which grew to be one of Florida's one hundred largest privately held companies. During this time, he was president or managing partner of 59 companies and partnerships.

He has written eight books, including the best-selling The Man in the Mirror, *which received the 1990 Gold Medallion Achievement Award in the Christian Living category.*

I am particularly impressed with Pat's desire to seek first the kingdom of God. In 1991, Pat sold his business and founded Man in the Mirror, a ministry to men.

Pat truly loves Christ. It has been my privilege to see him operate as a keen, astute businessman as a former member of the board of directors of Campus Crusade for Christ.

In reading his story, you will learn how he tried to fit the Bible into his own plans and discovered the disastrous results of being a cultural Christian instead of a biblical believer.

The silent hush of the pre-dawn darkness filled our home as I tiptoed through the house. Taking my seat at the kitchen table, I began to read the new Bible my wife had given me as a gift. I treasured those moments sitting quietly alone— reading, thinking, studying, meditating.

Soon I began to underline the passages that particularly registered with me, the ones that seemed to favor the direction in which I was maneuvering my life. When such a morsel of Scripture was found, I memorized it.

At the same time, when I spotted a passage of Scripture that ran counter to my plans, I would pull out a large mental eraser and figuratively smudge that verse right off the page.

One morning I discovered an especially troubling text: "Do not be a man who strikes hands in pledge or puts up security for debts; if you lack the means to pay, your very bed will be snatched from under you" (Proverbs 22:26,27, NIV).

This was not the truth I was looking for. In fact, to follow this principle would stop all of my plans dead in their tracks. I was building a real estate business, and everyone knows you can't do that without mortgage debt. That required personal liability—meaning that *all* of my assets were pledged to repay the debt, not just the asset against which the money was borrowed.

I tried everything to dilute the meaning of that verse. *Well, it's not a command,* I decided, *only a principle...It doesn't say I "will" have my bed snatched; it only says so if I can't pay. I'm smarter than the average Joe...I will be able to pay. This applies to another time and place. Our laws don't permit losing everything—"my very bed." The risks are different today.*

Oh, how I wished I had never seen that verse! It tortured my mind. God had spoken directly to me, but the best real estate deals all seemed to require personal liability. Then one day, when my resistance was low, I crossed the line and struck my hand in pledge. After that I signed regularly.

The whole problem, of course, was that my approach was man-centered, not God-centered. Instead of earnestly seeking God's agenda, I was zealously trying to help God discover my agenda.

Looking back, I see how easily I had slid into this position...

When I became a Christian, I sincerely did receive Christ as my Savior and Lord. Yet, in many ways, I just "added" Him to my life as another interest in an already busy and otherwise overcrowded schedule. I confess that many times I was more interested in the *benefits* of Jesus than in Jesus.

Slowly, I began to realize that there was not a one-to-one correlation between my *beliefs* and my *behavior.* I seemed to be Christian in spirit, but often secular in practice. Don't misunderstand—I was sincerely striving to be a moral, honest person. Oswald Chambers captured the crux of my problem when he wrote: "The majority of people have their morality well within their own grasp, they have no sense of the need of the gospel." Yet I had this lingering feeling that something wasn't quite right about my life. I was trying to have my cake and eat it too. I was living by a Christian life view part of the time, but I often formed plans, set priorities, solved problems, and made decisions in ways that reflected secular thinking.

In other words, I *syncretized* my life. I *added* Christian values and beliefs, but didn't *subtract* secular thinking. The result? Both Christian and secular ideas competed for control of the way I made decisions.

MANY TIMES I WAS MORE INTERESTED IN THE BENEFITS OF JESUS THAN IN JESUS.

To put it another way—I became a *cultural Christian*. I pursued the God I wanted, but did not really know the God who is. I wanted Him to be a gentle grandfather who would spoil me and let me have my own way. I found myself following the God I was underlining in my Bible. In short, I created a fifth gospel: Matthew, Mark, Luke, John, and Patrick.

Frankly, I did not intentionally or consciously set out to edit the Bible into my own version. Nevertheless, subtly, over time, through self-deceit and compromise, I "shoehorned" the Word of God (like the Proverbs passage on striking hands in pledge) into my plans.

My entire life was built around the principle of *plan, then pray.* In other words, I knew where I was going and worked diligently to push my plans through to gain the necessary approvals from "headquarters."

I ignored the biblical command of Jesus that says, "If anyone would come after Me, he must deny himself and take up his cross and follow Me" (Matthew 16:24, NIV). Instead, I denied myself little.

One day it occurred to me that there simply wasn't much difference between my lifestyle and the lifestyles of those who made no claim of having Christ in their lives. I began to despise my life. Instead of offering hope to a broken, hurting world, I was devoting my energies to my own plans—ones devised to let me stand at center stage for a few brief moments.

I longed to change my life—to be salt and light. But a caldron of selfish ambitions bubbled, seethed, and boiled within me. Like a tug-of-war, they pulled me in the other direction. For several years I wrestled daily with the compromises that had infiltrated my life.

Then one day the big idea finally struck me: There is a God we want, and there is a God who is—but they are not the same God. Nothing we think, say, or do can make God into someone He is not. God is who He is, and He is unchanging as He proclaims: "I the Lord do not change" (Malachi 3:6, NIV).

One morning in early 1986, the truth finally connected with my brain: "The world and its desires pass away, but the man who does the will of God lives forever" (1 John 2:17, NIV). So, after two-and-a-half years of struggling to understand what had happened to me, I surrendered. On the title page of my Bible I wrote, "I want to spend the rest of my earthly life for the will of God." It was my turning point.

The lesson I learned is profoundly simple: When we stop seeking the God we want, we can start seeking the God who is. Jeremiah explains, "'You will seek Me and find Me when you seek Me with all your heart. I will be found by you,' declares the LORD" (Jeremiah 29:13,14, NIV).

This turning point was the active choice to stop being a cultural Christian and to become a biblical Christian. And this commitment includes the decision to approach the Scriptures objectively, instead of looking for evidence to support the choices already made. It is the decision to *pray, then plan.* And it is the greatest lesson I have ever learned.

Lloyd J. Ogilvie

THE SECRET OF TRUE POWER

Dr. Lloyd J. Ogilvie has been Chaplain of the U.S. Senate since 1996. For over twenty years he was pastor of the historic First Presbyterian Church in Hollywood, California, where I received Jesus Christ as my Savior and Lord more than fifty-five years ago. He also hosted the nationally syndicated radio and television ministry "Let God Love You."

Dr. Ogilvie is the author of over forty books, including the daily devotional Silent Strength and Making Stress Work For You, winner of a Gold Medallion Book Award. He also served as general editor of several books of the thirty-two-volume Communicator's Commentary.

Dr. Ogilvie is in great demand as a speaker for conventions, conferences, and renewal retreats for clergy and laity. He is truly one of God's anointed, Spirit-filled servants, who always ministers to my heart whenever I hear him speak.

Here Dr. Ogilvie describes how he caught a vision of what a Christian is meant to be. This secret led him to a new boldness and joy and changed his ministry dramatically.

It was the last day of the prolonged, solitary retreat I had taken on a lonely beach during the summer after my first year as a Presbyterian pastor. I took a stick and wrote in the firm sand all of my needs, yearnings, and failures. Then I scratched out a list of the sad results of a powerless life and ministry. Though it was many years ago, I can remember that time as if it happened today...

I'd been a Christian for eight years. With seminary and post-graduate studies completed, I began my ordained ministry. My preaching was biblically sound and Christ-centered, and I taught good orthodox reformed theology. As a man "in Christ," I knew I was a recipient of salvation through the gift of His death and resurrection. I knew I was forgiven, that death had no power over me, and that I was alive forever. I tried to follow Christ to the best of my ability. Yet, I still had a problem.

Few lives were moved or changed as a result of my ministry. Something was wrong; something was lacking. Depending on human energy, talents, and personality, I had no power for a supernatural ministry. Popularity and outward success did not satisfy my gnawing, inner spiritual hunger—a real need and longing for authentic power. As a result, I became exhausted and frustrated.

This led me to my solitary retreat. I was alone with Christ, and He guided me to spend time studying the Gospel of John, chapters 14–16, along with Paul's letter to the Colossians.

Again and again, I stumbled over the Lord's words, "Apart from Me you can do nothing" (John 15:5, NIV). The words contradicted my aggressive, self-assertive addiction to human power. Repeatedly, I read Christ's promise that He would make His home in me, and I longed to experience His presence. Then I read these words in Colossians, "Christ in you, the hope of glory" (Colossians 1:27, NIV). They sounded like the blast of a trumpet.

"That's it!" I exclaimed. Suddenly, I had caught a vision of what a Christian is meant to be—the resurrection home of the risen Christ.

During those days, the secret of true power became real to me. The pre-existent, reigning, all-powerful Christ is also the indwelling Lord. The glory promised was a manifestation of Christ in me, a character transplant so that I could be like Him in attitude, action, and reaction. A liberating conviction captured my mind: *Christianity is not only life as Christ lived it; it is more than my life in Him; it is Christ living in me!*

I had read those Scriptures before. How had I missed the experience of these promises? The Lord wanted a surrender of all there was of me—mind, soul, will, and body—to Him. It took the crisis of powerlessness to make me ready to receive what was offered all along.

I got on my knees and asked Christ to indwell my total life. I prayed, "Lord, I've missed the secret. I've been ministering *for* You and have not allowed *You* to work *through me.* Come live Your life in me. I am empty and need to be filled. Love through me; care through me; preach through me; lead through me. All that I am or ever hope to be, I yield to You."

Christ's presence flooded my entire being, from the top of my head to the soles of my feet. I felt loved, forgiven, empowered. I don't know how long I was on my knees, but it must have been a long time because when I got up the tide had come in and washed away all I had written in the sand.

I returned home a different person, set free from my compulsive efforts to try to earn my status with the Lord. The experience replenished the parched places of my soul that had kept my Christian life a constant dry spell. The indwelling Christ gave me all that I had previously worked so hard to achieve, studied to understand, struggled to accomplish. Now I was free to love without restraint and felt a new boldness, an exuberant joyousness I couldn't contain.

One of the greatest changes was in my preaching. Instead of depending on human talent, rhetoric, and scholarship alone, I experienced wisdom beyond my understanding, knowledge beyond my learning, and discernment beyond my insight. I was amazed. Only Christ could have given me these gifts, and I give Him all the glory.

I began to preach each sermon as if never to preach again. The secret of true power that had been missing in my life and message, the power of the indwelling Christ, became the thrust of my preaching. My new theme was that nothing can happen *through* us until it happens *to* us. And there is no limit to what Christ will do in us if we yield our lives as a laboratory in which we discover what He wants to share with others through us.

But don't misread my enthusiasm for what happened so many years ago. It has had to be renewed every day, especially in each new challenge or difficulty. I have known my share of suffering and pain, disappointments and problems. And I've been called to attempt some humanly impossible tasks. Looking back, I can't imagine living through it all without the power of the indwelling Christ.

Over the years, the resiliency of His presence has given me a tireless expectancy. I've discovered that guidance is not something I must beg to receive, but something Christ signals within my mind and spirit. My task is only to pray for openness to let Him through, and then to marvel at what He says and does. Then each person I meet or work with gives me a fresh opportunity to let go and allow Christ to speak or love through me.

WE ARE MEANT

TO BE RIVERBEDS

FOR THE FLOW

OF HIS SPIRIT,

NOT-RESERVOIRS.

What a relief it is to no longer feel that I have to find answers and solve problems on my own! Christ is at work in me. I know that as surely as I feel my heart beat and my lungs breathe. Problems and difficulties are really gifts for new levels of depth in experiencing the limitless adequacy of what Christ can do.

And I know something else. We are meant to be riverbeds for the flow of His Spirit, not reservoirs. Christ's indwelling power is for servanthood, not for private, esoteric piety. When Christ takes up residency in us, He leads us into situations and to people who need Him most. And the more we serve, the more power He releases.

When I was asked to share my most beneficial lesson, my mind was flooded by magnificent things I've discovered in the trials and triumphs through the years. At first, it was difficult to select one that was the most beneficial. And then it hit me—all the experiences of growth through the years were but diminutive repetitions of the ultimate discovery there on the lonely beach where I was not alone. And each one brought me back to a renewal of the secret of the abundant life I experienced—that Christ in your heart is your only hope of glory.

Luis Palau

ANY OLD BUSH WILL DO

Luis Palau is one of the great evangelists of our time. During almost thirty-five years of ministry, he has spoken in person to more than thirteen million people in almost seventy nations and to millions more through his radio and television broadcasts.

Luis began his evangelistic career at the age of eighteen, preaching on weekends while he worked at an Argentine bank. Within a few years, he and several other young men organized a tent evangelism and radio ministry in Argentina.

Since that time, his ministry has continued to flourish. God has used him to bring multitudes to Jesus Christ in Central and South America, North America, Europe, the South Pacific, Asia, Africa, and the Soviet Union. Convinced of his love for our Lord and demonstrated integrity, I consider it a special delight, along with members of our staff, to cooperate with him in his various crusades.

In his account, Luis shows how he learned to depend on Christ alone. His story begins in his late teenage years with his search for a holy life.

Whenever a great preacher came to our church in Argentina, some of my friends and I would try to get an interview with him. Our questions were always the same. "How can we get victory over temptation? How can we live holy lives?"

Usually the visiting preacher would ask, "Are you reading the Bible?"

"Yes, we get up at five every morning before going to school or work. We read several chapters every day."

"Great! But are you testifying for Jesus?"

"Yes. We hand out tracts, teach children's classes, and even hold street meetings."

"That's terrific! But are you praying?" the preacher would ask. So we'd tell him about our all-night prayer meetings.

Our frustration must have been obvious. "What else do we need to do?" we'd ask.

"Well, pray some more, witness some more, read the Bible some more." So we did. And we just about killed ourselves, we were so eager to be holy.

I was on the verge of giving up, not because I saw a lack in God, but because I was weary of fighting and struggling and seeking on my own to persevere through sheer dedication.

When am I ever going to catch on? I wondered. *Will I give up now, after all I've been through?* I wanted to please and love and serve God. I wanted people to be saved. I would sing, "Oh, Jesus, I have promised to serve Thee to the end," and I would think, *even if it kills me.*

One day I was invited to view a brief film of Billy Graham speaking to Christian leaders in India. Although he spoke before an unbelievable crowd of tens of thousands, he seemed to be staring right into my eyes as he quoted Ephesians 5:18: "Do not get drunk on wine, which leads to debauchery. Instead, be filled with the Spirit" (NIV). It was as if the crowd in India didn't exist. He was looking right at me and shouting, "Are you filled with the Spirit?"

I knew that was my problem—I wasn't filled with the Holy Spirit. That was the reason for my up-and-down Christianity. That's why I had zeal and commitment, but little fruit or victory. When would it end? When would I find the answer?

I found it in the United States after several frustrating months of Bible school.

I came to the States through the patient prodding of Ray Stedman, pastor of Peninsula Bible Church in Palo Alto, California. The first two months, I lived in his home. I was argumentative and wanted to discuss theology and doctrine for hours. I had come to learn, but maybe I wasn't yet ready to admit that I didn't have all the answers.

After two months with the Stedmans, I went to Multnomah School of the Bible in Portland, Oregon. Multnomah is a demanding school and I found the first semester particularly rough.

Our Spiritual Life class professor, Dr. George Kehoe, only added to my frustration when he began *every* class period by quoting Galatians 2:20: "I have been crucified with Christ and I no longer live, but Christ lives in me. The life

I live in the body, I live by faith in the Son of God, who loved me and gave Himself for me" (NIV).

I was still frustrated with not being able to live the lifestyle I saw in men like Ray Stedman and several others at Peninsula Bible Church and at Multnomah. Their lives exhibited a joy and freedom that I found attractive. But the more I sought it, the more elusive it seemed.

My spiritual journey seemed like a climb up a tall cliff. I clawed every inch of the way only to slip and slide back down. Although I had experienced times of blessing and victory, for the most part I felt the struggle was impossible. I couldn't go on that way, especially when no one else knew about it. It was my secret, private death.

I felt like a hypocrite. If I were to describe myself in those days, I would have to say I was envious, jealous, too preoccupied and self-centered, and ambitious to a wrong degree. I was smug about other speakers, silently rating their illustrations or delivery against my own. That left me feeling mean and ugly and petty. No amount of wrestling with myself would rid me of those sins. And yet I tried. I felt despicable; I hated the idea that I was a hypocrite.

Maybe that's why I didn't like the constant reminder of Galatians 2:20 and was getting annoyed at Dr. Kehoe's quoting that verse every day. *It can't be a Bible verse that gets you so upset,* I told myself. *It must be you.* Rather than let that verse penetrate my pride, I decided that the verse was self-contradictory, hard to understand, and confusing, especially in English.

Shortly before Christmas break, Major Ian Thomas, founder and director of Torchbearers, the group that runs Capernwray Bible School in England, spoke at our chapel service. I usually sat in the back of the auditorium and dared the speaker to make me pay attention. If he was good, I'd honor him by listening. Otherwise I would daydream or peek at my class notes.

Ian Thomas talked about Moses and how it took this great man forty years in the wilderness to learn that he was nothing. Then one day Moses was confronted with a burning bush—likely a dry bunch of ugly little sticks that had hardly developed—yet Moses had to take off his shoes. Why? Because this was holy ground. Why was it holy ground? Because God was in the bush!

I WOULD LET

GOD BE GOD

AND LET LUIS

PALAU BE DEPEN-

DENT UPON-HIM.

Here was Major Thomas's point: God was telling Moses, "I don't need a pretty bush or an educated bush or an eloquent bush. *Any old bush will do, as long as I am in the bush.* If I am going to use you, I am going to use you. It will not be you doing something for Me, but Me doing something through you."

It suddenly hit me that I was that kind of bush—a worthless, useless bunch of dried-up sticks. I could do nothing for God. All my reading and studying, asking questions, and trying to model myself after others was worthless. Everything in my ministry was worthless, unless God was in the bush. Only He could make something happen.

Thomas told of many Christian workers who failed at first because they thought they had something to offer God. He himself had once imagined that because he was an aggressive, winsome, evangelistic sort, God would use him. But God didn't use him until he came to the end of himself. *That's exactly my situation,* I thought. *I am at the end of myself.*

Thomas closed his message by reading—you guessed it—Galatians 2:20. And then it all came together for me. "I have been crucified with Christ and *I no longer live, but Christ lives in me.*" My biggest spiritual struggle was finally over! I would let God be God and let Luis Palau be dependent upon Him.

I ran back to my room and in tears fell to my knees next to my bunk. "Lord, now I understand!" I prayed in my native Spanish. "The whole thing is 'not I, but Christ in me.' It's not what I'm going to do for You, but rather what You're going to do through me."

I stayed on my knees until lunchtime, an hour-and-a-half later. I asked the Lord's forgiveness for my pride.

Well, God still had a lot of burning to do, but He was finally in control of this bush. He wanted me to be grateful for all the small things He had put in my life, but He didn't want me to place my confidence in those opportunities to make me a better minister or preacher. He wanted me to depend not on myself or my breaks, but on Christ alone— the indwelling, resurrected almighty Lord Jesus.

That day marked the intellectual turning point in my spiritual life. The practical working out of that discovery would be lengthy and painful, but at last the realization had come. We have everything we need when we have Jesus Christ living in us. It's His power that controls our dispositions, enables us to serve, and corrects and directs us (Philippians 2:13). I could relax and rest in Him. He was going to do the work through me.

EXPERIENCING THE-POSITIVE POWER OF CHRIST

More than fifty years ago as a young Christian, I was challenged in my walk with Christ by Dr. Norman Vincent Peale when he spoke at the First Presbyterian Church in Hollywood where I was a member. Through the years as I came to know him better, his enthusiasm for our Savior continued to inspire me.

Some years ago, I was privileged to be invited to New York City for a special meeting with Dr. Peale and his wife, Ruth, to plan a strategy to help reach America for Christ. I was deeply moved by his sincere desire to communicate the gospel of our Lord Jesus Christ to the entire country.

Dr. and Mrs. Peale were co-editors and publishers of the popular Guideposts magazine. He wrote forty books, includ-ing The Power of Positive Thinking, *which sold more than* fifteen million copies. Dr. Peale also was the recipient of the Presidential Medal of Freedom. On Christmas Day, 1993, he went to meet his Savior face-to-face.

Dr. Peale's story is about a man who influenced his life in a dramatic way. The transformation in this man's life will inspire you to also experience—and share—the positive power of Christ.

❧

Sometimes an event occurs in a person's life with dramatic suddenness, and as a result that person is never the same again.

The experience may penetrate so deeply into the personality that it leaves a permanent impression which can change the individual for life.

Such an unforgettable and determinative experience happened to me one cold, February night when I was a small boy. It conditioned my thinking and living for a lifetime.

The snow lay deep around the white, steepled church in my small midwestern hometown. Light gleamed through the windows, welcoming the worshipers who struggled through the drifts to the door. Many, stamping off snow, entered the little church until it was filled to the last seat. Even more crowded in to stand.

The midwinter revival gatherings, which met every night for two weeks of evangelistic preaching, were called "protracted meetings." And the community's interest was intense—especially if the preacher, in this case my father, was well-known throughout the area as a powerful speaker motivated by a sincere faith and dedication to Jesus Christ.

Since in those days there was no radio or television to compete and no motion picture theater, the church was the focal point of interest. A special series of revival meetings, long anticipated, attracted not only regular churchgoers, but the irregular and non-religious as well. Few ignored the enthusiasm generated as the meetings progressed night after night.

Sitting near the front each night with my mother and younger brother, Bob, I felt the excitement and awareness of God's presence that developed as the revival series mounted in zeal. The content was controlled emotionally, however, for my father was suspicious of the emotionalism that sometimes prevailed at such meetings and often resulted in a falling away of people converted superficially. What he wanted was in-depth life change in which not only emotion but the mind combined in a commitment bringing spiritual growth and lifelong Christian discipleship. The anticipation of great things happening was in the air, and on one particular night something great did occur.

There was a man in the community, Dave Henderson, who was a rough, tough character. He would go on regular drunks. Nowadays he would be considered an alcoholic. His speech was profane, and he could easily be provoked into a fight. And he had a mean streak that was revealed in violent outbursts of temper. Rumor had it that he was a wife beater, but his sweet and dignified mate never let on that he was anything but a perfect husband.

Despite everything, something about Dave was likable, and my father, a "he-man" type of minister, was rather fond of him. I recall his saying, "There is something pretty fine in that man if he would only let the Lord bring it out." And Dave, in turn, liked my father. He would often come to church, sit in a rear pew, and afterward say to Father, "I like to hear you talk, Reverend." But still he went on with his lifestyle, which most charitably could be described, to use words prevalent in those days, as "wicked and evil." He was the bad man of the town.

Then came the unforgettable night. The meeting opened with the congregational singing of old revival hymns. Prayer was offered, the Scriptures read. Then Father went into his sermon. He was always tender and loving—most persuasive. He loved Jesus, and that love communicated itself impressively to the congregation. He told how powerful and loving Jesus is—that the Savior can do the most wonderful things in even the worst lives. The sermon was thoughtful, intelligent, and irrefutable in its logical presentation. And it was heightened by love. My father loved these people, and one by one, he had loved them into the Kingdom.

He finished his sermon by giving the invitation to all who wanted to be saved and know the Lord, to be converted and have their lives changed, to come forward to the altar and receive the power of Christ.

There was a moment of silence. Then I could almost feel the church shake a bit as a heavy man started down the aisle. Seated at the end of the pew, I looked back to see Dave walking with a kind of determined air, quite unconscious of the stir he was creating. Tears were streaming down his cheeks. Even though I was a small boy, I knew that this man was deeply moved.

Reaching the altar, Dave knelt. Father knelt with him and, as he later told us, said to him, "Dave, you have been struggling against God, and that is no good. God wants you, my dear friend, and if you surrender to Him, He will give you peace and joy, and your life will be wonderful forever."

Dave said quietly, "Reverend, I want Jesus. I can't do anything with my life. I don't want to be this way anymore."

Father put his hand on the big fellow's shoulder and said, "Receive Jesus Christ who forgives all your sins and makes you now His own."

I could not hear this conversation. It was spoken in low tones, and I report it here from memory as told to me by my father more than seventy years ago.

Then Dave rose and turned around to face the congregation, all of whom knew him for his bad qualities and actions. He said only, "Jesus! Thank You, Jesus!" But it was the look on his face that got me, and indeed, everyone else. It was a look that was other-worldly in its beauty. His countenance was transformed, illuminated. It was beautiful. It was so incredibly wonderful that tears welled up in my eyes. The feeling I had was one of wonderment, astonishment. How could this be?

"HE LED ME TO

CHRIST. WHAT

GREATER THING

CAN ONE MAN DO

FOR ANOTHER?"

Surely this wasn't happening to *this* man! And just what was happening? The answer is that the positive power of Jesus Christ was happening. A man was being transformed.

And Dave was changed. Some people said it wouldn't last. But it did. From that moment, this man was totally different. He broke instantly with all of his bad habits. He became a good, honorable, upright man of God. Literally, he became a saint—a rugged, loving saint. And if I were called upon to name the best men, the most Christlike men I have ever known, Dave Henderson would be right up there at the top of the list.

But still, even though I was only a small boy, I was confused. How could this be—a man walks into a church one sort of man and leaves the church totally different? "What happened, Father?" I asked. "What happened to Dave in that one minute of time?"

Father smiled. "It's wonderful, Norman; it's all very wonderful. The power happened to him. He received the power —the positive power of Jesus Christ. He is a new man in Christ."

I can recall to this day my father repeating that glorious line from Scripture: "If anyone is in Christ, he is a new creation; old things have passed away; behold, all things have become new" (2 Corinthians 5:17, NKJ). Then Father added, "The fact that Jesus Christ can do this to people is what made me a preacher."

And, I might add, it made me a preacher also.

So the years passed, and Dave kept the faith. He walked among men as a man of God. He was beloved, even venerated. He was a blessing to everyone he met. Eventually, his big head was crowned with snowy white hair. Love and kindness were written on his rugged countenance. Then he became ill, and I received word that the end was near. I immediately went from my home in New York back to the little town where he lived to see him once more. He lay in bed, his white hair against the pillow. His giant form was now emaciated. His big hand, now so thin, was white against the sheet, and the blue veins showed clearly. We talked of the old times, particularly of my father. "Greatest man I ever knew," said Dave. "He led me to Christ. And what greater thing can one man do for another?"

Then I asked Dave to pray for me. I knelt by the side of his bed and could feel his hand reaching for me. Presently, it rested on my head. I cannot recall now just what he said; I only know that this was a sacred experience. I felt cleansed and blessed. I felt the Holy Presence. It was one of the deepest and most beautiful spiritual experiences of my life.

Dennis Rainey

THE LEGACY OF A "GOOD NAME"

Dennis Rainey is cofounder and director of Campus Crusade for Christ's Family Ministry in Little Rock, Arkansas. As a featured speaker for Family Life Conferences, he has ministered throughout the United States and Canada, as well as South Africa, South Korea, and Singapore. He has also conducted marriage and family seminars for some of America's largest corporations.

Dennis is being used by God to influence tens of thousands of families. I am always excited when he shares the heartwarming reports of couples who are inspired to make our Lord the center of their marriages after attending a Family Life Conference.

With his wife, Barbara, Dennis is coauthor of the best-selling book Building Your Mate's Self-Esteem, *and he has also authored* Lonely Husbands, Lonely Wives *and various titles in the HomeBuilders Couples Series.*

His story begins in a small town in Missouri with his first attempt as a salesman. Through this experience and others, Dennis shares the seed of his character development, the integrity of his father.

Growing up in a small, rural community nestled in the Ozark Mountains of southern Missouri meant there were few secrets. As a teenager, I learned that mistakes made on Saturday night were Monday morning's headline news at the local barber shop. It was generally true both for children and adults: An individual's character and reputation were like laundry hanging outdoors on the clothesline—there for all to see.

By the time I was a senior in high school, I had become acutely aware of the negative side of our little community's efficient communication network. However, I didn't realize that it had its positive side until I began selling magazine subscriptions to raise money for our senior project.

As the contest began, I set my eyes on a small tape recorder and a teddy bear that would be my reward for selling a modest number of subscriptions. I immediately cashed in several sales to my numerous aunts and uncles.

However, it became increasingly difficult as I solicited subscriptions from my neighbors. I was still a good distance from my goal when I found myself going door to door in town. That strategy didn't break any sales records, so I headed out into the country. There I met considerable resistance while burning a tank of gas. Sales had ceased.

As I was driving home about to give up and settle for a

cheap, pint-sized, stuffed chipmunk, I impulsively turned off the gravel road into a driveway that led to a small, white farm house. As I got out of the car and walked up the steps, I thought to myself, *They probably can't afford to buy anyway.* My suspicions were inwardly confirmed when I was greeted by an elderly man in well-worn overalls standing behind the screened door.

I introduced myself and was hurriedly rattling off my canned sales pitch when the old man interrupted me: "Son, what did you say your name was?"

"Dennis Rainey, sir," I tried to say politely, wondering what that had to do with my sales presentation.

"Are you 'Hook' Rainey's son?" he asked with a slight grin.

The old man's etched face immediately brightened with my answer, "Why, yes sir. He's my dad."

"Well, come on in!" He beamed as he unlatched the screen door and swung it open. He went on and on about my father, telling stories of how Dad had sold him home heating fuel for years, how Dad had helped him and others when they couldn't pay their bills.

Then he bought two magazine subscriptions.

Driving away, I decided to see if this was a fluke or if others shared the same opinion about my dad. I stopped at the next little house on the edge of that country road and introduced myself. "Hello, I'm 'Hook' Rainey's son; my name is Dennis Rainey."

Eureka! The response was identical. Sales soared as I drove from house to house down every gravel road I could find. Not only did I win the tape recorder, but I also won thirteen huge stuffed animals—teddy bears, tigers, and dogs. I cleaned them out by winning first place and setting a record for sales.

For years I thought I had won that magazine sales contest. But it wasn't until Dad's death that I realized what had happened: it was his character that had made the difference. I had witnessed a living proverb: "A good name is to be more desired than great riches" (Proverbs 22:1, NASB).

My dad's good name was earned during sixty-six years lived within two miles of where he was born. His character was shaped as a boy when his father deserted him, his mother, and six other brothers and sisters. As a lad, Dad learned what it meant to be responsible as the family struggled to scratch out enough to feed eight in a drafty, two-room log cabin.

During his late teenage years, he picked up his nickname "Hook." Evidently, in his prime he was a pretty fair baseball pitcher—he even pitched a game against Dizzy Dean. As a lefty, he was known for having the most crooked curve ball around—a wicked "hook" that mystified batters.

But in contrast to his curve ball, Dad's life was as straight and powerful as a Nolan Ryan fastball. He was widely known and known well in the business community. As a single man, he started his own business pumping gas and, over a forty-four-year period, built a solid company. At his funeral, attended by about a third of the town, one man commented, "I never heard a negative word about 'Hook' Rainey."

At the heart of Dad's good name was his integrity. His word was good. His promises were sealed with a firm handshake. No contracts were needed to make certain he didn't become slippery in business.

His commitment to my mom in 1932 was sure until his death in 1976.

He made good on his promises to me to go fishing during busy times of the year. I remember thinking as a young boy that if I could only get him to say yes to something, then it was a done deal. His integrity permeated all that he did; his private life was no different from his public life.

Dad was a man of few words. He had a soft-spoken faith in God, but underneath was a bedrock of practical righteousness. He wasn't perfect, but he was never pompously pious.

Upon reflection, I sometimes feel that my dad's life was a lesson in character and integrity—just for me. As I go about trusting my heavenly Father, His Word, and His plan for my life, I've learned that the seeds of trust were planted there by an earthly father who was trustworthy. I agree with Alexander Pope when he said, "An honest man is the noblest work of God." It is from observing this noble work of God that I draw strength daily to live my life and lead my family.

As I ponder the greatest lesson my dad taught me, I'm grateful to God for a father who embodied the words of Charles Haddon Spurgeon: "A good character is the best tombstone. Those who loved you and were helped by you, remember you when forget-me-nots are withered. Carve your name on hearts, and not on marble."

The older I become, the more I am grateful to God for a dad who engraved integrity upon his son's heart. I pray that I will do the same.

Praise the Lord!
How blessed is the man who fears the Lord,
Who greatly delights in His commandments.
His descendants will be mighty on earth;
The generation of the upright will be blessed
(Psalm 112:1,2, NASB).

Adrian Rogers

THE SOUVENIRS OF-PAIN

Adrian Rogers is pastor of the 26,000-member Bellevue Baptist Church in Memphis, Tennessee. He has served three terms as president of the Southern Baptist Convention.

Adrian and I met more than thirty-five years ago when Campus Crusade for Christ conducted a Lay Institute for Evangelism in a church he was pastoring in Florida. We have continued our friendship, and through the years I have been tremendously impressed as he has powerfully proclaimed God's holy, inspired Word and faithfully exalted our Lord Jesus Christ, both in his personal life and his ministry.

Highly regarded as an evangelist and speaker, Adrian has taught in the Billy Graham Schools of Evangelism and held citywide crusades in the United States and abroad. In 1980 he brought a major address to a gathering of more than 500,000 assembled for the "Washington for Jesus" rally.

His greatest lesson came through a tragedy in his family. He reminds us of how Jesus suffered and of how His scars are mementos of the pain He endured for us.

Often when we visit a place, we bring back a souvenir. It's our way of saying, "I've been there." Our Lord brought back some souvenirs from His journey to Earth—the scars that He bears in His glorified body.

Indeed, the only manmade things in heaven are the scars that Jesus bears. After His resurrection, those scars convinced Thomas that He indeed had risen (John 20:24–29). The glorified body that brought Thomas to his knees still had "the print of the nails."

Jesus was a suffering God. His scars are memorials of excruciating pain. They are eternal reminders to me of the greatest lesson I've ever learned: God is faithful and trustworthy to turn our scars into ministry to others.

The world today is having great difficulty with the problem of pain. Some agonize in a dungeon of doubt because of indescribable and seemingly senseless suffering. How often have you asked God to remove a problem, and it seemed to get worse? Why is this, if God is love and all powerful?

Is it that God is love, but weak and powerless? Or that He is powerful, but without love and, therefore, cruel? Or even worse—is there no love or power because there is no God at all?

The answers to these questions lie in our response to an even greater issue. Can God suffer? Indeed, He can and does! And why does God Himself suffer?

Think about it. It's reasonable.

Does not a father suffer with his children? The story of the prodigal son is meant to teach, among other things, that a father suffers when his son does. We're told to "grieve not the holy Spirit of God" (Ephesians 4:30, KJV). "Grieve" is a love word. We can only grieve someone who loves us. Your lawn mower may vex you, but your children can grieve you. Yes, our loving heavenly Father is often grieved for His children.

Does not the head feel and register pain coming in from a wounded body? Jesus is the exalted head of the church, which is His body, and He, therefore, continues to "be touched with the feeling of our infirmities" (Hebrews 4:15, KJV).

Does not a loving groom grieve if his betrothed bride is unfaithful or indifferent to him? Surely, the heavenly Bridegroom, Jesus, is heartbroken over the church which sometimes proves to be a faithless and fickle bride.

But why would God suffer? He is God. He could choose not to suffer. Yes, but He allows Himself to suffer, and that brings us to the next question.

Why doesn't God just remove pain? Because pain is an absolutely necessary commodity in a world that has been cursed by sin.

Pain is God's way to remind us that this universe in which we live has a disease, and we indeed are part of it. It is His loving reminder that mankind needs the healing of redemption. The apostle Paul explains, "We know that the whole creation groaneth and travaileth in pain together until now. And not only they, but ourselves also...groan within ourselves, waiting for the adoption, to wit, the redemption of our body" (Romans 8:22,23, KJV).

A loving God could not remove the pain (a result of sin) until the last vestige of sin (the infection of our world) is dealt with and gone. The worst thing that could happen to fallen humanity would be to live blindly in "paradise" and never seek a Savior.

Thank God that our Lord does not remove pain. The scars, to the contrary, tell us that He shares the pain. Hebrews 4:15 assures us, "We have not an high priest which cannot be touched with the feeling of our infirmities; but was in all points tempted like as we are, yet without sin" (KJV).

The sad part is that we are a generation that blocks out pain at any cost. It's amazing what we have concocted to accomplish this: drugs, alcohol, sexual affairs, television, and amusements. Many are merely heading for a sedative to kill the pain instead of coming to the Savior to heal the infection.

When we come to Jesus, He may not remove all of the pain because, though we have been saved from the penalty of sin, we still need to be saved from the presence of sin. Therefore, He may not remove the painful thorn, but gives added grace and joy to help us endure it (2 Corinthians 12:1–10).

Our Lord did not have to suffer, but He invaded our sufferings so He could bear them and heal them. The prophet Isaiah proclaims, "He was wounded for our transgressions, he was bruised for our iniquities; the chastisement of our peace was upon him; and with his stripes we are healed" (Isaiah 53:5, KJV). Because of Calvary, we're saved. Not only did He die, but He arose again and lives forever to wear the scars.

The great lesson in all of this for me is that Jesus has some scars, and so will we if we are to be like Him. The apostle Paul says, "From henceforth let no man trouble me: for I bear in my body the marks of the Lord Jesus" (Galatians 6:17, KJV).

Remember that a scar is a wound that has healed. *We need to bring our wounds to Jesus,* let Him heal them, and then *use our scars for Jesus.*

Indeed, your scars may be your greatest ministry. Just as the scars of Jesus convinced Thomas, perhaps your scars will convince someone today.

After seminary, my wife, Joyce, and I were called back to Florida to a fine little church in Fort Pierce. By this time we had three children: Steve, Gayle, and Philip. Philip was only two months old when we settled into the new parsonage.

It happened on Mother's Day. It was a beautiful day, as the days in May so often are near the Florida coast. I had just preached a Mother's Day message on the blessings of a Christian home. Our small house was nestled right next door to the little white, cement block church. Joyce was out in the kitchen preparing our lunch after the service. And I was in the living room reading.

Suddenly I heard her distraught voice. "Adrian! Come here quickly! Something is wrong with Philip."

I leaped to my feet. She had our baby boy in her arms. He was not breathing. His face had a blue cast to it.

"What's wrong?" she cried.

"I don't know. You call the hospital and tell them I'm coming."

I put our little boy inside my coat to keep him warm. With eyes blinded by tears, I screeched out of our driveway and sped to the hospital emergency room. "Please help me," I cried to a waiting nurse as I burst through the heavy double entrance doors to the hospital. Kind hands took Philip and rushed him to a nearby room. I knelt outside the emergency room door and prayed for God's mercy, not caring who saw me or what they might think.

After a while, an attending doctor came out of the room and walked over to me. He laid his hand upon my shoulder and shook his head. "He's gone. There was nothing we could do. We tried."

It was one of those sudden "crib deaths."

Joyce was standing in the doorway of our house when I returned alone. The look on my face told the story. Mother's Day had turned into a day of incredible grief and confusion for us. The tragedy was so sudden and so stark. We did the only thing we knew to do. We knelt and called out to the Lord for help.

Then we turned to the Word of God. I wasn't sure just where to begin reading. Instead, the Lord Himself led us to the message we so sorely needed:

> Grace be to you and peace from God our Father, and from the Lord Jesus Christ. Blessed be God, even the Father of our Lord Jesus Christ, the Father of mercies, and the God of all comfort; who comforteth us in all our tribulation, that we may be able to comfort them which are in any trouble, by the comfort wherewith we ourselves are comforted of God (2 Corinthians 1:2–4, KJV).

I did not understand all that God was allowing to happen to us, but already He had made one thing abundantly clear. The Father of mercies was going to use our sorrow to make us a blessing to other people with broken hearts. He was going to heal us and then use our scars as a testimony.

Since that time, we have met so many who have suffered

the heartache of losing a little one. I have watched others as they have tried to give comfort, and their words have seemed like scant drops of water on a blazing desert.

Then I have seen my wife put her arm around a broken-hearted mother and cry with her. I have seen my wife tell this distraught and grieving mother that Jesus knows and cares and heals. Then I've seen that broken and crushed life unfold and be in the road to healing and restored joy. *Only someone with scars can minister like that.*

If you're hurting, don't block out the pain with sedatives and lock out God. He loves you so much. And if He has healed you, remember that *your scars may be your greatest ministry!*

Roy Rogers

MASTER OF
MY FATE

Roy and Dale Rogers were the most prominent of the famous Hollywood stars who joined with Dr. Henrietta Mears, Vonette, and me in starting the Hollywood Christian Group more than fifty years ago. Any time spent with Roy would make you sense, as I did, that you were speaking with a truly great man who possessed a genuine spirit of humility.

He grew up in a family in which music played an important role. He was strumming the guitar when he was eight and calling square dances at ten, meanwhile developing a fine singing voice and an unusual talent for yodeling.

Roy landed his first movie role in 1937 where he was cast as a singing cowboy. The King of Cowboys went on to star in eighty-seven musical westerns, becoming the number one box-office star in all westerns for twelve consecutive years.

In 1947 Roy married Dale Evans, his leading lady in thirty-five of his pictures. As one of America's most beloved *couples, they endeared themselves to millions around the world and experienced a full life of good times and tragic experiences. Roy died in 1998 from congestive heart failure at his home in California at age 86.*

In this story of his greatest lesson, Roy shares how God led him into his career and how he learned to cope with times of trial through our Lord's strength.

Looking back over my life, I can see how the Lord has had His hand on me for years, even when I made no effort to know Him in a personal way.

When I was a boy, my family lived on a farm twelve miles outside Portsmouth, Ohio. My mother was crippled from polio, and my dad worked at a shoe factory in the city—coming home only every other weekend. My three sisters and I did all the farm chores. And because of the Great Depression, we had very little money.

As a child I wanted to be a dentist, perhaps because dental care was practically non-existent where we lived. If you got a bad toothache, the tooth was pulled with hardly any effective anesthetic.

But because of hard times, I had to drop that and other dreams tied to a high school education and go to work alongside Dad in the shoe factory in Cincinnati. Later, our family visited my older sister in California and decided to move there.

One day she talked me into playing guitar, singing, and yodeling in a local talent contest. I was shy, so she literally had to push me on stage. I must have pleased somebody because I was asked to join a group that ultimately became "The Sons of the Pioneers." That was the start of my career in the entertainment business.

In those days I didn't go to church. I always believed in a power greater than myself, but knew nothing about a personal relationship with Jesus Christ. Yet God's hand guided me to the right places at the right times, and my career started to grow.

Republic Studios was looking for a new singing cowboy. They had tested different fellows all morning when the vice president just "happened" to walk through the casting office and see me sitting there with my guitar and Stetson. Immediately, he grabbed me and shoved me in front of the camera. I was on my way to stardom.

Five other singers auditioned at the same time. They were well-educated young men, not shy like me. And yet I was chosen. Why? I believe God had a work for me in family entertainment. He knew I was like "Popeye the Sailor Man" in the funny papers: "I yam what I yam and that's all I yam!" No facade, just me.

But first God had to change my heart, which wasn't until after I had met and married Dale Evans. It began one day when Dale shared a new excitement with me: "I've just made the greatest decision of my life. Today I dedicated my life to Jesus Christ. It's wonderful."

I was a skeptic about religion. But I smiled and listened as she went on and on about the new feelings she was experiencing. When she had quieted, I said, "I'm glad for you if it makes you happy. But be careful. Just don't go overboard, okay?"

Dale didn't pressure me to accept her faith. Instead, she gathered the family in the evenings for Bible reading and prayer. She even bought me a new Bible. I could see the change in Dale but didn't understand her new joy.

Finally, one Saturday night I stood looking out our bedroom window after an incident at a party we had given that had strained our relationship. I thought about my responsibilities to my family, and it occurred to me that any financial provisions I might be able to leave for my children would someday be gone. The fame of being a movie star wouldn't last forever. I realized that I wanted my kids to remember me for something special, something that mattered. I wanted them to remember me as a daddy who took them to church on Sundays and helped them learn how to live a good Christian life.

The next morning as Dale was preparing to take the children to Sunday school and church, I came downstairs and informed her, "If you are going to church, I am going with you."

As we sat in the service, I bowed my head for a long time, thinking about the decision I should make. At the invitation I sat up and turned to Dale. "Mama, I'm going down there." I did go, accepting Jesus Christ as my Savior.

The next Sunday our oldest daughter, Cheryl, accepted Jesus. Both of us were baptized Palm Sunday evening. And a spiritual bond was formed in our family which has never been broken.

I am so grateful that Dale worked with God to bring me something I had longed for all my life—peace. Materially speaking, for years I had nothing. Then for years I had much. But I soon learned that having too much is worse than having too little. Nothing ever seemed quite right. I was restless, confused, unsatisfied. But in my walk with the Lord, I've learned that the power of prayer and the feeling of spiritual blessedness and the love of Jesus have no price tags.

Over the years, my trail has been a great one, sometimes bumpy, sometimes stormy, sometimes smooth and beautiful. But when I asked Jesus Christ to be my Savior and Lord in 1948, He took me at my word and has been working out His will for me ever since.

I do not have to understand all the sorrow Dale and I have suffered in the loss of three children, friends, and parents. It is not for me to question, but to trust His overall plan for my life as the Bible teaches: "Trust in the Lord with all your heart, and lean not on your own understanding" (Proverbs 3:5, NKJ).

One of the tragedies we suffered was the death of our beautiful mongoloid daughter, Robin. For all of her problems, her frailty, and her handicaps, she was a happy, loving little girl who spread a warmth throughout our family that I will not even attempt to describe. Suffice it to say, Robin Elizabeth Rogers was someone special, and everyone in our home knew it. She was, as Dale has often said, more like an angel than a human being.

She brought a rare kind of peace to our home. I can remember so many evenings when I would come home from the studio, tired and not in the best mood, and go straight to see her. As I talked and played with her, everything would suddenly be okay.

Just before her second birthday, Robin went to be with the Lord. Making the funeral arrangements was one of the hardest things I've ever had to do. And as time passed, I became more and more aware of the magnificent things she had accomplished in her brief visit.

The deaths of our daughter, Debbie, and son, Sandy,

were equally hard. But through these experiences, we learned to trust God in all of our circumstances.

On the eve of my aorta surgery, my pastor prayed with me. When he finished, I told him, "I have had a long life and a good one. Whatever the Lord wants to do with me is all right."

God is a big, good God and makes no mistakes. I am grateful to Him for the blessings of my life, my country, my family, my career, and my many loyal friends. Even when I have stumbled and seemed to lose my way, He has come to my aid and brought my feet to a larger place of service. One of the greatest lessons I have learned in life is that He is the Master of my fate.

Robert H. Schuller

TOUGH PEOPLE LAST

What began as an outdoor church in a rented drive-in theater has fruitfully prospered into the 10,000-member Crystal Cathedral in Garden Grove, California, and the "Hour of Power" television ministry under its founding pastor, Dr. Robert Schuller.

Bob was actively involved in a Los Angeles Billy Graham Crusade when I first met him. He is a man with a great heart for God and a brilliant mind, who has been called to communicate to nonbelievers in what he often refers to as "pre-evangelism." He knows the language of the marketplace and has the ear of multitudes who would not normally listen to religious messages.

In December 1989, Bob became the first non-Soviet pastor ever to deliver a sermon on Soviet television, a message heard by an estimated 200 million Soviet people.

He is the popular author of more than thirty books,

including several that made the New York Times *Best Seller list.*

He learned his greatest lesson through the tragic motorcycle accident that injured his daughter, Carol. Her positive spirit in the midst of her trial will touch your heart, just as it did his.

My daughter, Carol, lost her leg in a motorcycle accident in 1978. At the time, my wife, Arvella, and I were in Korea. On the long trip back to Iowa, I searched for the right thing to say. What would my first words to Carol be?

When we arrived at the hospital, I was shocked. Carol lay in her bed in intensive care, her body bruised, broken, and disfigured. But her spirits were whole and healthy. Immediately she solved the problem of what to say by speaking first: "I know why it happened, Dad. God wants to use me to help others who have been hurt."

It was this spirit that carried her through seven months of hospitalization, intravenous feedings, and consequent collapsed veins. This positive attitude gave her the courage to fight a raging infection that threatened her life and to hang on until a new drug was released by the FDA. (It was the right drug at the right time—a real miracle.)

It was that same positive attitude that helped Carol make the transition from hospital patient to a "handicapped" family member and student—and to feel normal and whole again.

The last picture we have of Carol with both legs is one taken when she was in her softball uniform. The athlete of the family, Carol loves to play softball.

The summer after her accident, she shocked me by saying, "Dad, I'm going to sign up for softball again this year."

"That's great," I responded, not wanting to discourage her.

At that time, Carol's artificial leg was attached just below the knee, which was so stiff that she could barely bend it at a thirty-degree angle. She walked very stiffly; running was out of the question.

However, I took her to the local school where all the parents were lining up with their daughters to register for the girls' softball team. Carol signed up and went to check out her uniform.

As she swung her stiff plastic leg into the car and rested her jersey, socks, and cap in her lap, I turned to her and said, "Carol, how do you expect to play ball if you can't run?"

With flashing eyes, she snapped back, "I've got that all figured out, Dad! When you hit home runs, you don't have to run."

My daughter is tough. She's a survivor. She hit enough home runs that season to justify her presence on the team!

Carol inspired everyone with her tenacity, too. She had six surgeries after that first amputation. Later, she took up skiing and won a gold medal in the qualifying races that admitted her to that elite corps of skiers participating in the National Ski Championships. In March 1983, she pulled her goggles on and took her place among the champions of her country—at the young age of eighteen!

Yes, she still walked with a limp. She drew curious looks from strangers. But her positive attitude and determination helped her even with that.

Several years ago, our family was privileged to be guests of the American-Hawaiian Steamship Company on a one-week cruise of the Hawaiian Islands. It was absolutely beautiful. During the trip, Carol was not in the least ashamed to be seen in shorts or swimming attire although her artificial leg covered her stump to just below the hip. But she was very conscious of the fact that people looked at her out of the corners of their eyes and wondered what had happened to her.

"IT'S NOT HOW YOU WALK THAT COUNTS, BUT WHO WALKS WITH YOU."

On this cruise, it was customary on the last night to have a talent show in which the passengers participated. Carol, then seventeen years old, surprised us by saying, "I'm going to be in the talent show tonight." Now Carol doesn't sing, and of course she doesn't dance. So, naturally, I was curious as to what she would do.

Friday night, my wife and I sat in the lounge along with six hundred other people. The stage was set in the big glorified cocktail lounge. As you can imagine, it was a very secular scene. The first acts performed were typical of amateur talent shows. Then it was Carol's turn.

She came on stage wearing neither shorts nor Hawaiian garb, but a full-length dress. She looked beautiful. Walking up to the microphone, she said, "I really don't know what talent is, but I thought this would be a good chance for me to give what I think I owe you all—an explanation. I know you've been looking at me all week, wondering about my fake leg. I thought I should tell you what happened.

"I was in a motorcycle accident. I almost died, but the

doctors kept giving me blood, and my pulse came back. They amputated my leg below the knee, and later, they amputated through the knee. I spent seven months in the hospital—seven months with intravenous antibiotics to fight infection."

She paused a moment, then continued. "If I've one talent, it's this: During that time, my faith became very real to me."

Suddenly a hush swept over the lounge. The waitresses stopped serving drinks. The glasses stopped clinking. Every eye was focused on this tall seventeen-year-old blonde.

She said, "I look at you girls who walk without a limp, and I wish I could walk that way. I can't, but this is what I've learned, and I want to leave it with you: It's not how you walk that counts, but who walks with you and with whom you walk."

Then she paused and said, "I'd like to sing a song about my friend, my Lord." And she sang.

> And He walks with me,
> and He talks with me,
> And He tells me I am His own,
> And the joy we share
> in our time of prayer (originally "as we tarry there")
> None other has ever known.[1]

"Thank you." And she stepped down.

There was not a dry eye, not a life that wasn't touched that night.

By holding on, digging in, and making the most of what happened to her, Carol taught me one of the greatest lessons I've ever learned: tough times never last, but tough people do.

THE GREATEST LESSON I'VE EVER LEARNED

When tough times come, we need to take tough action, to hold on until the tide turns for the better, to tenaciously dig in and bloom where we are planted, and to inspire people with our cheerful and positive attitude. In the process, other people will be stimulated to choose noble and positive outlooks for their lives too.

William E. Simon

JOINING THE FIGHT

William E. Simon possessed one of the most brilliant financial minds in our country, demonstrated by his phenomenal success in the business world. He founded William E. Simon & Sons Inc. in 1988, and was chairman of the board until his death in June 2000. He also served in many high-ranking posts in government and in the private sector.

Bill was appointed Deputy Secretary of the U.S. Treasury in 1973 and later that year became the first administrator of the Federal Energy office. In 1974 he was appointed Secretary of the Treasury and held that cabinet post for three years.

A former president of the U.S. Olympic Committee, Bill also chaired the U.S. Olympic Foundation from 1985 to 1997 and served on the board of several sports organizations.

Even though Bill had a long list of accomplishments, what impressed me even more was the earnest prayer from his sincere heart, "Lord, help me to know and obey Your will. I want to know Your plan for my life." His story shows how dramatically the Lord led through that prayer.

Suddenly a telephone call came that would change my life. It was from the White House. Out of the blue, I was being asked to fly immediately to Washington, D.C., to meet with newly re-elected President Nixon. The President, it seemed, was going to offer me a senior position in his administration.

The year was 1972. I was a senior partner at Salomon Brothers, one of the leading investment houses in New York. My wife, Carol, and I were blessed with seven beautiful children. And we had just built our dream house in New Vernon, New Jersey.

In short, we were a close and happy family, and we wanted for nothing. We had reached the point where we had always longed to be.

I remember putting down the phone and looking at Carol. She had exactly the same reactions that were tugging inside of me.

Certainly I felt pride, excitement and, above all, gratitude at the prospect of being asked to serve my country, especially during that critical time in our history. Divisive forces from the war in Vietnam and an increasingly unstable economy were tearing at the fabric of our country's freedom, prosperity, and goodwill.

But I also felt some apprehension and foreboding. After all, why should I interrupt a successful career and uproot my family to venture into that political snake pit in Washington?

I vastly preferred the free-wheeling, rough-and-tumble of the business world to the encrusted and too often cryptic cocoon of bureaucratic life in government. What's more, the contrast between modern-day Washington and the city built as a proud trademark to the ideals of the Founding Fathers filled me with sorrow.

In my view, Washington had become an elitist, self-absorbed city that cared little for the values of everyday Americans who believe deeply in the work ethic and in family, freedom, and faith in God. And behind those majestic monuments in the back rooms of Congress, I knew that self-serving politicians were busily spending and borrowing America ever deeper into debt.

Yet in the end, all those reservations only reinforced the consideration Carol and I came to see as critical: if you truly fear for your country and if you fear for freedom, then how can you stand by and see the battle lost without joining the fight?

I knew that I couldn't stand by. I had to join the fray. And I also believed fervently that when your President asks you to serve, it is your duty to do so.

So I did. I met with President Nixon and gratefully accepted his offer. In early 1973, our family packed our bags, said goodbye to New Jersey, and headed south to a new adventure.

And what an adventure it was!

Little did I realize that when I accepted the President's offer, I would land in the eye of two economic cyclones that swept over the country during my years in office.

I was the "energy czar" during the OPEC oil embargo that sent prices soaring at the gas pumps. For the first time, Americans realized that they had lost their energy independence.

And I was treasury secretary under President Ford during the worst peacetime inflation and recession to rock the country in forty years.

Not a bad political baptism! I worked eighteen-hour

days, devoured thousands of briefing papers, appeared before more than three hundred congressional committees, and learned more about energy and the economy in my first four months on each job than I had during four years in college.

I was determined to do everything humanly possible to break the insane cycle of boom and bust that had begun with the decade that encompassed the Great Society and led to steadily worsening inflation, recession, economic dislocations, and instability. Our mission was to get America off that disastrous economic roller coaster.

THERE IS NO HIGHER DUTY, NOR GREATER HONOR, THAN SERVING YOUR COUNTRY.

Although we worked as a team, I came to appreciate that true leadership is lonely. Certainly it was lonely for great men like Washington, Lincoln, and Eisenhower.

And it was lonely for President Ford as well. Especially when he vetoed sixty-six bills in two years—and made fifty-four vetoes stick—in his unflinching quest to break the back of big government accompanied by out-of-control spending.

The media ridiculed us. Our opponents demagogued us.

There were days when my secret thoughts drifted back to our quiet and happy times in New Jersey. But, in retrospect, I would never trade that experience in Washington for all the material comforts and security in the world. As our country pulled together and we overcame the aftermath of Vietnam and the tragedy of Watergate, the Ford administration ended in January 1977 with America's spirits uplifted and our nation back on track. Inflation was down dramatically, our economy was growing again with renewed vigor, and through it all, the principles of freedom—and the inextricable link between personal, political, and economic freedom—were raised up and reaffirmed.

This gave me a tremendous feeling of satisfaction. I had responded to my country's call and served America in her hour of need.

So, for me, the greatest lesson will always be that alongside one's devotion to family, there is no higher duty, nor greater honor, than serving your country—not just in a governmental position, but also in our military, in our communities, and in our neighborhoods.

Life is not a dress rehearsal, and rarely are we given the opportunity to do something twice. I'm not sure where my life would have led had I declined the President's request and stayed on the well-traveled road I was following on Wall Street. But by listening to my instincts, taking a risk, and beginning a new journey on an unknown road, I learned more about life, discovered more about myself, stretched my horizons farther, and savored experiences far richer than I would otherwise have ever known.

Some people might call it fate. Some might call it luck. But some of us would call it God's plan.

Kenneth Taylor

TWO LIFE-CHANGING EVENTS

Daily my life is enriched because of the creative, brilliant mind and dedicated heart of Dr. Kenneth Taylor, translator of The Living Bible. *Though I possess and study God's Word from many translations, my favorite is this culturally relevant paraphrase that God has used in the lives of tens of millions around the world.*

Dr. Taylor is a noted scholar, author, and publisher. Currently he serves as chairman of the board of Tyndale House Publishers and as international chairman emeritus of Living Bibles International. He is also a member of the advisory board for the Christian Embassy, a ministry of Campus Crusade for Christ.

Kenneth is the author of many books including My First Bible in Pictures, *which won an Angel Award in 1990. He has also been inducted into the Christian Booksellers Association Hall of Fame.*

Kenneth tells about two turning points in his life, one when he was a young man and the other when he was older. Both demonstrate his openness to the Lord's leading that I have observed in his life.

Instead of one lesson, I'm going to relate two. One took place during my college days, and the other when I was forty-five years old.

During college vacations, I worked in the hay fields near Portland, Oregon, my childhood home. But Sunday work was not allowed in our family, so on a certain Sunday afternoon, while the baling crew was sweating through the hot, ten-hour day, I went to church. After our family dinner, I picked up a book from my father's library and spent the afternoon reading it.

The book looked interesting, for it was a biography of another college student, Bill Borden of Yale University, class of 1909. I became fascinated as I read because he had such a love for God and for his fellow human beings. Those were qualities I longed to have in my own life. I was eager to see how he got that way so I could follow his example.

Bill Borden came from a wealthy home. His father had left him a million dollars—currently worth at least ten times that much. But Bill didn't try to keep his inheritance because he had given himself to God, and he felt that everything he had was a trust from God. So he gave away hundreds of thousands of dollars.

I was aghast. Since childhood I had considered becoming a millionaire to be one of life's highest goals, even though in my case it was impossible to reach.

But here was Bill Borden, a college senior, giving great riches away. He was a spiritual giant in other ways, too. He frequently talked with his classmates about God—that He had a plan for their lives, including the forgiveness of their sins through faith in Jesus Christ. At that time, I don't think I had ever talked with an unbeliever about Christ, and the thought terrified me. Perhaps this was a reaction to my father's almost embarrassing readiness to tell others about the Savior. Yet here was my hero, Bill Borden, starting a gospel mission to preach to poor street people. He would go there on Saturday nights and put his arm around men who came forward, telling them about Christ's willingness to forgive and help them.

I also admired Bill's experience on the Yale wrestling team; he knew some of the agonies I had experienced when pinned to the mat.

But as I read further about this millionaire, athlete, and spiritual giant, I became uneasy. He was thinking of becoming a missionary! Now that was something I knew I would never be—not because I had prayed and decided on the basis of God's will, but because I just didn't want to go. I didn't want to give up the good things of life in America, and I didn't want Bill Borden to do it either!

But he did just that. After Yale University he attended Princeton Seminary and became greatly concerned about Chinese Muslims, for whom it seemed little was being done by mission societies. After being ordained in Moody Church, his home church in Chicago, he applied to and was accepted by the China Inland Mission. The mission board assigned him to a western province in China heavily populated by Muslims. In preparation, he went to Egypt to study the Arabic language and Muslim literature.

As I read, I became increasingly uncomfortable. Suppose God called me to be a missionary. Would I go? I wasn't willing to face the question and tried to put it out of my mind.

Then I read that Bill became ill after only a few weeks in Egypt. But I had read missionary stories before, and I knew of wonderful miracles of healing because people trusted in God. Well, I was entirely unprepared as I turned the page to find that Bill's fever grew higher and higher. "Dear God," I prayed as I followed the story, "*don't* let him die."

But he did die. God let Bill Borden die. I was overwhelmed by shock. Then a cold, hard resolution gripped me. "If that is the way God treats a man wholly devoted to Him, then I want no more of such a God." It was a terrible moment as I deliberately turned my back on God. It was as if I were stepping off a cliff and plunging to the rocks below.

IT WAS A TERRIBLE MOMENT AS I DELIBERATELY TURNED MY BACK ON GOD.

But God was gracious beyond expression. He reached out and grabbed me and pulled me back. I can't explain what happened—apart from God—but suddenly I found myself on my knees beside the chair where I had been sitting. I was praying in deep contrition, "Lord, here is my life. Take it and use it in any way You want to."

I have never turned back from that decision—a decision that completely changed my direction in life. It was a decision that made it possible for God to lead me on a guided tour for the rest of my life.

I also experienced another life-changing event. Many years later as an adult, I attended a Campus Crusade seminar for business people. When I arrived, I found out to my horror that part of the program was to leave the conference grounds and tell someone the Good News concerning Christ dying for our sins and redeeming us for heaven. I literally clenched my teeth to make myself carry out the assignment. I started out across a nearby park to find someone I could talk to, hoping against hope that no one would be there! But of course, there was! A young black man was sitting against a tree. I sat down beside him and tried to open a conversation with a few pleasantries about the weather. But he didn't seem to notice me and had little responsiveness to my overtures. Finally I took courage and asked him if he ever read the Bible.

He said no.

So I told him about some things in Scripture, especially about its promises to those who believe. The young man was somewhat interested but not to the point of making a life-changing decision.

As I left him, I had mingled emotions: sadness because of his little chance for happiness, hope that the tiny seed I had planted would grow, and elation that I had carried out a hard task. That experience was, in fact, a turning point in my life. I had discovered that telling a stranger about our Lord—though not easy—was not an impossible thing for me to do, and after that it became simpler to witness to others about God's love.

John F. Walvoord

GOD IS FAITHFUL

Dr. John F. Walvoord is the chancellor and professor emeritus of systematic theology at Dallas Theological Seminary where he served as president for thirty-four years. He impressed me many years ago with his brilliant theological mind and burning heart for Christ.

Through the years he has helped to give a strong emphasis to the authority and inerrancy of God's holy, inspired Word, for which I am personally indebted, as is the whole Body of Christ.

Dr. Walvoord is the author of many books, including The Prophecy Knowledge Handbook; What We Believe: Discovering the Truths of Scripture; and the best-selling Armageddon, Oil and the Middle East Crisis. He also served as co-editor for the Old and New Testament editions of The Bible Knowledge Commentary and was a member of the revision committee for the New Scofield Reference Edition of the Bible.

Throughout his lifetime, Dr. Walvoord has experienced the touch of God on his work and in his family life. He *shares how God has led him into exciting ministry opportunities and faith-stretching circumstances, including the accidental death of one of his sons.*

God's faithfulness to me started early—even before I was born. My mother had been chronically ill, and the doctor advised an abortion to preserve her health as well as to avoid an abnormal baby. As a committed Christian, however, she would have nothing to do with this suggestion. Her prayers were answered when I was born a perfectly normal child. Indeed, her own health improved, and she lived almost to the age of 102.

After several years of catechism, I joined the church at age 9. When I was 12 years old, I decided to be a minister of the gospel. But at age 15 catastrophe struck. My father suddenly lost his job as superintendent of schools in our town because he had forbidden the sale of beer at the high school dances. His stand was too much for the German community in which we lived. The beer interests raised a political fund and elected a board of education that fired him. It seemed like the end of the world to us at the time. But, in fact, this incident led to an event that would transform my life.

We moved to Racine, Wisconsin, where my father had found new employment. That first fall I joined a Bible class taught by Dr. William McCarrell of the Cicero Bible Church. The class was held in the Sixth Avenue Methodist Church which was rented for the occasion. On the second night, as he was teaching Galatians, Dr. McCarrell said, "You can't be good enough to be saved." These words hit me like a lightning bolt. After all, I wasn't bad; I did the best I could.

Wasn't that enough? He then explained that Christ had to die for our sins. Immediately I accepted this truth. The next morning I realized something had happened to me: I had been spiritually born again.

Upon graduating from high school I had to decide which college to attend. My brother and sister had gone to a denominational school which was at least nominally religious. But some of my friends were going to Wheaton College, a small, struggling school which had just been accredited. I went to Wheaton. The first Sunday night after my arrival, Percy Crawford, an upperclassman, led an evangelistic meeting and gave an appeal for complete surrender to Christ. Determined to make the will of God the rule of my life, I went forward. The commitment I made that night has never wavered.

Upon my graduation from Wheaton, the choice of seminary was before me. In the East a prestigious seminary with a long history, large faculty, and a great reputation was open, but I had heard about a new school in Dallas, later to be called Dallas Theological Seminary. It was obviously evangelical and had sixty-five students and only a few faculty members, none of them with earned doctorates. In my confusion I went to Dr. J. Oliver Buswell, president of Wheaton College, for guidance. He listened to my story and said quietly, "I think you'll get a good education at Dallas." That settled the matter for me.

My experience at Dallas was a happy one. More than a fourth of the entering class of twenty-five had been fellow classmates at Wheaton. But upon approaching seminary graduation, I faced the necessity of applying to a mission board.

I had long believed that I was called to be a missionary

in China, so I sent a letter asking for an application form to the China Inland Mission. When the application arrived, I spread it on my bed, got down on my knees, and asked the Lord for guidance. He very definitely said I should not send it in. Thinking I had chosen the wrong country, I asked for an application for India from another mission board. God again said no. Apparently, for reasons beyond my understanding, He did not want me on the mission field.

As a result, I remained at Dallas and enrolled in the doctoral program. As I neared the completion of this degree, I began to look for a pastoral position. In the first church in which I candidated, I discovered that the world was not waiting for me even though I was a Dallas Seminary graduate. The congregation showed no interest whatsoever.

The next church was located in the midst of a booming oil field and was the only church permitted within a ten-mile radius. The area had a population of 8,000 people. I spoke to crowded meetings Sunday morning and Sunday night and was asked to become the pastor. This was it—a mission field right in my own country. But the Lord said no. It seemed to me that I would not have a better opportunity to minister as a pastor than what was just offered to me. What was I to do?

I recalled that, the year before, I had been offered the job as registrar at Dallas Seminary but had no interest in it. I told the Lord that if He wanted me to take this position, President Lewis Sperry Chafer would have to renew the invitation. Within ten days President Chafer called me into his office. This time he offered not only the registrar's position, which was really heading up all the educational programs of the seminary, but also half of the theology department which he taught. During our meeting, he solemnly set me apart in prayer for what proved to be fifty years of faculty service, the last thirty-three years as president.

On my departure that day, he announced that I would receive a salary of $100 per month. But I didn't pay any attention to his words because I knew the seminary could not afford it. Six months later my salary was raised, but I didn't know about it for three years. What I have learned in life, however, is that God is faithful. I never had a financial obligation I could not pay and never suffered a lack of anything that I really needed.

Three years after I began on the seminary's faculty, I married a wonderful helpmate, Geraldine, for whom I have been daffy grateful ever since. Our first son, John, was born three years later and proved to be an unusually precocious and bright child. Later, he earned a Ph.D. from Dallas Theological Seminary and a Ph.D. from Columbia University.

> WHAT I HAVE
> LEARNED IN LIFE
> IS THAT GOD IS
> FAITHFUL.

Our second son, James, was born three years after John. He was slightly handicapped, both mentally and physically, and was not able to walk until two years of age. We placed him in special schools from the time he was three, but he has never been able to function completely on his own and presently is living at the Marbridge Ranch near Austin, Texas, with about a hundred other men who are also slightly handicapped. He is a knowledgeable Christian with an outgoing personality who thoroughly enjoys life.

Our third son, Timothy, was born some years later. He turned out to have unusual ability. In his large high school, he was chosen to be one of thirty honor students given special privileges in choosing the courses they wanted. Moving on to Wheaton College, he completed the four-year course in two years and nine months and graduated in the top two percent of his class. Consequently he had no difficulty getting into the medical school he wanted in Texas. After his first year, he married Dawn, a college classmate. Upon graduating from medical school, he immediately took his state board exams and passed them with flying colors.

During his senior year in medical school, Timothy taught a high school Bible class and a college-age Bible class at a little Baptist church near the school. Because of the church's regard for Timothy, they gave a special send-off service one Sunday. The following Sunday they held a memorial service for him—he had been instantly killed by a large truck which had moved suddenly into his path on an interstate highway.

One may ask, "Why?" Of the thousand letters we received from sympathetic friends, Dr. W. A. Criswell's expressed it simply: "Some Christians get ready for heaven sooner than others."

Our fourth child, Paul, was hopelessly retarded, mentally and physically, and has spent most of his years in a state school where he will stay for the rest of his life.

What is the greatest lesson I've learned? That God sustains us. In times of triumph, in times of sorrow, in times of achievement, in times of disappointment—our God is faithful.

Pat Williams

THE SECRET TO
SUCCESS IN THE
MARKETPLACE

Pat Williams became a part of our lives more than thirty years ago when one of our staff introduced him to Christ through the Four Spiritual Laws *gospel presentation. Over the years, our paths have crossed, and with each meeting our hearts have been drawn closer together. As chairman of the fundraising committee, Pat played a significant role in helping Campus Crusade for Christ relocate its international headquarters from San Bernardino, California, to Orlando, Florida.*

Pat is senior executive vice president of the Orlando Magic, the National Basketball Association (NBA) franchise in Orlando. He is widely recognized throughout the sports world as a consummate promoter and astute talent scout.

While he enjoys a widespread reputation in worldwide

sporting circles, many consider him to be one of this country's premier motivational and humorous speakers. He is the author of a number of motivational books offering inspiration and wit, among which are Making Magic, The Power Within You, Rekindled, *and* Love Her…Like Him.

From his years as a successful businessman, Pat has learned many lessons about conducting himself in a godly manner. Here he gives us the rules he goes by to pattern his life after biblical principles.

For men, all too often the biggest three-letter word in our vocabulary is *ego.*

Have you ever noticed that the first thing we ask a man we meet is not, "How are you as a father?" or, "What kind of husband are you?" but rather, "What do you do?"

Particularly with a man, too often the job becomes the number one priority. I'm convinced our ego makes this so. We feel that if we are not succeeding in our work, we're not succeeding at all.

But everything goes out of whack when that happens, so it's worth a daily struggle, if necessary, to keep our priorities in order.

This doesn't mean that during the time you're being paid, you're giving less than total effort. Your paycheck is housing you, clothing you, feeding your family. You owe your employer a great deal for that. And the greatest trade for your paycheck is yourself. Your character is a gift to your boss. It makes you what you are, determines whether you'll be a success, and charts how valuable you are to the company.

When I was in Spartanburg, South Carolina, with the Phillies organization, one of the owners of the ball club was Mr. R. E. Littlejohn. He was a committed Christian. He knew the Lord, loved and served Him, and believed that God, not man, has control in the affairs of men. He believed that our sovereign God has a plan for the world, and that He is ordering history according to that plan. He made a tremendous impact on me and from him I learned some of my greatest lessons in life.

What made him so special? Christlikeness. That's not an attribute anyone should throw around lightly. And I don't. I realize what I'm saying when I say a human being is like Christ. It's the highest compliment that can be paid. The way Mr. Littlejohn conducted himself in his personal life and his business affairs made me want to emulate him.

Over dinner one day, I reminded Mr. Littlejohn of the many things I'd learned from him and suggested we try to get his principles down on paper. A couple of hours of brainstorming produced what I like to call The Littlejohn Rules for Success in the Marketplace. You'll find that they're based on reverse-style, paradoxical living. I trust that his advice will be as valuable to you as it is to me.

The Littlejohn Rules for Success in the Marketplace

1. Have faith in God, and seek divine guidance in every decision, no matter how big or small.
2. Sell yourself to others. They must have confidence in you so they can depend on you, trust you, believe you, and confide in you. You only get one chance to make a good first impression.
3. Never give the other fellow the impression that you think you know more than he does. If you do, you will

break his spirit and destroy your influence with him, losing your ability to communicate properly.

4. Seek information from other people who are more experienced and be willing to listen to their advice. Be humble and willing to learn from anyone—regardless of his station in life. One good way to measure a person's character is to observe the way he treats people who can't possibly do him any good.

5. Work hard. Put first things first. Work as if you would live forever; live as if you would die tomorrow. Be willing to sacrifice some pleasures in order to do what has to be done.

6. Remember that everything you do in life leaves an impression on somebody. You are being observed every minute of each day, and every move is being recorded in someone's mind, either as a plus or a minus.

7. Don't expect everyone to agree with your ideas, but if the majority of people disagree on a subject, it's wise to make a new appraisal of your position.

8. It is necessary to control the things you have control over, no matter how small they may seem.

9. If you don't have a good feeling about a decision, don't make it. Never make an important decision without sleeping on it for two nights.

10. Don't make things complicated. Most good things in life are simple and practical.

11. Learn to manage your own personal affairs before expecting anyone to trust you with operating the affairs of their business.

12. To build loyalty and cooperation, take a personal interest in the feelings and welfare of other people you are working with.

13. Don't run from problems. A real problem gives you an opportunity to sell yourself to others. It's not the problem that matters so much, but how you react to it. The gem cannot be polished without friction, nor the child of God cleansed without adversity.

14. Surround yourself with successful people. The greatness of a man shows when he is able to see the greatness in others.

15. Be a good listener. Ask questions and get the other fellow to express his opinion first.

16. Gain experience. Pay your dues. You can't start at the top. You must learn at all levels to become an effective executive.

Mr. Littlejohn patterned his life after these biblical principles. Some might say that his are the rules of a weak, non-assertive type. They're wrong. He was a successful businessman, a successful baseball club owner, a successful husband and father, a successful employer. And he was also a successful, witnessing Christian.

THE CHILD OF GOD CANNOT BE CLEANSED WITHOUT ADVERSITY.

The best advice from such an outstanding example of a Christian? He would say not to look at him. Look to Christ, the author of unconditional love who said, "Greater love hath no man than this, that a man lay down his life for his friends" (John 15:13, KJV). That, Mr. Littlejohn would tell you, is the example we should follow.

Ralph D. Winter

REDISCOVERING
THE BIBLE

Highly regarded as a missions scholar, Dr. Ralph D. Winter is the founder and director of the United States Center for World Mission (USCWM). Its purpose is to help existing missions agencies focus their own strategies and mobilization efforts to reach the "hidden peoples"—those populations where no indigenous church exists.

My friendship with Ralph goes back to the days when we were students together at Princeton and later at Fuller Theological Seminary. He has always stood out among the crowd with his vision, creative ideas, and dedication to helping fulfill the Great Commission. His concern for the world caused him to launch a prayer campaign called Frontier Fellowship, which sought to involve a million people in praying for the 12,000 unreached people groups of the world.

In this account, Ralph provides thought-provoking insights into the historical significance of the Bible.

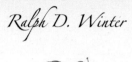

A few years ago I learned an amazing lesson that I often refer to as "the greatest intellectual revolution in my life." It took me completely by surprise. The lesson did not even soak in fully for a number of months. But it catapulted me into extraordinary consternation and anxious research.

For years, I had known about certain passages in the Old Testament that echoed in advance the Great Commission of our Lord recorded in Matthew 28:18–20; namely, sharing the knowledge of God with all the nations and tribes and tongues of the earth. This idea is found in a number of places in the Old Testament.

But somehow I had gotten the basic impression that the Old Testament was "outmoded" by the New Testament. For example, people didn't exactly get "born again" in the Old Testament. They did not go around witnessing for Christ. Nor did they form mission societies to send people to the ends of the earth. The people of God of the Old Testament mainly struggled with their own personal, family, and national problems.

Up to this time, I had heard many different views of the Bible's significance:

- *The Medicine Chest Bible:* Early as a Christian, I thought of the Old Testament and the Bible in general as something like a medicine chest—where you look when something goes wrong. If your marriage is in trouble, see page xxx. If you have aches and pains, see page xxx. That's why it made sense to put all those suggestions in the front of Gideon Bibles placed in hotels.

- *The Snack Bar Bible:* Later, I began to discover all the good, positive, and inspiring things in the Bible. Sunday school teachers hauled out this verse. The pastor's sermon highlighted that one. Great stuff. Like reaching into a well-stocked refrigerator—good things on every shelf.

- *The Crystal Ball Bible:* Pretty soon, most of the really good verses became well known to me. But there still remained the possibility of getting fascinated by biblical prophecy. For some people that is the ultimate in the Bible. They ransack every reference to the future to find out what is going to happen.

But in all of this, the Old Testament was not a whole lot more than a source book—a grab-bag of stories for children and a book of sermon illustrations for adults.

However, the first 75 percent of the Bible, the Old Testament, did tell the continuous story of a nation. I finally got Israel's history straight in my mind:

- Abraham coming over from Kuwait to Israel
- His descendants getting carried off to Egypt for four hundred years
- Moses bringing the survivors back to Palestine, with a big interlude in the desert
- The rocky period of the Judges, the Kings, and the two kingdoms
- The dispersion of the northern group
- The exile of the Judean group
- The trickling back of these Judeans (Jews) under Ezra and Nehemiah
- The Greek and Roman domination of the politics and culture of the hardy survivors

And finally the bright, blue yonder opens up and God strategically intervenes in human history as Jesus, His only Son, appears among men.

Wow! This is so important. Why bother about all that detailed background? Isn't that for seminary students? Or for sermonizers to mine for practical applications and illustrations for their messages? How important is the Old Testament if the New Testament is so *new?*

Actually, the terms *Old* and *New*, as handy and familiar as they are, don't tell the full story. The New Testament, in an important sense, begins with Genesis 12! Abraham was the first Gentile proselyte, the beginning of God's outreach to the whole world.

The Old Testament is thus not just the description of what preceded Jesus' arrival. From Abraham on, the major portion of the Bible is the story of what happened in an unfolding plan that has, from 2000 B.C. until now, been the single major event of relentless missionary outreach to the nationalities, tribes, and tongues of the world.

Every commentator on Genesis breaks the book at Genesis chapter 12. In fact, a Bible could be published in which Genesis 1–11 would be called the Introduction; Genesis 12–50 labeled chapter 1; Exodus, chapter 2; Leviticus, chapter 3, and so on. The title of this new edition could be *The Kingdom Strikes Back.*

For example, Genesis 1–11 portrays: 1) the goodness of God's creation, 2) the gruesome entrance of evil, and 3) the hopelessness of the result—"every intent of the thoughts of [man's] heart was only evil continually" (Genesis 6:5, NKJ). What an introduction!

But what is next? What does God do now?

Well, Genesis 12 (the beginning of our new chapter 1)

opens with—and initiates—the astounding plan where God chooses one man and one nation through whom He can reclaim all mankind. The Lord informs Abraham that He has decided to make him a child of God by faith—right then and there! "I will bless you" in verse 2 means adoption, including all of the New Testament concept of reconciliation. Jesus reaffirmed this when He said, "Abraham rejoiced to see My day, and he saw it and was glad" (John 8:56, NKJ). Abraham's sins were covered by the blood of Christ.

God also tells Abraham that not only his own lineage, but all of the peoples of the earth, will also be blessed (adopted) —beginning right then and there! The Book of Revelation assures us that some from every tribe and tongue and nation will participate in this adoptive reconciliation (Revelation 5:9).

Okay, okay, okay, why is this so significantly different? Why did this mean so much to me? Because the great bulk of the Bible is no longer an up-and-down story of what happened before the sparks began to fly, before God's major plan began to move forward. *It is the story of a nation that received a commission and did not fully live up to it.*

Note well: If one nation received the blessing of heavenly inheritance and could and should pass it on to all other peoples, how did this chosen nation do? The Old Testament tells us the gripping story of Israel *under orders*, a commission it partially carried out and then handed on to other nations.

Now, all of a sudden, I understand why God moved Abraham and his family from Kuwait to Israel: because that was the land-bridge connecting Europe and Asia and Africa—a better place from which to reach out to the whole world.

Now I see God gently pushing this budding nation into

238

Egypt *as a missionary operation.*

Now I understand that the Mosaic Exodus brought God's people out of Egypt *so they could reach out to all the peoples of the earth*—even though their self-centered struggles blinded them to this continuing obligation and privilege. (Check Jonah's inability to get it straight.)

Now I view the "dispersion" of the northern group as not just a punishment, but as part of *God's missionary concern to reach out to other nations.* The same goes for the Judean exile: the Jews' longing to return to their land clashed with God's purposes for sending them—"You should be My salvation *to the ends of the earth!*" (Isaiah 49:6, NKJ).

Now I also understand Jesus' anger at the moneychangers who took up the space intended as *the court of the Gentiles* in "a house of prayer for all nations" (Matthew 21:12; Isaiah 56:7, NKJ).

But a new thought really clinched the matter for me. The absence of evidence that Abraham's descendants took the Great Commission seriously prior to the appearance of Christ is no more proof that the clear commission in Genesis 12:2,3 was not yet in force than it would be proof that the New Testament repetition of the Great Commission was not yet in force just because the vast majority of God's people paid virtually no attention to it in the eighteen centuries following the New Testament!

Where is the Great Commission in Chrysostom's sermons, or Tertullian's, or Augustine's? Or where is it to be seen in the Nicean Creed, the Chalcedonian creed, the Augsburg (Lutheran) Confession, or the Westminster Confession? *Its absence does not prove Jesus intended it for later attention* in modern times—by, say, William Carey.

Suddenly I saw the history of the United States, the history of Russia, and recently the history of Korea—and of every other nation that has heard the gospel—as stories of nations under this commission. That is, the Old Testament experience is a dynamic, full blown *parallel* (not a preface) to our own national experience and to other similarly "blessed" nations.

But now that our people (of the United States) have received that same blessing, how are we doing? Is our nation foggy on this point? Do the 137 languages spoken in Los Angeles have a clear missionary significance to Americans, or even American evangelicals? Are we unaware that God is a missionary God from start to finish?

ARE WE UNAWARE THAT GOD IS A MISSIONARY GOD FROM START TO FINISH?

Now I understood completely. Instead of being the story of a nation not yet commissioned but merely exhorted to "behave," the Bible is a new, exciting book, full of insights, missionary strategy, and up-to-date applications of how God wants to teach and use His people to finish the Great Commission.

For me, this is the greatest lesson I have ever learned.

Bill Bright

HOW TO LOVE
THE-UNLOVABLE

Like the rest of the authors of this book, I have made many important discoveries and learned many valuable lessons in the course of my almost eighty years.

I could have written of my days of agnosticism when as a happy pagan I finally heard the Good News for the first time and fell in love with Jesus Christ.

I could have told about the days when I first experienced the reality of the person and ministry of the Holy Spirit.

I could have shared my discovery of how to introduce others to Christ as a way of life, or my realization that everybody hungers for God, even the so-called atheists, because God created us that way (Romans 1:19,20).

However, having considered all of these possibilities, I have chosen to write about how I learned to love people who sometimes are difficult to love.

Why was this lesson important to me? Because God places

a very strong emphasis on love in His Word. In fact, our Lord teaches us to "love the Lord your God with all your heart, soul, and mind" and to "love your neighbor as much as you love yourself. All the other commandments and all the demands of the prophets stem from these two laws and are fulfilled if you obey them" (Matthew 22:37–40, TLB).

Jesus reminds us in John 13:35, "By this all men will know that you are my disciples, if you love one another" (NIV).

And the Holy Spirit spoke through the apostle Paul, as he records in 1 Corinthians 13, that no matter what else we might accomplish in life, regardless of what we may contribute that is good and commendable, apart from love it is of no value whatsoever.

Further, I was sobered by the message that God sent to the church at Ephesus. This church was mightily used by God to touch the wicked city of Ephesus. However, approximately thirty years after the apostle Paul was martyred for his Christian faith, the church had left its first love. God threatened to remove their candlestick from its place among the churches unless they repented and returned to that first love (Revelation 2:1–7).

With such emphasis in God's Word on loving Christ and one another, I finally concluded that the most important contribution I can make to this book is the revolutionary discovery I made many years ago on how to love by faith.

Is there someone in your life whom you have difficulty loving? Have you ever experienced a conflict with another person that left you with bitter or angry feelings?

There was a period in my ministry when I was faced with such a challenge. Several men in whom I had placed great confidence, who were in positions of leadership in Campus Crusade for Christ, were unfaithful to that trust. This resulted in misunderstandings all across the nation of what our ministry was about. The situation was fraught with tremendous crises and had a potential for anger, resentment, discord, and conflict. A godly resolution required a full measure of my love for these men.

For years I had spoken on the subject of love. I had a simple four-point outline:

1. God loves you unconditionally.
2. You are commanded to love others—God, your neighbors, your enemies.
3. You are incapable of loving others in your own strength.
4. You can love others with God's love.

But, as in the case of most sermons on love, something was missing. I still did not grasp one essential ingredient for enabling God to love through me despite the circumstances.

One night at the beginning of this crisis, I was awakened at 2 A.M. I knew that God had something to say to me. I felt impressed to get out of bed, take my Bible, and go into another room so I wouldn't disturb my wife, Vonette. I fell to my knees and read and prayed for the next couple of hours.

What I discovered that night has since enriched my life and the lives of tens of thousands of others. I had never heard anyone speak on the lesson God revealed to me. Yet it was so simple, so biblical, and so revolutionary. The discovery? *Christians can love by faith.*

As a result of applying this lesson, the situation that had such a vast potential for destruction was resolved. And God never allowed me to have any resentment or antagonism toward my brothers. In fact, I continue to love them to this day.

Truly, love is the greatest privilege and power known to man. When Christ came into my life and I became a Christian, God gave me the resources to be a different person. He gave me the ability to love. But I did not discover how to make that love a practical reality in my life until that night on my knees.

Everything in the Christian life, I knew, was based on faith. God's holy Word says, "*Without faith* it is impossible to please God" (Hebrews 11:6, NIV). "The just shall live *by faith*" (Romans 1:17, NKJ) and "everything that does not come *from faith* is sin" (Romans 14:23, NIV). Then, that memorable night, God showed me that we love by faith just as we received Christ by faith, just as we are filled with the Holy Spirit by faith, and just as we walk in the Spirit by faith. Likewise, there can be no demonstration of God's love apart from faith.

It is God's will for us to love. Jesus *commands*, "Love each other as much as I love you" (John 15:12, TLB). He would not command us to do anything that He will not enable us to do if only we trust and obey Him. In 1 John 5:14,15, God *promises,* "If we ask anything according to His will, He hears us. And if we know that He hears us—whatever we ask—we know that we have what we asked of Him" (NIV). Relating this *promise* to God's *command* to love, I discovered: *We can claim by faith the privilege of loving with His love.* In order to experience and share this love, we must claim it by faith; that is, trust His promise that He will give us all that we need to do His will on the basis of

His *command* and *promise*.

Love is an act of our will and not of our emotions. Because we are obeying a command of God, we are not being hypocritical when we say, "I love you," even though we may not feel loving.

This truth is not new. It has been recorded in God's Word for two thousand years. But it was a revolutionary discovery to me that early morning some years ago and, since that time, to many thousands of other Christians with whom I have shared it. When I began to practice loving others by faith, I found that problems of tension with other individuals seemed to disappear, often miraculously.

> LOVE IS AN ACT
>
> OF OUR WILL
>
> AND NOT OF
>
> OUR EMOTIONS.

In one instance, I was having difficulty loving a fellow staff member. This troubled me. I wanted to love him. I knew that God's Word commanded me to love him. Yet, because of certain areas of inconsistency and personality differences, I found it difficult to love him. But the Lord reminded me of 1 Peter 5:7: "Let Him have all your worries and cares, for He is always thinking about you and watching everything that concerns you" (TLB). I decided to give this problem to Him and love this man *by faith*. When I claimed God's love for the man by faith, my concern lifted. I knew the matter was in God's hands.

An hour later, I found a letter under my door from that very man, who had no possible way of knowing what I had just experienced. In fact, his letter had been written the day before. The Lord had foreseen the change in me. This friend and I met that afternoon and had the most wonderful time of prayer and fellowship we had ever experienced together. Loving with God's love by faith had changed our relationship.

I have seen this principle at work in many situations since then. For example, two gifted attorneys had great professional animosity, even hatred for each other. Even though they were distinguished members of the same firm, they were constantly criticizing each other, making the other's life miserable.

One of the men received Christ through our ministry and some months later came to me for counsel.

"I have hated and criticized my partner for years," he said, "and he has been equally antagonistic toward me. But now that I am a Christian, I don't feel right about continuing our warfare. What shall I do?"

"Why not ask your partner to forgive you and tell him that you love him?" I suggested.

"I could never do that!" he exclaimed. "That would be hypocritical. I *don't* love him. How could I tell him I love him when I don't?"

I explained the greatest lesson I had ever learned: God commands His children to love even their enemies, and His supernatural, unconditional love is an expression not of our emotions, but of our will, which we exercise by faith.

Together we knelt to pray, and my friend asked God's forgiveness for his critical attitude toward his law partner and claimed God's love for him by faith.

Early the next morning, my friend walked into his partner's office and announced, "Something wonderful has happened to me. I have become a Christian. And I have come to ask you to forgive me for all that I have done to hurt you in the past and to tell you that I love you."

His partner was so surprised and convicted of his own sin that he responded by asking my friend to forgive him. Then, to my friend's surprise, his partner said, "I would like to become a Christian, too. Would you show me what I need to do?"

After my friend shared how to receive Christ as Savior and Lord, they knelt together to pray. Then they both came to tell me of this marvelous miracle of God's love in their lives and in their relationship.

Perhaps you have been in a similar situation and have wondered, "How can I really love that person?" No doubt you have found certain people hard to tolerate.

I encourage you to make a list of those whom you don't like and begin to love them by faith. Perhaps your boss, a coworker, your spouse, your children, or your father or mother are on the list. Confess any wrong attitudes you have about them to the Lord. Ask the Holy Spirit to fill you with Christ's love for each of them. Draw upon God's limitless, inexhaustible, overwhelming love for them by faith. Love every one of your "enemies" by faith—those who anger you, ignore you, bore you, or frustrate you. Then, as God enables you, claiming the power of the Holy Spirit, go to the individuals with whom you have discord and conflict. Tell them that you love them.

You will discover, as I have, that we can never run out of opportunities to love by faith. People are desperately waiting to be loved with God's love. And God has an unending supply of His divine, supernatural love for everyone. It is for us to claim, to grow on, to spread to others, and thus to reach everyone around us with the love that counts—the love that will bring them to Jesus Christ.

Bringing It All Together

A very remarkable experience in my life took place years ago in St. Louis, Missouri. I had finished my speaking engagements and rushed to the airport to catch a plane to Arrowhead Springs to be with Vonette and our sons, Zac and Brad. My travel schedule had been unusually busy so I had not spent as much time with them as I wanted and was especially eager to return home.

As I sped to the airport, I noticed storm clouds gathering rapidly. On arrival, I rushed to the counter to purchase my ticket for the first plane leaving, only to find that all planes were grounded because of the weather.

Dismayed, I caught a bus back to the hotel. At first I was sad and terribly disappointed, but as I bumped along in the bus the Holy Spirit seemed to say, "I have something very important for you to do."

As I entered the hotel lobby, I joined other discouraged passengers waiting in line for rooms and struck up a conversation with one of them.

In the course of our conversation, he told me that he and his wife had been searching for God for the past two years. They had attended different churches every Sunday. But they had not found Him.

248

You can imagine my excitement and delight! I pulled a copy of the *Four Spiritual Laws* booklet from my pocket and used it as a tool to explain to him how he could know God in a personal way.

His response was enthusiastic; he was ready and eager to receive Christ. We found a quiet place and bowed together in prayer. As soon as we had finished praying, he asked, "What do you do for a living?"

When I explained that I had dedicated my life to telling others the Good News I had just shared with him, he responded with words I shall never forget: "Surely, you must bring a lot of happiness into this world!" With eyes filled with tears of gratitude, he asked if he could keep the *Four Spiritual Laws* booklet to share with his wife who was as hungry for God as he was. Of course I gladly gave it to him.

> "SURELY, YOU MUST BRING A LOT OF HAPPINESS INTO THIS WORLD!"

I went to bed that night with a joyful heart, singing praises to our wonderful Lord for allowing me to have the privilege of introducing this businessman to our Savior. As I went to sleep, his words played like an unbroken refrain in my mind: "You must bring a lot of happiness into this world."

For more than fifty-five years I have had the joyful privilege of not only knowing Jesus Christ in a vital, personal way, but also of helping to share the Good News with millions of others around the world.

Perhaps you are on a spiritual journey like my friend in St. Louis. You may still be seeking to know God in a personal way.

If so, reading the next few pages may be the most important thing you ever do. Let me share four principles that, if applied, will enable you to know the reality of God in your life. And if you have already made the discovery of knowing Christ personally, may I encourage you to send a copy of this book to all your friends who are not believers.

Notes

Bill Armstrong

1. I relied on the *Four Spiritual Laws* with great confidence, having used this effective ministry tool on many previous occasions. This little tract was instrumental in my own conversion a number of years earlier. Since then, I have quoted the "laws" (really the distilled essence of the New Testament) in hundreds of speeches and personal conversations. Instead of shrouding the gospel in complex and forbidding verbiage, this pamphlet is simple and direct. In my opinion, it is divinely inspired and the best ministry tool of its kind of which I am aware.

Ted W. Engstrom

1. New Life 2000 is a registered servicemark of Campus Crusade for Christ, Inc.

Jack Hayford

1. Song-making and song-writing are two different things entirely. I do not even generally encourage people to think of the songs they sing spontaneously as songs to be written for others to sing. Of course, occasionally that will occur, but if the focus of worship-song becomes "song-writing," the pure simplicity of the practice becomes lost in one's preoccupation with memorability, the effect the song may have on others, the quality of the melody, the refinement of the lyric, etc. Song-writing for widespread use is a gift God gives to relatively few; song-making is a gift potential He has given to everyone.

Robert H. Schuller

1. From the song, "In the Garden," words and music by C. Austin Miles, © 1912 by Hall Mack Co.

I would like to thank the publishers for granting their authors permission to adapt material from the following books for use in this volume:

The God of Stones and Spiders by Charles Colson (Wheaton, IL: Crossway Books, 1990).

10 Years of God's Miracles by Paul Crouch (Santa Ana, California: nd).

The Gospel and the Briefcase by Ted DeMoss (Chattanooga, TN: Christian Business Men's Committee of USA, 1987).

Turning Hearts Toward Home by Rolf Zettersten (Irving, TX: Word Inc., 1989).

Sandy: A Heart for God by Leighton Ford (Downers Grove, IL: InterVarsity Press, 1985).

Worship His Majesty by Jack Hayford (Irving, TX: Word, Inc., 1987).

The Man in the Mirror and *I Surrender* by Pat Morley (Brentwood, TN: Wolgemuth and Hyatt, Inc., 1989 and 1990).

Say, "Yes!": How to Renew Your Spiritual Passion by Luis Palau (Portland, OR: Multnomah Press, 1991).

The Positive Power of Jesus Christ by Norman Vincent Peale (Wheaton, IL: Tyndale House Publishers, 1980).

Happy Trails by Roy Rogers and Dale Evans (Irving, TX: Word Inc., 1979).

Tough Times Never Last, But Tough People Do by Robert Schuller (Nashville, TN: Thomas Nelson Inc., 1983).

BOOK 2

*To my husband, Bill, who is a constant
encouragement, and
to all of these women who have been
open and honest in sharing their greatest
lessons to make this book possible*

To the Reader

Elise and Patrick were married in a beautiful traditional Christian ceremony, which ended with the lighting of a single candle. They took candles, which their mothers had previously lit to represent each of their families, and joined their flames to light the wick of the single candle that signified the beginning of their lives together. Each then blew out the flame of his own candle.

During the wedding reception, the father of the bride asked the guests to come to the microphone and share with the young couple any admonition, memories, funny stories, or comments they desired. He also asked that they would say a prayer of blessing for the bride and groom after their remarks.

I have attended a thousand or more weddings, but this was a new and very interesting approach to launching a young couple in the formation of a new home.

As the bride and groom listened to each statement—some humorous, some serious, but all very meaningful—and as person after person prayed God's blessing upon them, I began to consider how different, and even bizarre, this experience could seem to many people who know little or nothing about the biblical approach to marriage.

It also has become strange to some people to approach solutions to problems from a biblical point of view. "The Bible says…" is not as known or relevant in our "enlightened" age as it once was. The standards of the Bible are at odds with the standards of the world.

I became all the more aware of this recently when I was reading the Beatitudes that Jesus gave in His Sermon on the Mount, recorded in Matthew 5: "'Humble men are very fortunate!' he told them, 'for the Kingdom of Heaven is given to them. Those who mourn are fortunate! for they shall be comforted. The meek and lowly are fortunate! for the whole wide world belongs to them. Happy are those who long to be just and good, for they shall be completely satisfied. Happy are the kind and merciful, for they shall be shown mercy. Happy are those whose hearts are pure, for they shall see God. Happy are those who strive for peace— they shall be called the sons of God. Happy are those who are persecuted because they are good, for the Kingdom of Heaven is theirs'" (Matthew 5:3–10).

The footnote in the *Life Application Bible* says this:

> Jesus began His sermon with words that seemed to contradict each other. But God's way of living usually contradicts the world's. If you want to live for God, you must be ready to say and do what seems strange to the world. You must be willing to give when others take, to love when others hate, to help when others abuse. In doing this you will one day receive everything, while the others will end up with nothing.

The book you now hold contains living examples of women who have chosen to live within the boundaries of God's textbook to mankind, the Bible.

Why listen to people like this? These women of experience have found answers to human needs, to which so often there seems to be no answer. And don't we *all* have needs! A need for love, a need for security, a need for forgiveness, a need for self-esteem, a need for wisdom!

In sharing with you how they coped with real-life situations, these women give you examples of how to live from their knowledge of the Bible and their walk with God. I trust they will bless your life as they have mine.

Vonette Zachary Bright,
Editor

Ney Bailey

IS MY GOD BIGGER THAN MY HURT?

A former adoption agency case worker in New Orleans, Ney Bailey has been a staff member with Campus Crusade for Christ for nearly forty years. Presently, she is an international traveling representative with this ministry.

After serving on campus at the University of Arizona, she founded and directed Campus Crusade's personnel department for six years. She has spoken extensively on university campuses, at weekend conferences and retreats, and to civic groups. Ney has also addressed congressional wives, ambassadors, and diplomats.

She participated in the founding of Campus Crusade's Family Ministry and Keystone Kaper Singles' Conference, initiated Campus Crusade's Alumni Ministry, and has served on the faculty of the Institute of Biblical Studies. She also serves on the board of directors of Insight for Living, Dr. Charles R. Swindoll's ministry.

She is listed in The World Who's Who of Women *and is the author of the best-selling book* Faith Is Not a Feeling.

A good listener, wise counselor, and excellent speaker, Ney readily identifies with her audience whether it be one person or thousands.

I was barely three feet tall and standing on the edge of the municipal swimming pool.

"Jump, Ney Ann!" coaxed my father, his arms outstretched. "I'll catch you!"

The water was over my head where he was standing in the pool and I was petrified about jumping in.

Trembling, I called out, "No, I can't do it."

"Yes, you can," he shouted. "Jump, and I'll catch you!"

Finally, I jumped. My head went under the water and I came up sputtering and thrashing. My father wasn't there. He had moved back in the water, hoping I would swim to him. I began to cry.

"Daddy, you moved! You said you wouldn't!"

I heard him laughing.

"Ney Ann, you've gotten upset over nothing. You know I wouldn't let anything happen to you. I was just trying to teach you to swim."

That experience had a devastating effect on my tender, young mind. I had trusted Daddy with everything that my little heart could muster—he had said he would catch me, but he didn't. He had let me down.

This experience represents how I began to feel about

my father as I grew older. I began to realize that some of the deepest hurts we'll ever know come from those we care most about, hurts that often result in bruised relationships within our families. And those relationships are often the hardest to heal. With many other experiences to fuel my feelings and attitudes, my bitterness toward my father became deeply rooted—and was fully grown—by the time I entered college.

In later years, my hostility turned to a subtle rebellion. I thought, *You go your way and I'll go mine. You don't bother me and I won't bother you.* If Dad yelled at me, I wished I could yell back. If he ignored me, I ignored him. If he hurt my feelings, I'd try to hurt his. I wanted to give him what I thought he deserved.

When I was fifteen, I invited Jesus Christ to become my Savior, but it wasn't until I had graduated from college and was working in New Orleans that I truly gave my life to Christ. At twenty-five, I joined the staff of Campus Crusade for Christ.

As I became an adult, my relationship with my dad was not characterized by open hostility, but it did lack warmth and understanding. We politely went our separate ways. I felt no guilt or loss. I assume he didn't either.

Later, my discovery of the meaning of faith was a catalyst that led to the improvement in my relationship with my dad.

One summer I was taking a class on the Book of Romans. One of my assignments was to go through Romans and find everything Paul said about faith.

As I moved through the chapters, the word "faith" appeared almost too many times to count. As I pondered the word, I found myself asking, "What is it? Faith is probably the most important thing in my life, but how do I define it?"

I thought, *Lord, how would You define it?*

Immediately a story came to mind in which Jesus had said to someone, "Not even in Israel have I found such great faith." I became quite curious. What was it that Jesus Himself called "great faith"?

I quickly looked up the passage in Luke 7, and learned that He equated great faith with someone who was simply willing to take Him at His word.

I wondered if such a "definition" would be confirmed elsewhere in Scripture. Since Hebrews 11 is often referred to as "faith's hall of fame," I turned there.

For example, God told Noah to build an ark.

Noah took God at His word and built the ark. Therefore, Hebrews 11:7 begins, "By faith Noah…" Throughout the chapter it appeared that regardless of the circumstances, despite arguments of logic and reason—even regardless of how he felt—each person believed God, took Him at His word, and chose to be obedient.

By now, my homework had become far more exciting than I could have imagined.

On the basis of all I observed in these passages, I had arrived at a simple, workable definition of faith! I wasn't sure if I would ever finish the assignment on all that the Book of Romans said about faith, but in my own heart I knew I had learned something that would prove to be very significant in my walk with God.

But I had one more question: If faith is a matter of taking God at His word, what does God say *about* His Word? I found the answer in Scripture itself:

"The word of the Lord abides forever" (1 Peter 1:25).

"The grass withers, the flower fades, but the word of our God stands forever" (Isaiah 40:8).

"Heaven and earth will pass away, but My words shall not pass away" (Matthew 24:35).

Everything in life may change, I observed, but God's Word remains constant! That means:

- God's Word is truer than anything I feel.
- God's Word is truer than anything I experience.
- God's Word is truer than any circumstance I will ever face.
- God's Word is truer than anything in the world.

I began to see clearly that faith is not a feeling, it is a choice we have—to take God at His word. As a result, I made a lifetime commitment to bank my life on God's Word.

I was beginning to catch a glimpse of how this could affect me, and for the first time in my life, I began to think about the impact of my faith on my relationship with my father.

I had always heard that I was supposed to love other people with a 1 Corinthians 13 kind of love. Someone suggested that I test my love for others by inserting my name wherever the chapter mentions "love." For example: "Ney is patient, Ney is kind, Ney is not provoked…" I failed the test! Then I remembered 1 John 4:16 says that God is love. And since 1 Corinthians 13 explains what love is, I decided to put God's name beside the word "love" and relate it to myself:

- God's love toward me is patient,
- God's love toward me is kind,
- God's love toward me is not provoked,

- God's love toward me does not take into account a wrong suffered,
- God's love toward me would bear all things,
- believe all things,
- hope all things,
- endure all things.
- God's love toward me would never fail.

It was overwhelming to think that He loved me in that way. And I was struck with amazement to realize that He loved my father in the very same way.

I thought, *If God loves my father just the way he is, who am I not to love him also?* My love had been conditional, based on his performance. I had been waiting for him to change. Then, if he changed, I would begin to love him.

My love had said, "Daddy, I'll love you if you do this and if you do that." Yet God's love simply said, "I love you, *period*." No "if's" about it.

I was driving up the mountain road to my home with tears streaming down my face as the reality of this truth began touching my heart. For the first time in my life, I decided to take God at His word and love and accept my father just as he was.

I was grateful for this new understanding as I pulled the car into my driveway. It seemed as if the Lord had done something new in my life. But I knew the real test was yet to come.

Not knowing where to begin, I began to pray that God would give me an opportunity to make things right with my father. I knew it would be difficult and that I would not feel like doing it, but I needed to take the first step.

The next time I visited my folks, I had an attitude of

love and acceptance rather than one of being critical and judgmental. As I was nice to my father, he was nice to me. He must have sensed God's Spirit working in me.

Later, I remember thinking, *If my dad were to die, would I have any regrets at his funeral?* The answer was "Yes." I would regret that I had never asked him to forgive me for some of my ugly ways while I was growing up.

So, I purposed in my heart to ask his forgiveness. It was very scary to talk to him because he was a bullheaded lawyer, by his own description, and I imagined myself prostrate on the ground, crying my eyes out, unable to say a word.

On the weekend I went home, I knew enough not to talk to him during the football game, so I waited for half-time and for my mother to leave the room. When he and I were alone I said, "Daddy, I've been thinking about my growing-up years—how unloving, ungrateful, and unkind I was. Will you forgive me?"

IF GOD LOVES MY FATHER JUST THE WAY HE IS, WHO AM I NOT TO LOVE HIM ALSO?

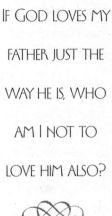

As he turned and looked at me with a twinkle in his eye, he said, "No." Pausing, he added, "I don't remember all those things except for the time…" And then he named one.

Knowing the importance of his response, I asked, "Will you forgive me for what you can remember?"

"Yes," he answered.

From that time on he was warmer and kinder than ever before.

Without warning, a few years later my father became

critically ill.

As I was leaving his bedside in the intensive care unit, I said, "Well, Daddy, I'd better go now and let Brenda [my sister] come in. She's out in the hall waiting. I love you, Daddy."

"I love you, too, honey, whether you're in here or whether you're out in the hall waiting to come in." Those were to be his last words to me.

A few days later as the family gathered at the funeral home, I looked out and saw the casket. I remembered that when I did not feel like it, I chose with my will to forgive my father. I was so glad as I was sitting there that I did not have any regrets. The only regret I did have was that I had not done it sooner.

I realized that when I am hurt I need to ask myself the question, "Is my God bigger than my hurt or is my hurt bigger than my God?" I am the one who gets to choose. There are many things that are inexcusable, but nothing is unforgivable. Someone has said, "To forgive is to set the prisoner free only to discover that the prisoner was you." I am not most like Christ when I am perfect, but I am most like Christ when I am forgiving.

My dad never asked me to forgive him, but God asked that of me and it made all the difference.[1]

Jill Briscoe

THE ULTRA-SUEDE LADIES

Jill Briscoe is real, practical, down-to-earth, and disarmingly honest with a well-adjusted, healthy outlook on her gifts, family, and ministry.

Born in Liverpool, England, and educated at Homerton College in Cambridge, she is an advisor to the women's ministries at the Elmbrook Church in Brookfield, Wisconsin, where her husband, Stuart, is the pastor. They minister together through their "Telling the Truth" media outreach.

Jill is executive editor of Just Between Us, *a magazine for ministry wives and women in leadership, and advises numerous non-profit organizations.*

Because of her heart for God, she is helping women wherever she travels to overcome their feelings of inadequacy. She joyfully helps them do the things they never believed they could do and be the people they never thought they could be. The following story relates how she overcame her own lack of

self-confidence and how God began to develop in her a new sense of well-being.

"I had tea with the Queen," the beautiful lady informed me.

"Queen who?" I wanted to ask facetiously. But I knew "who." Queen Elizabeth, of course. *My* queen! This polished American lady who was to share the platform with me at a women's retreat was telling me all about her tea party with the Queen of England herself! After describing the event in detail, the lady added another story of yet one more "queenly" interview in another European capital, where she had been able to actually talk to "Her Majesty" about the Lord!

Settling back in the big black limousine that was speeding us toward the retreat center, I thought of how I had never even seen the Queen in person, never mind had tea with her. How absolutely marvelous! I envisioned myself in Buckingham Palace, standing in this huge room under a gigantic chandelier, holding a white Bible in my hand. I would know *just* the right thing to say to the royal relatives; I would be in complete charge of myself and the situation. Carried away with such fantasies, I could see the Royal Guards bowing their black fuzzy hats in prayer as they stood in their compact little boxes outside the palace gate.

I was brought back to earth by the beautiful lady inquiring, "And just where have *you* been lately?"

I gazed at her, completely lost for words. I wanted to say casually, "Oh, Washington, D.C., a little Bible study meeting with the congressmen's wives, and then on to the Florida Hilton, before dropping in for a quick meeting at the governor's mansion!" I wanted to say it but couldn't—though all of those invitations had been given to me, I hadn't accepted them. Looking at my beautiful ultra-suede companion, I felt the old familiar struggle all over again. *I wanted to be like her!*

Ultra-suede ladies, especially the ultra-ultra ones, frightened me out of my mind. I had already decided there was absolutely no way that God could use me to reach "the up and outers."

Just look at me, I mumbled quietly as I slumped against the upholstery in a self-conscious heap. *Here I am in my forties, suffering from a teenage bad self-image syndrome.* I wanted to shout at my Maker, "Why don't You recall all those 1935 models with defects [like me] and make us right! For a start, You could give me new hair."

My hair was the fine baby type that convinced me I faced premature baldness. Often I was tempted to get on a plane with a plastic bag over my head so the wind wouldn't mess up my painstakingly arranged hairdo. It was years before I could travel comfortably.

Sitting in the speeding limousine beside my American friend, I also pondered why the Eternal hadn't made my metabolism so that I could eat all those sweet, sticky, energy-giving cakes and hot fudge sundaes that I wanted and still stay slim and trim! I found myself starving after each speech, craving for an extra shot of energy to meet a demanding traveling schedule. When I stayed in a private home, people were just too kind in their care of me. How do you refuse your hostess's lovingly prepared caloric recipes without offending her? And anyway, who *wants* to refuse?

Glancing sideways in the semi-dark cab, I acknowledged the super-trim shape of my companion with something akin to gloom and despair. How would I ever gain the ear of the ultra, ultra-suede ladies unless I looked like a size-eight model?

"And then, Lord, there is the money problem," I sighed. "How could I ever afford to dress ultra-suede to match my audience, or on the other hand cope with the trouble arising if I did?" For one thing, the ultra, ultra-suede who seemed to put such store in appearance might not listen if I didn't match up dress-wise, but then the "sub-suede" in the audience (like me!) might consider an ultra-suede outfit a gross misuse of the Lord's money!

I remembered with a shudder the time I found myself a guest in an incredible "villa." We were to change for dinner in a "small" bedroom (about half the size of our entire house). The other ladies were pouring themselves into their exclusive outfits and throwing around the casual remarks about Dior's latest show! With my little bit of starched cotton dress hanging limply from my hand, I encountered a fabulous-looking creature who remarked kindly, "That looks like a pretty little creation, Jill." She had focused the attention of the entire roomful of women onto my apparel. I didn't need to say it, but I did anyway. "Sears," I whispered, as if I'd just been caught shoplifting! *Why did I do that?* I asked myself furiously. Why couldn't I just smile and say "thank you," because it *was* a pretty dress and quite as lovely as all the rest, just not as expensive.

I knew in my heart, of course, that my reaction was a guilty confession to these women that, because of the way I looked, I felt totally out of place among them. How could it be that I still believed those ultra, ultra-suede ladies would hear what I had to say only if I dressed in ultra-suede? Maybe the fact of the matter was that this woman's ministry just wasn't my "cup of tea," as we say in England.

If your husband is a speaker, the public expects you to follow suit. *All* sorts of doors of opportunity had opened up to me as soon as I arrived in the States, simply because of Stuart's already well-established ministry.

"But I don't *want* to speak to ladies," I had complained to the Eternal. He knew I never had liked it when lots of women were compressed together in a confined space. What a row they made for starters! But having learned not to be a Jonah and run away from my responsibility to speak to people whom I didn't particularly like, I had answered the invitations and gone anyway.

It really doesn't matter that I don't like them very much, I thought. *After all, they needn't know!*

Like Jonah, I marched into Nineveh (the situation I would like to have stayed away from) and preached my heart out —retiring like that same angry prophet to my hill of disdain once the engagement was over. But God apparently used the message and I received requests to return.

One day I went to Memphis, Tennessee. Verla met me at the airport. She was a speaker and teacher, ran a rescue mission, talked to up-and-outers and down-and-outers, and was totally relaxed with both. She gave me an uncomfortable feeling in the pit of my conscience the moment I saw her warm touch with the women. Her whole approach and ministry served to rebuke me outright, saying louder than any verbal complaint: "Jill, you are technically a good speaker, but *you do not love these women!*"

Being with her was like telling me my slip was showing, only this was the slip of disobedience, and it was hanging down several inches. I knew that love was a conscious decision, and where these women were concerned I had definitely decided against love.

The Eternal had long since shown me that love was not just a feeling too big for words. Jesus had said to His followers, "A new commandment I give unto you, that ye love one another" (John 13:34). I knew that you couldn't command a feeling, and so had come to the conclusion that if love was a command, I must be able to obey it. This took love out of the realm of emotions and into the arena of loving actions. And that would involve me in the lives of people I didn't "feel" I liked!

I HAD COME TO THE-CONCLUSION THAT IF LOVE WAS A COMMAND, I MUST BE ABLE TO OBEY IT.

God could help me to love them, I decided, but *that* wasn't the issue. The problem was, would they love *me*, and most important, would they listen to what I had to tell them?

Once I was on my feet with my Bible open and a message prepared, I felt fine. It was the before and after small talk, the winning-of-the-ladies-to-myself-that-I-might-win-them-to-Him part that got to me!

What I was like *off* the platform was a question those women had every right to ask. If they knew my insecurities, if they heard my foolish attempts at making classy conversation, I knew they would dislike me.

As our limousine continued toward our destination, I groaned inwardly, thinking of the disappointment the women were in for as they found out there was "nothing to me" after all!

Stuart had encouraged me to take this particular invitation. He had reminded me of the apostle Paul counting himself in debt to the Jew and the Greek, barbarian and free. That, he explained, meant we all had a debt to pay—that of sharing the knowledge of salvation with all types of people, including the sophisticated as well as the unsophisticated. Believing it, I had simply come to pay my debt.

All too soon, the taxi arrived. The meetings came and went, and I returned home just as unsure of everything as I had been when I set out.

In the days that followed, I asked myself if it was simply my Britishness that forbade the crossing of the "class" line, or if my problem was just inverted pride. Perhaps it was false humility or a despising of the gifts that others saw in me. I didn't know what was so dreadfully wrong, so I continued to travel and speak and wonder afterward how on earth I'd had the nerve!

Then one day the Eternal decided it was time to set me free. I was in Coral Gables, Florida, among some of the *nouveau riche* young ladies who populate that classy area of Miami. Observing them as they entered the club restaurant where we were dining, each one seemed a beauty in her own lovely right.

Sitting at a table with three of the most elegant females, I felt fat, forty, and somewhat futile! Why, oh, why had I come?

I looked around at the beautiful exclusive-looking creature who had just made her entrance from an exclusive car into that exclusive place and was about to order some of their exclusive food at a definitely exclusive price! Suddenly and unexpectedly the Eternal inquired of me, "Why do you think everyone is so tense?"

"Competition," I replied with sudden comprehension.

"That's right," He answered.

It was very, very still in my heart, so I distinctly heard the Eternal's next words: "Jill, you'll *never* be competition."

That was it—I was *free!* Oh, the joy of it. I could be a big sister to them, a friendly mother to them, an ugly aunt to them. But certainly I could relax, knowing I would never threaten one of them! They were bound to listen to me for the very reason I had believed them bound not to! What an incredible release!

God had made me just right for my vocation, and that was all that mattered. He had gifted me with ordinary and acceptable good looks. Everywhere I went, someone would always come up to me and tell me I was like their daughter, cousin, or Great Aunt Susan. Now I could see how comfortable that made everybody feel.

I thanked God for dressing me well enough to hold my own, but not too well to distract or cause envy, freeing me to wear an outfit twice in a row if I desired. For the first time I was able to be glad for my fine hair, realizing that because it curled so easily I could always bully it into shape.

I began to make a mental list of my best qualities. I had a sort of pleasant voice (that made a long talk part-way enjoyable), an expressive face (useful for dramatic emphasis), and a metabolism that could be mastered by diet and discipline. To discover you are "just right" in His eyes is enough. *He* is the lover of our souls, and to despise the way He has assembled our bodies, dressed our heads, or arranged our features is to miss the point. To be able to say, "I am free, not to be the me that *I* would choose to be, but the me *He* has already chosen me to be," is freedom indeed.

Set free on the outside, I was about to be set free on the

inside as well!

It was Christmas time and as I opened the Gospel of Luke I read the words of Zacharias. He prayed for all others, like himself, whose mouths had been closed by fear and doubt, by that dreadful and strangling sense of the inadequacy, when faced with God's expectations of them. He was interceding for those of us who would come to know the liberty of a God-confident self-acceptance: "May God grant that we, being delivered out of the hand of our enemies, might *serve Him without fear*." God was about to grant me just that.

I had fought this battle for so long, without victory. I had prayed earnestly for the fear to be removed, but without avail. I had even tried to dig into my subconscious to find reasons for my anxieties. I worried in preparing a talk whether it would be interesting enough. I dreaded being asked questions that I presumably wouldn't be able to answer. I also was afraid of success. Just what might praise or appreciation do to my head and therefore to my sweet relationship with the Lord?

Letters began to come from editors inviting me to write. Immediately, I felt suffocated with fear. Why write articles *nobody* will read? Hot on the heels of that anxiety came a worse dread: People would rip them apart doctrinally or write nasty letters to the editor that *everybody* would read!

With the memory of Coral Gables fresh in my mind, I took time out to listen to God. Again the Eternal applied His Word to my heart. He visited me with the written Word as He had visited Zacharias with the Living Word, and it proved to be sweeter than honey, finer than gold, more precious than rubies. He reminded me of the way He had overcome my fear of losing friends, of sharing my faith, of being attacked on the back streets of Liverpool, of something happening to the children or to Stuart and the horror of rejection and death. He had dealt with my awful fear of flying.

Even my fearful obediences had brought me great reward. They had led to marvelous adventures that I wouldn't have missed for anything. But now I knew that the promise to serve Him *without fear* was for me and had everything to do with the ultra-suede ladies.

As I knelt, the Father dressed my spirit with an incredibly tender anticipation of heavenly delight. I told the Lord Jesus how much I loved Him for it all—He who must have been tempted to be afraid many, many times; He who had refused to doubt His Father's faithfulness to Him; He who could have decided not to be a suffering servant for fear that what He went through wouldn't make a difference. But He came anyway and didn't shudder at the rejection of the world or the agony of the cross. He feared His Father first! *The fear of God, rather than the fear of man, was the key*—fear in the sense of reverent trust, coupled with hatred of sin.

Shuffling through my invitations with a quickening excitement, I chose three of the most challenging I had ever been given and wrote an eager acceptance. Surprised by a feeling of peace and an incredible new hope, I breathed, *West Point, Princeton, Washington...ultra, ultra-suede ladies, here we come!* And as I went, it was with the prayer of Psalm 19 uppermost in my thinking.

> May the words of my mouth and the meditation of my heart be acceptable *in thy sight,* oh Lord, my Rock and my Redeemer! (Psalm 19:14)

As I stood on platforms here and there and felt wooden planks or shiny bricks underneath my feet, I somehow knew I would begin to feel another substance undergirding my obedience: "my Rock." That new confidence in my Redeemer's promises would begin to work in me a new sense of well-being with myself.

My ministry took on a new swing—an exuberance, a depth of satisfaction and sureness I'd never known before. As I left a huge convention to catch a plane to the next assignment, I smiled at the jumble of cars and at my frantic hostess running around like a scalded cat—she couldn't remember where she'd parked. I was reminded of my husband's quip, "Women don't park cars, they abandon them!"

The next time some dear little blue-haired ladies in tennis shoes came and whispered in my ear, "We couldn't hear you," and I asked, "Where were you sitting?" and they answered me, "On the back row and we're all deaf you know," I found a sweet warmth and loving concern instead of the old irritation as I patiently suggested they sit on the front row next time!

It was all different. Women were everywhere. In my head, in my heart, in my plans, in my schedules and spare moments, in my tears and in my laughter—they were part of me and I was part of them. And I was *glad, glad, glad*— we were women together![1]

Barbara Bush

EVERYONE HAS
SOMETHING TO GIVE

Barbara Pierce Bush, wife of former President George Bush and the thirty-eighth First Lady, has lived a life that reflects her husband's varied career in business and public service.

The Bushes have lived in seventeen cities and twenty-nine homes since their marriage in 1945. The demands of his service as a member of Congress, U.S. Representative to the United Nations, Chairman of the Republican National Committee, Chief of the United States Liaison Office in the People's Republic of China, Director of the CIA, and Vice President and President of the United States, have truly made them public servants.

Mrs. Bush has chosen the promotion of literacy as her special area of focus. She is honorary chairperson of the Barbara Bush Foundation for Family Literacy, an organization whose mission is to establish literacy as a value in every

family in America, to support the development of family literacy programs, and to break the intergenerational cycle of illiteracy.

Mrs. Bush also serves as the honorary chairperson of a number of other organizations, councils, foundations, and groups relating to education, literacy, learning disabilities, child abuse, hunger, health, and adoption.

She has received the honorary degree of Doctor of Humane Letters from several institutions, including Smith College in Northampton, Massachusetts; Bennett College in Greensboro, North Carolina; and Morehouse School of Medicine in Atlanta, Georgia.

The mother of five children and grandmother of twelve, Mrs. Bush is an exercise enthusiast and enjoys reading, gardening, and being with her family.

To celebrate the National Day of Prayer their first year in office, President and Mrs. Bush honored the National Prayer Committee at a breakfast in the White House State Dining Room. They were honorary co-chairmen for 1990.

I believe history will regard her as one of our nation's all-time great First Ladies. (America loves you, Barbara.)

Her contribution to this book reflects her heart for people and captures her refreshing philosophy of life.

During his presidency, George Bush, one of the smartest people I know, challenged the people of our great country to open their hearts to one another.

That is the way George has lived his life, and he made it a theme of his presidency when he said in a speech, "From now on, any definition of a successful life must include service to others."

It's no wonder, then, that being married to George Bush has been instrumental in teaching me what I consider my most important lesson: Caring for and sharing with others is life's biggest reward.

It is a lesson I never quit learning—sometimes through the large, significant incidents in my life; more often, through small, daily reminders such as an offhand remark or a handshake. I would like to share a few such incidents with you.

In 1953, George and I were living in Midland, Texas. We thought we were on top of the world. We were young, full of energy and ambition, with our whole lives stretching before us. George was working long hours establishing himself in the oil business. I was busy having babies and raising them. Everything seemed so right.

Then our world broke apart. One bright spring day, a doctor told us that our precious three-year-old daughter, Robin, had leukemia and would not live. Despite a brave battle and the care of many doctors, she died seven months later.

The time of her illness and death was one of the most difficult periods of my life. The death of a child is so painful, both emotionally and spiritually, that I truly wondered if my own heart and spirit would ever heal.

But our strong faith in God and our wonderful family and friends pulled us through. Everywhere we looked there were helping hands: those of good friends and family, and those of strangers—the doctors and nurses and hospital volunteers who saw our pain and reached out to us.

Through them, I soon learned that I could help myself best by helping others.

George and I came from families dedicated to volunteerism and public service, but it wasn't until Robin died that I truly threw myself into volunteer work. That precious little girl left our family a great legacy: I know George and I care more for every living person because of her. We learned firsthand the importance of reaching out to help because others had reached out to us during that crucial time.

I SOON LEARNED THAT I COULD HELP-MYSELF BEST BY HELPING OTHERS.

Since then, my strong belief in volunteerism and the spirit of caring has been reinforced almost daily by the wonderful people I have met. I am talking about the "silent" heroes, the thousands of people who work hard behind the scenes to make life better for others. You will never see their names in the headlines or their faces on the evening news.

Instead, they are the people who live right next door to us, kneel next to us in church, or have children who go to school with our children and grandchildren.

They are the people who provide shelter for the homeless or take in babies afflicted with the AIDS virus. They are volunteers in hospitals and nursing homes; the tutors for children who have trouble learning and for adults who never learned to read or write.

They are the neighborhood women who get together and cook a meal for a new mother, the talented fundraiser who can find the necessary pennies for all the right causes, the class of fourth-graders who once a week make cheese sandwiches at the homeless shelter downtown.

When people ask me how they can help, what they can

possibly do to make a difference (so many people worry that they don't have the time, talent, or resources), I tell them about all of these "silent" heroes.

One of my favorites is a man I don't even know.

Not long ago, while visiting a school in Boston, I saw a blind man teaching two young boys how to read. I will never forget him—and I hope you don't either. For that very brief encounter helped remind me in a very special way of life's most important lesson: Caring and sharing is everything—and everyone has something to give.

Evelyn Christenson

"Before You Know the Outcome, Here Is My Peace"

Evelyn Christenson is the wife of a pastor turned college administrator. She reared three children while being involved in church and denominational activities in support of her husband's ministry.

As a Bible teacher who observed firsthand what can happen when women pray, she saw the need for a united prayer movement.

I first met Evelyn when she and her husband came to Arrowhead Springs for a conference. It was early 1972, just as I was launching a movement to encourage united prayer in our nation. I shared with her how I was sure prayer could bring our nation back to a greater moral and spiritual foundation. Our hearts were immediately united, and she invited me to be one of the speakers for Bethel College Founder's Week.

Now Evelyn is the founder and chairman of the board of United Prayer Ministries in St. Paul, Minnesota. Under her direction, the ministry operates a prayer chain in the Twin City area, furnishes Christian material to missionaries around the world and to prisoners in the United States, and sponsors broadcasts into China, India, and Spanish-speaking lands.

Evelyn is the author of several books, including What Happens When Women Pray, *which has sold more than two million copies and was on the best-seller list for four consecutive years. She is one of the original members of the National Prayer Committee and co-chair of AD2000 North American Women's Track. Although in great demand as a speaker around the world, she still gives priority to her now-retired husband and loves being a grandmother.*

Her story is one of God's abiding peace in the face of cancer and how His purpose for our lives is unchangeable even when life's circumstances become difficult.

For many generations no word has struck terror in human hearts more than the word *cancer*. Somehow, pronouncing it evokes—rightly or wrongly—visions of suffering, chemotherapy, and death. Through the years, hearing it diagnosed has gripped hearts of patients and loved ones alike with icy fingers.

I struggled with that word myself. In a routine checkup, my husband's doctor found "a little lump." Later on the biopsy report was that word: *cancer.*

We had to wait several more days—until the following Monday—for his bone marrow, CT scan, and blood tests to see if the cancer had spread to other parts of his body, knowing full well what it meant if it had.

On Friday Chris and I drove to Illinois for a prayer seminar with that word hanging over us like a thick, menacing cloud. *Cancer.*

While Chris took his turn to nap and I drove, I talked to God about the word *promises* in Hebrews 6:12, which He had impressed upon me the month before:

> That you may not be sluggish, but imitators of those who through faith and patience inherit the promises.

Why did the Lord place this word so heavily on my heart? What did He mean? Was He about to promise me something? Was He speaking to me about my ministry or my personal life? I didn't have the faintest idea.

I prayed fervently, pleading with God to give me more insight. Then clearly and firmly the answer came to my mind: "Romans 8:28." It was as though He were saying, "I, God, am working all things together for your good because you love Me and are called according to My purpose."

Disappointed and almost frustrated with God, I cried, "Oh God, not *that* old one again."

When I was just twenty-three years old, I lost my first three pregnancies. At that time, God had spoken words of comfort and assurance to me through Romans 8:28.

Having taken this verse then as my philosophy of life, I had lived it and God had proven faithful to it for forty-two years. But now, in the face of my husband's cancer, I wanted —and thought I needed—something new and powerful.

But as I drove, God began to impress on my heart why He had again chosen this particular promise. *Up to this time,* He said into my heart, *you have been experiencing, teaching, and writing about how I work out all things for your good because you love Me. But I want to expand your understanding of this verse. You have thought that you will see Me working all things for your good, sometimes while here on earth when you are going through a trial, and other times when you get to heaven and view things from My perspective. But I'm telling you in advance—before Chris even takes the tests next Monday—that I am working for your good whatever the outcome is.*

With tears streaming down my face, I could hardly see to drive. A great peace settled over me. Before Chris even took the tests, God was telling me that whatever the results, however good or bad the verdict, He was working it for our good.

Sunday morning, still before Chris's tests, God drew me back to the Hebrews 6 portion once again. At first, I was puzzled that He would keep me devotionally in one portion of Scripture for so long. Then I saw His reason in verse 17:

> In the same way God, desiring even more to show to the heirs of the promise the unchangeableness of His purpose...

I wrote "me" by the word *heirs*. He wanted to show me, an heir of the promise, what? The unchangeableness of His purpose. God was telling me that His purpose for me had not changed since I was twenty-three. He had it all planned from before the foundation of the earth. And just because circumstances changed, which they have over and over again, His purpose for me is still unchangeable.

Chris's test results on Monday did not show that the cancer had spread. Surgery was scheduled and people prayed. I realized through this traumatic experience that God was still working out His purpose in our lives. He was teaching us some eternal values.

Let me share several:

First, *we cannot take answers to prayer for granted.* With a constant flow of answers to multitudes of prayers in our lives, it is easy to take some of them for granted. But watching God work in Chris in answer to prayers from people all-over the country has brought a fresh awareness to me of the power of prayer.

Second, *we must maintain an "attitude of gratitude."* In my hectic schedule, I had not only taken answers to prayer for granted, I had also let my "attitude of gratitude" slip. Chris and I are now experiencing a continuous, unbelievably deep sense of gratitude to God that Chris's doctor decided to check "a few more things" during a routine exam—and that he found that little lump early enough to get it all. Surgery was 100 percent successful!

HAVING FACED ETERNITY, WE HAVE A-NEW SENSE OF COMMITMENT TO WHAT GOD STILL HAS-FOR US TO DO.

I continue to praise God that the cancer was detected before it could spread to any other part of Chris's body. If it had, the outcome would have been completely different.

I stand in awe at how God continues to answer prayer for Chris. His recovery has been truly remarkable with no complications to date.

Third, *we must keep our commitment to Christ fresh.* Having encountered the possibility of facing eternity, Chris and I have a new sense of commitment to what God still has for us to do. The uneasy experience of his retirement has changed to expectancy and thankful waiting upon God for new assignments.

These lessons helped me not only through my husband's bout with cancer, but also gave me strong assurance that God was indeed working out His purpose in my life when I also underwent a cancer test just three weeks after Chris's surgery.

As I lay in bed on the morning of my mammogram, God gently spoke into my heart His time-tested promise in Isaiah 26:3:

> Thou wilt keep him in perfect peace whose mind is stayed on Thee.

Immediately all the tension drained from my body as His peace flooded me. I felt the incredible sense of being completely engulfed in a soft spherical capsule, in the rare atmosphere of God Himself.

As I write this, I haven't received the results of my mammogram.* But God is here. My common sense says, "It's just another exam like all the others." But God is saying, "Before you know the outcome, here is My peace."

There is a word, I have discovered, that transcends all human words, even *cancer*. That word is *God*.

*Editor's note: Evelyn's mammogram showed no signs of cancer.

Sallie Clingman

LESSONS ON A FIRE ESCAPE

A staff member of Campus Crusade for more than thirty years, Sallie Clingman served with the Christian Embassy in Washington, D.C. where, for many years, she led weekly Bible studies with senate, congressional, and cabinet members' wives. Sallie is now a speaker and consultant to various women's ministries, helping women become more effective ambassadors for Christ.

She also has served as the national women's coordinator for Campus Crusade, spoken at 150 colleges and universities in this country, and traveled in Asia, Africa, and Europe.

She holds a B.S. degree in biology from Centenary College in Louisiana. She also did graduate work in biochemistry at Louisiana State University School of Medicine in New Orleans and worked as a research associate for the university.

Sallie shares her struggle with low self-esteem and the lessons God taught her while sitting on a fire escape at Cam-

pus Crusade headquarters as she prepared to join staff. These lessons helped transform her into a joyful, fruitful servant of the Lord. I know they will encourage your faith as well.

I had never been that lonely in my whole life.

There were 1,251 conferees attending the Institute of Biblical Studies at Arrowhead Springs, at that time the international headquarters for Campus Crusade for Christ. The population for that four-and-a-half-week session consisted primarily of college students and staff of Campus Crusade. I stood out like a sore thumb. I was the "1" of the 1,251.

I had never in my life seen such beautiful people. Every young man looked like the proverbial football hero or president of the student body—or both. Every young woman looked like the head cheerleader or "voted most likely to succeed"—or both. And they were so friendly and cool and comfortable with each other and with God. They prayed for a friend back in Georgia as they stood in line to eat, and they prayed for the professor as they walked to class. They talked to each other freely and talked about Jesus freely. Life seemed natural and easy for them.

I had spent the last six years of my life in a library or a chemistry lab. I was not exactly up on the latest fashions. My social skills were in mothballs, or chloroform, and I was twenty-seven years old. In that crowd I was on the verge of middle age.

I didn't know one other person at the conference. The only one who knew me was Ney Bailey, who at that time was the director of personnel for Campus Crusade. She was from my hometown. Bless her, she took me out to dinner a couple of nights and spoke to me warmly when she saw me.

I was a lonely, out-of-place, miserable misfit. But I knew God wanted me there. My Christian life was new and God had my attention. Only two years earlier, one night in my apartment in New Orleans, I had knelt to invite Jesus Christ to come into my heart. A whole new world had opened up to me and for the first time in my life I knew that I was right with God. I understood that it was not because my good deeds outweighed my bad deeds, but that I had put my faith in Jesus Christ for that "rightness" with God. My assurance was so solid that I desperately wanted to be able to tell other people what I had discovered and what was available to them if they wanted it. That was my motive in going to this conference. Someone had told me that Campus Crusade could teach me to articulate my faith. It was a high priority for me.

Before this trip, someone had commented that my hair had potential but needed some help. So, following their advice, I had colored my hair to—mind you—bring out the "red highlights." Well, my hair looked like an explosion in a Brillo factory—before explosions in Brillo factories were appropriate hair styles.

My twenty-seven-year-old skin looked like thirteen-year-old skin after a chocolate-covered-french-fries frenzy.

My clothes were utterly awful. Lab coats had covered a multitude of fashion sins back in New Orleans, but here I was without my protective layer and I knew I was a disaster.

All of this contributed to the world's worst self-image!

There were about five hundred in my class on the Book

of John. It was a stimulating, thrilling experience for me. However, my loneliness and my misery were so great that I would get to class early to get a seat in the back row near the door so I could escape unnoticed when my next wave of nausea came.

I would have conversations with people and the whole time I was thinking, *All they see is the outside.* They were delightful, caring people, but there was no way they could have known how much I wanted to cry, or how much I envied their apparent lack of pain.

My roommate situation was not any help, either. You could not have assembled four more different people in one room. It was so hot (this was July in Southern California) in our fourth floor, furnaced room that I would climb out onto the fire escape with my pillow to sleep—waiting for a breeze, a stir in the air, a rain shower, anything! One night I was attacked by birds, which only confirmed to me that things were not going to get any better for me at this conference.

We had classes all day. There was the Book of John, New Testament Survey, and Basic Doctrine. At night we heard a series of messages by Dr. Bill Bright. I devoured it all. It's interesting how teachable I get with a little pain. The wisdom I recognized in God's Word was cleansing and my faith was confirmed and encouraged hour after hour. And all the while I carried my fragile emotions from class to class, from meal to meal, and from sleep to sleep.

One night, Dr. Bright spoke from James 1:2–4 and 1 Thessalonians 5:16. He explained that it is an expression of faith or confidence in God to thank Him in trials. This made sense to me. I was certainly getting no relief by *not* thanking God for the discomfort I was having.

I went back to my fourth floor hotbox, climbed out on the fire escape for privacy and cool air, and sat there for what seemed like an eternity—just hurting. The words of James rang in my head. "Consider it all joy, my brethren, when you encounter various trials, knowing that the testing of your faith produces endurance. And let endurance have its perfect result, that you may be perfect and complete, lacking in nothing."

Finally, with a sense of desperate submission to God and His will for my life and character, I leaned my head against the cool iron railing of the fire escape and prayed.

I prayed in a choked whisper punctuated with deep lung-filling and emptying sighs. My prayer was so critical at that point that I remember it word for word:

> God, I want to thank You for all the discomfort I have experienced these weeks. Thank You for the loneliness, thank You for the lousy self-image. You know what You are doing. I trust You.

> (Long pause.)

> And now I want to tell You that I am willing to have ugly hair, bad skin, to wear unfashionable clothes, and to be alone for the rest of my life—as long as You don't leave me. Amen.

Then my thoughts turned away from me and my pitiful state to the wonder and wisdom of God. My mind raced over the incredible things I had been learning about God in my classes. My heart sensed that God was present and aware of this little person huddled on the fire escape 1,600 miles from home. My lips tried new words of praise and worship to express my new confidence in Him.

There were many lessons to learn from that moment on

the fire escape.

First, my uncomfortable circumstance was not invisible to God.

Second, God's Word, when trusted and obeyed, really changed my life.

Third, God used this rough spot in my life to teach me how subsequent rough spots could be treated.

Fourth, trusting God turned out to be the most important contribution I could make to my own mental and emotional health.

TRUSTING GOD WAS THE MOST IMPORTANT CONTRIBUTION TO MY MENTAL AND EMOTIONAL HEALTH.

Fifth, God changed my life without changing anything about my circumstances.

I came face to face with the character development God was engineering in my life. He was more concerned that my values be right and that my character be Christlike than that I would be comfortable. The great victory for me was that I agreed with God about this and was willing for Him to do what He knew was best.

When I left that conference a week later, I was not asked to be on the cover of *Vogue*, nor was I invited to be on the Johnny Carson Show. I was no Cinderella. But on the inside I was different.

God and I had a secret. We had had an intimate encounter. He had met with me. I knew He had because of the confidence I now had that this was not the last chapter in the story of my life.

I sensed that the conference was a launching pad for

knowing and loving God like I had never dared to dream. I had experienced a glimpse into what really mattered in life. That has prompted me many times in the years since to obey God's Words to "consider it *all* joy."

I had put my faith in God and His Word, and He had worked a miracle in my heart, teaching me that *He is able* to set me free on the inside when there is no escape on the outside.

Sally Conway

LOVE IS STRONGER THAN LIFE'S CIRCUMSTANCES

Sally Conway and her husband, Jim, a former pastor, established a ministry called Mid-Life Dimensions, conducting counseling sessions and seminars for mid-life adults and their families. Together, they touched a nerve in today's fast-paced world.

Sally battled cancer very bravely for several years and maintained a radiant testimony for our Lord before her death in 1998.

Because of her ability to combine wit, understanding, and a firm biblical foundation in a fun and upbeat approach to mid-life crisis, Sally was always in great demand as a speaker. She appeared on local and nationwide radio and TV programs and was considered one of America's foremost family experts.

The mother of three daughters and grandmother of several, Sally authored many books and was an adjunct professor at Talbot Theological Seminary for five years.

Bill and I met the Conways many years ago, before midlife crisis for men was even a consideration. I am not aware that my husband has had one, or that every man does, but Sally shares insight into how to cope with the situation.

My husband angrily grabbed his coat and slammed out the door. My heart sank to my feet where it had been so often lately. I thought we had been doing better recently. Yes, he still seemed depressed and confused much of the time, but generally he didn't blame me so much anymore.

As I watched Jim walk away down the snowy drive, I realized I had been off guard this evening. I had nagged a little bit here and there and had even questioned an insignificant decision he'd made. Until a few months ago he would have let those careless remarks go unchallenged. He was the one with the wide shoulders and the uncritical spirit. But now he had become hypersensitive, and I had to measure my words and reactions carefully. At times he would partially come out of his depression and be stronger emotionally, and then the slightest thing would trigger his anger and another down cycle.

I knew how much he hated the snow and cold, and since he wasn't adequately dressed, I didn't expect him to stay out long. Besides, this was the night before Thanksgiving and one of our daughters had arrived home from college only minutes before. We were planning a special welcome-home supper.

But Jim didn't return in time to eat with the family. We have a strong family tradition of waiting for everyone to gather before we eat. But each of the girls had other, previously arranged commitments, so they finally nibbled on something and went their ways. This kind of situation had never occurred before in our family. The special meal and I waited. I reset the table for two with special placemats and candles.

Eventually Jim did come home. He accepted my apology and seemed amiable as we ate our meal together by candlelight. Little did I know how much was still raging within him—some anger toward me, but mostly confusion and terror from the deeper struggles he couldn't understand within himself. We went to bed, and he spent the night in a furious battle with himself and God that I didn't know about until morning. I didn't know at the time how close that came to being our last night together in our bed.

Jim was in the throes of a gigantic mid-life crisis that lasted more than three years. He wanted to run from all his responsibilities. He was depressed. He swung back and forth between being sullen and fomenting with anger.

He declared that he had lost all feelings for me. In fact, he said, "I've never really loved you. It was a mistake for us to have married."

This was so unlike the optimistic, loving, Christ-centered man with whom I had already spent over twenty-three years of life and ministry. His perception about his world was totally off balance.

During the days that became weeks, months, and years of Jim's turmoil, I kept remembering a scene from my childhood. Part of the backbone I needed to enable me to help my husband through his mid-life crisis was provided by that earlier experience.

My family and I were heartsick! A hailstorm had just demolished our expected income. My mother stood beside me outside our small, white farmhouse after the devastating summer storm had passed. We leaned on the rain-dampened fence that separated our little yard of grass and flowers from the rest of the farmyard. Our house was on a hill with barns and pens of dairy cows, pigs, sheep, and chickens situated here and there down the hillside.

We were looking across a small valley to the next hill where our corn crop had just been shredded by hail. A big portion of our year's income lay pounded into a sickening mass on the ground over on that hill.

I knew Mother grieved over the work and expense that had gone into that cornfield. This was about 1944 and my parents hadn't completely recovered from the Great Depression. Nebraska farmers were never too far from disaster anyway. Within a few moments, hail or windstorms could completely wipe out all hopes of catching up with past years' deficits. If it wasn't the weather, it might be insects or diseases or a drop in grain and livestock prices.

Mother and Daddy had been married about twelve years before they felt they could afford to buy their own farm. On the day this hailstorm hit, they still owed a large debt. We needed every crop, each animal, the eggs, and cream from our dairy cows to pay for our farm and to cover our other expenses. Sometimes the success or failure of just one of these income sources determined whether or not we would lose the farm.

That day as we viewed our ruined crop, Mother probably said something about her fears and the wasted work and money. I don't remember. What I do remember is her arm around my shoulder and her words, "You know, honey, a husband and wife can take anything that comes in life as long as they love each other."

In the years that followed, my parents were good models of a loving couple who can "take anything." That tough bond lasted until Daddy's death at age eighty-three, and Mother still carries her part to this day.

I am a long way from that little farm now, which, by the way, we were able to keep in spite of many more storms and losses. I grew up there, graduated from high school, went away to college, and came back to be married in the little church in our nearest town.

I married a man who was called into Christian ministry. Jim and I went off to seminary as newlyweds. Over a period of thirty years we pastored part-time student churches and three full-time churches. We learned so much as we hurt with our people when they hurt and rejoiced when they rejoiced. During that time God gave us three daughters to nurture. They are now grown, married, launched into people-helping pursuits, and raising children of their own.

A few years ago, God moved Jim and me from a local church ministry to teaching in a seminary and pastoring the nation's hurting mid-life couples. We know firsthand what mid-lifers experience.

My own mid-life crisis a few years before Jim's was one of the first hard tests that directly affected our marriage. I went through a great deal of confusion, feeling unneeded and unappreciated, while Jim was busy with his important work of "winning the world."

Jim wisely saw that I needed to establish my own identity and sense of value. He knew I enjoyed being a pastor's wife and mother, but he encouraged me to combine those callings with going back to school and finding a ministry within our church that fit my God-given talents. His committed love helped me balance my life so I could once again "bloom where I was planted."

Trials to test our marriage bond have also come in other ways. For years our family experienced a wide gamut of physical problems—surgeries, broken bones, stitches, life-threatening reactions to bee stings, four out of five of us having mononucleosis, and the list goes on.

One fall while our daughter Brenda was still recovering from mono, she was hospitalized in her college health center with a viral infection. Her older sister, Barbara, was brought into the center with a severely fractured collar bone from a bike accident. As Brenda got out of bed to go comfort Barbara, she fainted and hit her head; she was taken to a city hospital where X-rays revealed a concussion.

Leaving Jim at home in the worst trough of his mid-life crisis, I drove to the college and eventually brought Barbara home because she couldn't use either arm. We didn't know at the time that in spite of an upper-body cast and several kinds of treatments, her collar bone would not heal for over a year.

We simply went on to the next health problem that fall. In a few days our youngest daughter, Becki, was to have a second biopsy of a tumor in her left leg. By spring the lab test results and many experts' opinions concluded that her tumor was a rare malignancy that required drastic action. Tragically, her leg had to be amputated above mid-thigh.

Jim had thoroughly believed that God would heal Becki's leg. When the miracle didn't come through, he nearly went off the deep end completely. "When Becki lost her leg, I lost God!" he cried many times later. I stood by him as he wrestled with why God would allow such a thing to happen to his vivacious sixteen-year-old daughter. He eventually arrived at a place of peace where he could "let God be God."

Other strains in our lives have included two times in the last few years when we have felt that God was leading us into a certain direction in our ministry and both ended in failure. Failure is an awful word, and it took me a long time to be able to say it in regard to our plans.

LOVE MEANS WE VALUE THE OTHER, EVEN WHEN THAT ONE IS NOT LOVING IN RETURN.

In both cases we went into personal debt for thousands of dollars. In fact, every time I look at our threadbare, outdated living room furniture, I am reminded that we could have had a nicely decorated house for ourselves and furniture for a lot of other people, too, if we hadn't lost that money in what we thought was God's will for our ministry. Worse than the financial loss, though, was the loss of esteem we each felt from having to withdraw from these projects.

Probably the most difficult path we have had to walk, however, has come in recent years. Quite unexpectedly, Jim has begun a journey of recalling his troubled childhood. Actually, now that he is able to bring it to the surface, the going is easier than it was.

While all the boyhood pain and neglect have been bubbling out, we have both had to call on every ounce of devotion we had for each other. Sometimes I have been mistaken for the unfair, judgmental authority figure that squelched

his personhood as a boy. He has reacted like the hurt little four-year-old, the selfish seven-year-old, or the sassy ten-year-old that he never got to be at those ages.

Jim has agonized over the realization that for decades he had buried the awful secret of his dysfunctional family, a secret that has extended its ugly tentacles in many directions with sad consequences for innocent people. Once he could face the truth about his family, he began to find freedom from his shame. It has not been easy, however.

As we face our own places of pain and as we work with mid-life couples whose long-term marriages are breaking or nearly broken, I keep hearing my mother's words, "A husband and wife can take anything that comes in life as long as they love each other."

Together Jim and I have learned that if a husband and wife love each other, they *are* able to "take everything" that happens in life. We've also learned that love is not simply a feeling. Love isn't over when the feelings aren't there. Lasting love is not something we fall into and out of.

Love is a commitment, a determination to contribute all that we can to the building of something beautiful and satisfying for both of us. Love means we value the other, even when that one is not loving in return. In spite of all the hurts and bashings that life can give, a marriage relationship can last.

Many people have taught me lots of valuable lessons—by word and by example. But the greatest lesson I learned has been used day in and day out for thirty-six years of my marriage and as Jim and I work to help other marriages survive. How innocently it took place that evening when Mother pointed out that love in a marriage relationship is stronger than life's circumstances.[1]

Joy Dawson

WHAT IT MEANS TO FEAR THE LORD

Joy Dawson has been traveling and teaching the Bible internationally since 1970, mostly at spiritual leadership conferences. A woman with a world vision, her missionary journeys have taken her to fifty-five nations spanning every continent. She has taught extensively on television and radio, and countless lives have been eternally touched through the worldwide distribution of her books and audio and video tapes. The character and ways of God are the biblical basis of her penetrating teachings. She is author of numerous books, including Intimate Friendship with God.

A woman of prayer, Joy is vivacious and "wound tight" to make her small in stature but tall in word and deed. It was a pleasure to work with her as a member of the National Day of Prayer Committee.

Joy has been a great encouragement to me. Ask her counsel and you will always receive a biblical answer. The Scrip-

tures are her authority, as you will see from what she shares
in this lesson.

By the time I was a young wife and mother, I was painfully aware of my lack of wisdom. Consequently, I tried
several ways to remedy this weakness in my character.

One was to listen to what wise people said, hoping to
gather up their pearls of wisdom and then use them at the
appropriate moments when conversing with others. But for
some inexplicable reasons, I never seemed to successfully
match the pearls with the right moments!

Then I observed that the people whom I considered
wise were mostly silent. So I tried that tactic and found the
frustration wasn't worth the effort. The family from which
I came were all strongly opinionated and had a lot to say. I
didn't seem to fit the silent mold. All too frequently I had
to humble myself and ask forgiveness for having said the
wrong thing.

Wisdom, it seemed, just wasn't my thing.

There were other areas in my life where I found it difficult to make necessary changes. Although I would confess
my sins to God, I would not always get to the place of real
repentance.

All of this troubled me because I had a deep and sincere
desire for intimate friendship with God. But I had no workable solutions—*until* the Holy Spirit sovereignly drew my
attention to the many verses in the Bible on the subject of
the fear of the Lord. What a gold mine of truth I discovered.
Let me share some of the lessons I learned.

First, "The fear of the Lord is to *hate* evil" (Proverbs 8:13). That means having God's attitude toward sin at all times. If I hated sin, it would be easy for me to choose not to sin. I would not do the things I hated unless forced to by a higher authority. This brought me to conclude that the reason I had chosen to sin was because I had a love for that sin in my heart. The love for the sin needed to be replaced with a hatred for it. *The fear of the Lord* would give me that hatred.

This simple but profound truth was reinforced by finding Proverbs 16:6: "Through the fear of the Lord a man *avoids* evil." What an incredible discovery this became to me. The reason I was not repenting of the sins I had so often confessed was because I lacked the fear of the Lord.

Day after day as I read the Word of God, I would write down more verses on the subject in a big notebook I titled *The Character and the Ways of God*. It was my personal concordance of verses which related to that title from my devotional readings. The more I meditated on what I wrote down on *the fear of the Lord* (which amounted to sixty-six verses), the more I realized that it was the answer to every area of weakness in my character.

Second, "The fear of the Lord is the *beginning* of wisdom" and "the *beginning* of knowledge" (Proverbs 9:10; 1:7). In Job 28:12, Job asked, "Where can wisdom be found? Where does understanding dwell?" I certainly could identify with that question. Obviously he understood my inquiry at a deep level.

No amount of wealth, Job said, can purchase wisdom or be compared with its value. It is hidden from man's understanding, but "God understands the way to it and he alone knows where it dwells" (Job 28:23). Then came a brilliant burst of truth: "And he [God] said to man, 'The fear of the Lord—that is wisdom, and to shun evil is understanding'" (Job 28:28).

I decided to make an in-depth study of *the fear of the Lord* and apply it to every area of my life.

I was encouraged to know that at least I was *beginning* to act upon a truth that would revolutionize my life more than any other.

Third, "The fear of the Lord is the *instruction* of wisdom" (Proverbs 15:33). I saw that I could have as much wisdom as I chose to be holy. The light bulbs of truth were being switched on in my mind and spirit. What release to submit to the Person of the Holy Spirit to work this in me and then through me to others.

From then on I repeatedly asked God for *the fear of the Lord* and received it by faith. The change in my life was as perceptible as a butterfly coming out of a chrysalis. The truth was setting me free. Not only did I experience a whole new hatred of sin in thought, word, and deed, but God's wisdom began to replace my human wisdom which at its best was embarrassing!

Fourth, "Come, my children, listen to me; I will *teach* you the fear of the Lord" (Psalm 34:11). I continued to write out each verse on *the fear of the Lord* as it appeared in my daily Bible reading and to meditate on each aspect of this truth. This led to the further discovery of God's special school on this subject as recorded in Psalm 34:11–13.

I pictured myself as a small child in a kindergarten, sitting on my little chair along with others in God's family, being taught by my fascinating teacher, God. It was a cozy scene and I was excited to learn.

How interesting to find that the first lesson in my kindergarten related to the discipline of the tongue (v. 13). I would learn that we can soon tell to what degree people fear the Lord by just listening to what they say—or just as important, what they don't say.

I pondered deeply at the high standard God set in His Word about 100 percent honesty, 100 percent of the time: "Keep your lips from speaking deceit" (Psalm 34:13). I realized there would have to be changes—no overstating, no understating, no misquoting someone by reporting what he or she said out of context. I started to think about the many times I had said, "I'd love to, but…" when declining invitations to do things or go places, when I didn't really want to be involved at all. Unless I really did want to, I learned to eliminate the words "I'd love to."

WHEN SIN HOLDS NO FASCINATION FOR US, WE NEED NOT FEAR THE STRONGEST TEMPTATIONS.

I thought about the times I had believed that as long as I said some facts that were truthful about a given situation, *that* was speaking the truth. The more I pursued *the fear of the Lord,* the more I realized that the truth is stated only when we have given enough facts to convey truth.

Fifth, *the fear of the Lord* is the only way to be released from the fear of man, which Proverbs 29:25 says will prove to be a snare. I had experienced the bondage that comes from being more impressed with man's reactions to my actions than with God's reaction.

The more God-conscious I became, the less self-conscious I was. The more concern I had for God's approval in every situation, the more confidence He released in me to act with His authority. *The fear of the Lord* brought freedom.

Sixth, it was wonderful to discover that when sin holds no fascination for us because we hate it, we need not fear the strongest or the most subtle temptations. Isaiah prophesied that when Jesus came He would "delight in the fear of the Lord." To me this suggests experiencing the joyous freedom that comes from living a holy life in thought, word, and deed. Free to be natural, open, loving, and honest with nothing to hide.

Although there was a lot to learn, it was not complicated. To obtain *the fear of the Lord* and maintain it, I discovered, I must desire it deeply, continually ask God for it and receive it by faith, keep studying the subject from His Word, and act upon the truth He reveals.

Living in *the fear of the Lord* not only became a liberating way of life but an exciting adventure.

Judy Douglass

SEARCHING FOR SIGNIFICANCE

A Campus Crusade for Christ staff member for more than thirty-five years, Judy Douglass served as editor of Collegiate Challenge *and* Worldwide Challenge *magazines and director of the publications department. She is currently a consulting editor for* Worldwide Challenge, *a freelance writer, and the author of three books that address issues facing singles and young mothers.*

Judy assists her husband, Steve, in leading the U.S. Ministries of Campus Crusade. She is a frequent speaker at college campus and church women's groups, retreats, missions conferences, and singles gatherings. She also has taught at writers' workshops.

She and her husband have two daughters. When her first child was born, Judy went home to "be a mom" and found that transition one of the more challenging adjustments of her life. You will be blessed as Judy describes her search for significance and how she discovered it.

My daughters, Debbie and Michelle, placed the array of angels on our table—two bright silver ones, a shiny brass angel, a lovely ceramic bell—while Steve lighted the elegant angel candle. I dished up peach cobbler for each of us. We were preparing to "celebrate with the angels."

"Yesterday Mom spoke to a group of women about Jesus," my husband, Steve, began. "Three of them said they wanted to invite Jesus into their lives as their Savior."

"You had a part in those women receiving Christ," I reminded the girls, "because you allowed me to go and share with them and because you prayed that God would use me in a special way. Now there are three new children in the family of God."

"What are the angels doing?" Steve asked.

"They're having a party!" Michelle exclaimed.

"They're celebrating because people asked Jesus into their hearts!" Debbie added.

All four of us prayed, thanking God for the privilege of helping introduce people to Christ, thanking Him for these new sisters in the Lord, and praying for them as they began their new lives in Christ. Then we ate our cobbler.

The "celebrate with the angels" party has become a cherished tradition in our home every time one of us is involved in the birth of a new believer. Every time we do that, God reminds us of the incredible privilege it is to tell people about His love. At those times I feel very significant. I feel that every little thing I do is important.

But I don't always feel that way. I particularly remember a conference one summer evening several years ago.

"The hour is urgent," the speaker was saying. "The world needs the Lord Jesus Christ. The world is hungry for God. This is no time for business as usual. Our lives must be supernatural. We must be spiritual revolutionaries."

"Sure," I thought to myself. "When will I ever do anything significant for the Lord again?"

Certainly I had achieved some significant accomplishments. At eight years of age I had decided I wanted to become a writer. When I received Christ at the age of fifteen, I had a definite sense that God had something special He wanted me to do. How thrilled I was that what He wanted me to do was write and edit for Him.

For fourteen years I had the privilege of working in the publications department of Campus Crusade for Christ, writing and editing—to touch lives for Christ. I had seen God do wonderful things in my life and through my life. I felt very much as though I were living a supernatural life, as though I were making a significant contribution to the cause of Christ.

But now I had a very active fourteen-month-old. Just maintaining daily life overwhelmed me. And I was pregnant. When would I ever find the time to reach out and minister to even one other person, much less do anything truly significant or satisfying?

My diminished sense of significance or self-worth shouldn't have been a surprise. Rather, it's a common response to the demands of mothering. But knowing that didn't lessen my frustration or simplify my search.

Psychologist Bruce Narramore tells us that most psychologists agree on which basic conditions in life contribute to our sense of significance or value. Five of the most important criteria for personal worth and significance are security, confidence, a sense of belonging, a feeling of being loved, and a sense of purpose.

In my career I had experienced personal worth in all of these areas. I felt secure in my job, primarily because I was sure I was doing what God had called me to do.

I had confidence. I had been doing my work long enough to know I was doing a good job and was comfortable with it.

I definitely had a sense of belonging. My co-workers and I were very close and had an excellent working relationship.

I felt loved by those I worked with as well as by my husband and other important people in my life.

And the assurance that my writing and editing touched lives for the Lord gave a tremendous purpose to my life.

My new role of motherhood, however, gave me little assurance of value in any of these areas.

Security. I did feel secure in this job. There was no one else to do it, though there were times I felt like giving the responsibility to someone else. I often did not feel sure of my health or my sanity. And my "just surviving" mentality hardly gave me a sense of real security.

Confidence. I did not find mothering easy and I had almost no confidence that I was doing an adequate job. I read a lot of books, and sometimes they helped, but too often they caused me to feel that I was inferior or a failure.

Belonging. Yes, there was a sense that I belonged to this child. But I had little opportunity to belong anywhere else. I often missed the camaraderie of the office.

Being loved. I was still certain of my husband's love, though I didn't feel lovely very often. As for my wonderful little daughter, she generally made demands rather than returning love to me.

Purpose. I knew that what I was doing in Debbie's life had great, long-term significance and purpose. But because there was little tangible evidence of results in those early days, it was hard to recognize any purpose.

Fortunately, God did not leave me hanging in frustration and insignificance. Nor did He allow me to shut myself away from the significant opportunities He had for me. Through study of His Word, extensive conversations with my husband, and the counsel of godly mothers, God provided His perspective on my life as a mother.

First, He dealt with my lost sense of significance. He reminded me that He, and He alone, was the source of my personal value and worth.

He reminded me that He loved me unconditionally (Romans 5:8), eternally (Jeremiah 31:3), and sacrificially (John 15:13).

He made me aware that my security had to be in Him, and that in Him I was truly safe. Jesus said, "No one can snatch them [my sheep] out of my hand" (John 10:28).

He reminded me that in Him—and only in Him—I can have confidence. I am a special person, created in God's image (Genesis 1:26,27). I am the crown of creation (Psalm 8:4,5). I am capable of great accomplishments (Philippians 4:13). God is my source of and reason for confidence.

God reminded me that I belong in the greatest group of all—His own family. He adopted me and made me His own child (Ephesians 1:4–6; John 1:12).

Then He showed me that I have a significant purpose.

His primary purpose in my life is to make me like Jesus (Romans 8:28,29). As I become more and more like Christ, I will fulfill His purpose for me by reflecting the glory of God (1 Peter 2:9).

God has other specific purposes for my life as well. One is to bear good fruit: "You did not choose Me, but I chose you, and appointed you, that you should go and bear fruit, and that your fruit should remain" (John 15:16). Also, God has prepared good works for me: "For we are God's workmanship, created in Christ Jesus to do good works, which God prepared in advance for us to do" (Ephesians 2:10). In the parable of the talents (Matthew 25:14–30), Christ tells us that we are to be good stewards of all that He gives us in life.

GOD REMINDED ME THAT HE, AND HE ALONE, WAS THE SOURCE OF MY PERSONAL VALUE AND WORTH.

As I understood that all I have is because I have Jesus, I began to recognize that it was not meeting all these important criteria in my life—in my career and ministry, or as a mother— that brought fulfillment. Rather it arose out of my relationship with God through Jesus Christ. He alone could give me the love, security, confidence, sense of belonging, and purpose for my life that I needed.

Thus, over time, God restored my sense of significance, unrelated to my mothering or any ministry I might have. He provided for my need for significance.

And then, when I clearly understood the true source of my significance, He began increasingly to unfold for me the significant opportunities He had for me. I gained a strong vision for the incredibly important—and significant—job I had as a mother. And step by step He led me into creative ways of touching lives for Him—ways that fit me, my abilities, and the needs of my family.

When I focus on Christ, He fills me with a true sense of significance. And that frees me to do the significant works He has planned for me.

Colleen Townsend Evans

LEARNING TO SAY NO

Colleen Evans served for 16 years on the board of directors of World Vision, U.S., and is a board member of Presbyterians for Renewal. She is on the advisory boards of International Justice Mission, a Christian witness for justice around the world, and Women at the Well, a ministry for women.

Colleen and her husband, Louis, are partners in renewal ministries, which involve men's/women's retreats, pastor/spouse retreats, and marriage and family conferences, as well as efforts aimed at improving cross-cultural relationships, and other ministries.

In 1987 she was named "Churchwoman of the Year" by Religious Heritage of America. She has received honorary doctorates from New York's King's College and Eastern College in St. David's, Pennsylvania.

After playing parts in several movies in the 1940s, "Coke" (as she is known to her closest friends) set aside a promising

film career to marry Louis H. Evans, Jr. in 1950.

The first years of their marriage were spent at San Francisco Theological Seminary, followed by two years at New College, University of Edinburgh, Scotland. She and her husband served the Bel Air Presbyterian Church and the La Jolla Presbyterian Church in California, and the National Presbyterian Church in Washington, D.C. They are now back in California at Menlo Park Presbyterian Church.

The Evanses have three sons and a daughter, and nine grandchildren.

Colleen is the author of nine books and with her husband is the co-author of a book on marriage.

When I asked Colleen to share the "greatest lesson" in her life, she thought of the many important things she has discovered over the years. What you are about to read was perhaps not her greatest lesson, but it certainly was one of the most practical. Had she not learned it, she most likely would not have been here to respond to my request. Here is her story.

It all began in the late 1950s. So much in my life was new then: I was a relatively new Christian; I became a new wife—then a new mother—and finally, when my husband finished seminary and graduate school, we were called to start a new church.

It was heady wine for someone who had always loved people and had a deep desire to serve. But to be honest, that was not the whole picture. I also wanted to please people and to have them care about me in return.

The new church that Louie, my husband, had been asked

to start was in Bel Air, an area in the hills above Los Angeles. It was an exciting new challenge for us, and we both dived in with energy and enthusiasm.

The church had nowhere to meet except in the living room of our low, gray, California-style frame house on Roscomare Road. This didn't present a problem for me—at first. We kept 150 folding chairs (our first furniture, other than beds!) in the garage for our constant stream of meetings and used the front bedroom for a church office.

After awhile, the growing congregation was able to rent the local elementary school auditorium for Sunday worship, but all the other meetings continued to be held in our home. It was almost a full-time job—setting up chairs, greeting people, taking down chairs, keeping the house in order, baking cookies, making punch, keeping the coffee pot on for meetings and drop-in callers at all times of the day and night.

In addition to all the church activities in our home, I also felt compelled to be involved in things outside our home. A community activist by nature, I seemed constitutionally unable to turn down requests to serve worthwhile causes. So I became chairperson for the Beverly Hills Bel Air Community Chest drive—which, looking back, was insane for me to chair during that season of my life.

By this time, I was no longer a "new" mother. We now had four babies, all under the age of five. It seemed that I could never quite finish folding one load of clean diapers before it was time to begin another.

After a church meeting one night, when the last lingering parishioner had headed home, I dragged myself to our bedroom and fell into bed utterly exhausted. The rest felt unbelievably good, but it was short-lived. A stirring from the cradle put me on notice that our youngest was ready for his midnight feeding. Almost automatically, I stumbled out of bed, picked him up, sat down in my rocker and began to nurse him. It was then that I looked over at Louie sleeping soundly.

The light of a full moon streamed through a crack between our draperies, looking like an eerie iridescent spotlight focused on the handsome face of my husband. He looked *so* comfortable, *so* rested, *so* like a Greek god in repose. And I felt a sudden flood of envy. No, more than envy: resentment, tinged with anger. Why couldn't he be more help, especially in the middle of the night?

Well, of course, I knew he couldn't nurse the baby. But at that moment I was in no mood to be logical. I was angry and I was tired and I had to blame somebody for something.

My attitude at that moment did not honor God, but it was honest (and God honors our honesty). It also served a purpose, for it let me know that I was in trouble and needed help. That fact was confirmed when I went to see my doctor, who also was a close family friend, for a checkup a few days later.

"To be frank, I'm really tired," I told him when he asked how I'd been feeling.

"No wonder!" he exclaimed, reading the lab report in front of him. "You're really anemic. I should put you in the hospital to see if we can build you up a bit."

"But Frosty," I sputtered to our longtime friend, "who would take care of Louie and the children, cook for the two prayer breakfasts each week, keep our home ready for all the church meetings, take over my responsibilities with the Community Chest fund drive, and…?"

I was about to run out of breath. "Frosty, you just *can't*

put me in the hospital!"

He just sat there shaking his head. "Do you have any household help?"

I laughed. "Help? On a new church development salary? No way!"

If I expected sympathy from my good friend, I was dead wrong. He looked at me with his intensely blue eyes, and without a tinge of "There, there," let me have it.

"Coke, you're crazy. Absolutely crazy. You're trying to be superwife, supermom, superfriend to everyone. And the truth is, you're becoming a supermartyr who doesn't know how to take care of herself. I know how much you want to serve the Lord and the whole world, but if you keep this up, you won't be able to serve anybody.

"Four babies—all that church stuff—and you still say yes to everybody who asks you to do anything. If you don't learn how to say *no*—and fast—you'll be burned out before you're thirty-five!"

I was stunned. His no-nonsense lecture got through to me. I knew that if I didn't make some immediate changes in my life, Frosty would be forced to make them for me.

As I left his office and drove home through the heavy Los Angeles traffic, I felt depressed. I feared Louie would be disappointed in me when I told him things were going to have to change, that I was going to have to cut back. But I was wrong.

Louie was wonderfully supportive, and this gave me a ray of insight. *He* was not the one pushing me to do so many things; *I* was. It wasn't Louie or the Lord driving me into an unhealthy lifestyle. It was my own expectations for myself. What Louie *really* wanted was for me to be the person God created me to be, and to enjoy him and the children. And so I began to relax—and pray in earnest.

"God, guide me. Show me how to live. Tell me what I must cut out of my schedule. Lord, please, with all of my heart, I want *You* to become the Lord of my daily routine."

HAVING NURTURED OUR RELATION-SHIPS AT HOME, WE COULD REACH OUT-TO A BRO-KEN WORLD FROM A-SOLID BASE.

I confess there were moments when I thought, *Maybe God will send me a maid. Most of my neighbors have maids and I need help as much as they do.* But God's wisdom prevailed, and that never happened. If God had supplied a maid, I would have continued in the disobedience of an unhealthy schedule. And Christ would never have been allowed to control the comings and goings of my life.

Instead, God continued to give me needed insight into myself. My priorities were wrong. For this season of my life, I was not to be out saving the world. There would be time for that later. But for now, I was to stay at home to care for my family and for myself. Most of all, I was to concentrate on nurturing my relationship with Christ, with my very special partner in life, and with the four tiny, beautiful human beings with whom God was trusting us for a brief time.

With radical clarity, God revealed to me that Louie and I could not continue ministering to needy people until we learned to minister in Christ's name to one another. Then, having nurtured our relationships at home, we could reach out to a broken world from a solid base.

So it wasn't a maid I needed. It was a realigning of priorities, a judicious pruning of activities. But that was not as easily done as said, for it meant giving up my dream of trying to please everybody. It meant making some people angry as I turned down their telephone requests, or sent out polite but firm notes of resignation. It was tough, but my mind was made up. In my new way of thinking, it had to be God's opinion that mattered most—and it had to be Christ, *not other people*, who ruled my life.

Consequently, I learned the lesson Frosty said I must learn to survive. And I began to say no to a lot of very good things—good, but not God's best for that season of my life. At the same time, I learned to say yes to people who had been wanting to help me with all sorts of things. And that opened the door to let some very gracious people into my life.

In the months that followed, when someone asked me to take on a responsibility I believed was not God's best, I felt increasingly free to say, "Thanks for thinking of me, but this isn't the time for that kind of involvement."

I was in the process of being liberated from my terrible need to be superwoman. I discovered that I didn't feel guilty for turning people down. I was able to stop condemning myself and chomping at the bit because of the limitations of my strength and circumstances. God was doing a real and much-needed work in me, and I was experiencing a joy and satisfaction in my daily life that I hadn't known in years. There is no question that learning to say no was a turning point in my life.

Now, many years later, the joy remains. Indeed, it has grown. And I am so deeply grateful to God for teaching me the importance of learning to say no through that painful experience. It is a lesson that has served me well. And amazingly, some of the very things I had to say no to in earlier seasons have returned as opportunities for a new season in my life.

If you are caught, as I was, in the barrenness of a too-busy life, look to Jesus. The Gospels reveal Him as a man who had learned the importance of saying no. There were times when He said no to the demands and requests made of Him, times when He said no to the crowd and got away to be alone with His disciples, times when He left the disciples to be alone with His Father.

Jesus looked to God for guidance and direction for His days. He listened for that one voice over the roar of all other voices calling for His time and energy and help. And so must we. For Jesus that meant that sometimes He did not get to those close to Him in their time of need. He did not get to His cousin John in prison before Herod took off his head, nor did He heed the call of Mary and Martha to be with Lazarus as he lay ill and dying. (And can't you just see Martha pacing the floor and muttering, "Where's that Jesus when we need Him most?")

And so we, like Jesus, must listen for that one voice above every other, and let God guide us in every aspect of our daily lives. But that will mean learning the important lesson of being willing to say *no* to people in order to say *yes* to God.

Then, and only then, will our great and loving Lord be able to reveal His greater plan through us, as He did to Mary and Martha in the resurrection of Lazarus.

Mary Graham

A LONGING TO BE-ACCEPTED

Mary Graham is president of Women of Faith, *a ministry that hosts conferences for women throughout the country.*

A native of Oklahoma, Mary earned a sociology degree from California State University in Fresno. Motivated by a desire to work with students, she joined the Campus Crusade for Christ staff in 1969, and has served the Lord at the Universities of New Mexico, Kansas, and Utah.

Mary worked for three years as Director of International Ministries with Insight for Living, *Dr. Charles Swindoll's radio ministry. She currently serves on its board of directors. Mary also was the executive producer and director of* Women Today With Vonette Bright, *a daily radio program.*

Being the youngest in a family of eight children has profoundly affected her life, giving her wisdom, humor, and insight that make her one of the most delightful and spiritually mature persons I have known.

"Little House on the Prairie" it was not. Yet, in many ways, growing up in our home in Picher, Oklahoma, was almost as ideal: a little house, a small community, and a loving family. The children were taught strong moral values, fierce family loyalty, and a commitment to the work ethic and the American way.

My father expressed his philosophy of child-rearing in these terms: "Tell them they can't do something and they will prove to you they can," and, "Never tell them they did well or they won't try to do better." There was no question about his heart's desire. He wanted his children to be hard-working, high-achieving, and well-accomplished adults who made positive contributions to life.

My mother's philosophy was equally demanding. She said it simply: "Stay out of trouble."

So often I recall their challenge to me, "Be something." And, "Behave."

Success in life was thus well-defined and I thought easily attained. But being the youngest of eight children, I had too many sidewalk captains giving me orders. Nothing was easy.

My parents had four girls, then three boys, then me. They described it like this: "First we had the girls, then we had the boys, then we had Mary." The female side of the family was always referred to as "the girls and Mary."

I'll never forget the day I phoned home and my dad answered, "Hi, honey." I could hear Mother in the background, "Is that one of the girls?" Without a second thought he answered, "No, it's Mary. You want to talk to her?"

The "girls" were all teenagers by the time I learned to walk and talk. They were not interested in my being one of them, and the boys—a small band of terrorists looking for someone to attack—were not interested in having their baby sister among their ranks either. That didn't diminish my popularity, unfortunately, as the candidate for their numerous shenanigans.

During those growing-up years, my heart longed to be wanted. I tried everything to fill this need. I pestered everyone. In an effort to appease me, Mother forced the boys to include me in their games—unless I cried. Countless times I heard her say, "I cannot make them play with you if you cry." Thus they learned quickly that getting rid of me was simple: Make her cry. If tears stunted growth, I'd be about an inch tall.

The boys were dreadful. They entertained themselves, and each other, with whatever was close at hand—like walking on old oil drums. As they balanced themselves on those big barrels and danced their little feet backwards and forwards, they looked like circus clowns. So agile. So gifted. So enviable. I wanted to do that.

"Never!" they declared. "Girls can't do this. You have to do two things at once, balance yourself and walk. Girls can only do one thing at a time—one or the other. Never both."

"Why?" I asked.

"Because they're girls," they insisted.

But I didn't give up. Finally, one of the boys responded to my persistent plea. "Okay, here's what you can do. Take the barrel up the hill. Get on it and balance yourself. That's all. Just one thing. The barrel will move down the hill on its own; you will not need to walk. It will roll itself."

Great! I thought. Well, not quite great. The barrel rolled on its own all right. It threw me off, then ran over me. I cried. My brothers were in complete unsympathetic hysterics.

"Girls!" they muttered. "Hmpf!"

Although the boys were mean to me, it was easy to see that they liked each other. My sisters liked each other, too. Clearly, the boys and the girls were friends, comrades, teams —at least with each other. So, to be included, I resolved to be like them.

Whatever they did, I did. Or at least tried. Life became adventuresome, albeit tiring. My energies were extremely focused: Perform. Their edict, my marching orders.

And so it went throughout my life. I earned a master's degree in the "performing arts." I learned to please people—my parents, my siblings, my teachers, peers, friends— everybody. I performed and lived on their agendas. It worked well for me. I looked and felt successful.

My theme in life could have been summed up in four words: "I can do that." Wherever I went, whatever need I perceived, no matter the cost, my response was always the same: "Oh, I can do that. No problem."

As a high school student, I was on the debate team. My partner, Bob, was clearly one of the best, most highly acclaimed debaters in the state. He was two years my senior and far outdistanced me in ability and experience. It was an honor to be on his team.

Anyone with as little experience as I was crazy to compete in his league. Not I. I was so accustomed to reaching beyond my own limitations, so attuned to trying harder and reaching higher that I rose to the challenge.

Although I was over my head by anyone's standard, this didn't stop me. I said whatever was necessary to win. I performed well, and we won. It was as simple as that. I knew no other way. The anxiety and stress I felt was at times tremendous, but never overwhelming. Such experiences defined and amplified my entire life.

Then I gave my heart to Christ.

As a junior in college, I discovered His love for me and received His forgiveness. I trusted Him to take absolute and irrevocable control of my life. My heart's desire was to please and honor Him. I learned that the only way to do that was "by faith."

Those who discipled me as a new believer were careful to instruct me in that faith. They consistently taught and modeled the biblical perspective: "God is not as concerned with your performance as He is with the attitude of your heart. He's not as interested in what you do as who you are inside." This was diametrically opposed to every standard I had ever known.

GOD IS NOT AS INTERESTED IN WHAT YOU DO AS-WHO YOU ARE-INSIDE.

With all of my being, I wanted to believe these truths. I wanted to understand God's grace. I wanted to experience His unconditional love for me. I wanted to believe His promise in John 15:9, "Just as the Father has loved Me, I have also loved you." And in Romans 15:7, "I have accepted you." And in Matthew 6:33, "I will care for you."

In my mind, I grasped the truth of these promises and clung as tightly as possible to their reliability. But somehow I could not always make them work in my life. They needed to go deeper into the foundation of my soul, to find solid ground. I needed an emotional framework to turn theory into practice.

"Unmerited favor," a definition of God's grace, was simply not in my vocabulary. Total acceptance and unconditional love were only terminology to me. I struggled to apply those terms personally.

Eventually, my performance orientation took its toll. I simply could not keep up with the demand.

I then made a very unfortunate transition. No longer did I try to live up to the expectations of others. Having internalized this driving force, I began making these harsh requirements of myself.

I sought the counsel of a very wise person who helped me understand how I had gotten myself into such a dilemma and how to unravel the confusion.

I began to search the Scriptures carefully and purposefully. The apostle Paul made it clear in Ephesians 2:8 that it is "by grace" that we have been saved. He spent most of his time in the Book of Galatians explaining that just as we are saved by God's grace, we are also perfected (brought to maturity) by His grace.

As I focused my mind on this, I began to comprehend that grace means God accepts me just as I am. He does not require or insist that I measure up to someone else's standard of performance. He loves me completely, thoroughly, and perfectly. There's nothing I can do to add to or detract from that love. He forgives me. Nothing I have ever done or will ever do is beyond the reach of His mercy and grace to forgive.

Even as I began to understand His grace, my mind still needed deprogramming. Its "software" had received inaccurate data. During the formative years of my life, I assumed God's demands were similar to but greater than those of my colleagues, friends, and family. I tried hard to please people and even harder to please Him. Yet, my self-effort, though well-intentioned, was thwarting my spiritual growth.

I needed first to understand and experience His grace. Once I grasped that, I could pursue and enjoy healthy relationships that reflected God's love. I stopped needing to perform.

Isn't it interesting that we are products of our early years? If someone is consistently lied to as a child, he will have difficulty trusting as an adult. If one is molested in childhood, she will not easily experience intimacy as an adult. If abandoned as a child, it is very hard to experience security in adult relationships.

Unwilling to let His children stay trapped in those liabilities, the Lord often engineers circumstances to reveal deep needs and provides people and insight to cause healing and growth. This is what He did for me. I performed as a child in order to be accepted. As an adult I did the same. Even in my relationship with the Lord, I assumed I would win His approval by my achievements—even though, intellectually, I knew better.

Eventually, as I was able to define my problem, determine my own misconceptions, realize why I had them and ultimately put my faith in the trustworthiness of a loving God, I began to grow and change. I actually felt it in my person, in my soul.

With those changes came an ability to experience not only His love and acceptance, but also a freedom that I had never known before. Paul said, "It was for freedom that Christ set us free" (Galatians 5:1). What a verse! Christ did not set us free from one thing so we could be enslaved by another. He set us free so we could enjoy freedom in Him.

God not only used my experience to show me that performance does not work, He gave me His Word to help me overcome my human tendencies. He surrounded me with a body of caring, supportive believers who genuinely loved me for who I am, not for what I can do. They were consistent, faithful, and devoted to me.

At last, I am on my way to freedom: Freedom from the demands and expectations of others; freedom from my fear of failure; freedom from the need to perform; freedom from concern about my own acceptance. I'm learning to experience God's grace, to accept others where they are and let them be who God wants them to be. I'm discovering that I am not responsible for running the world. And best of all, I'm finding the freedom to enjoy freedom.

I learned many wonderful things from my family, and I am indebted to them for all they taught me. But it was God who helped me realize that His grace, His acceptance, is what gives my life meaning. He has been my greatest teacher and has taught me my greatest lesson: He loves me just as I am.

Ruth Bell Graham

WORRY AND WORSHIP CANNOT LIVE IN THE SAME HEART

Ruth Bell Graham and her evangelist husband, Billy, have made their mark for the glory of God upon the entire world.

Born in China to Dr. and Mrs. L. Nelson Bell, medical missionaries at the Presbyterian Hospital three hundred miles north of Shanghai, Ruth met Billy while a student at Wheaton College. In 1943, after graduating from Wheaton, they were married.

Ruth became a pastor's wife for a brief period in Western Springs, Illinois. When Dr. Graham became a full-time evangelist, the Grahams made their home in Montreat, North Carolina. They have five children, nineteen grandchildren, and numerous great-grandchildren.

Ruth is the author of several books and an avid reader.

Because she has so much to share, she is in great demand as a speaker. But she mostly defers to her husband, saying, "One speaker in the family is enough."

The Bible says the older women should teach younger women.[1] Though Ruth is not that much older than I, she is one of the women I have most admired, observed, and loved. Never have I known a wiser, more Christlike woman ready to share her husband and herself with the world. She is a modern Proverbs 31 woman, a model for me and millions of others.

This account of her personal dependence upon God in the "storms" of life is typical of how she copes with daily encounters.

The rumble of thunder was only a distant threat. But the wind in the firs beside the stream, and the oaks and pines between the bedroom window and the street, announced the storm was on its way.

All my life I have loved storms. But then, I have only experienced them from the shelter of a solidly built house, and as a child, with the warm conviction that with Mother and Daddy near, nothing really bad could happen.

The wind rose menacingly, and there was a sudden crack of thunder directly overhead. Soon I heard the patter of little feet and sensed a small presence in the room. I heard a whispered "Mother?" That was all.

The covers were thrown back in comforting welcome as one or more small, night-clad forms would slip in (depending on the severity of the storm). There, lovingly encircled, we snuggled safely together under the covers, listening to the storm, unafraid. As nature once more grew quiet, we drifted off to sleep.

In later years, when I knew they were all enduring their own individual storms, I would lie awake wishing I could share them.

At night, it was as if I could hear a whispered "Mother?" Only there was no one there. I sensed the distant thunder, and all I could do was pray.

Then came the time when the Lord taught me to utilize more fully these times of prayer in the early hours of the day.

It was early in the morning in another country. Exhausted as I was, I awoke around three o'clock. The name of someone I loved dearly flashed into my mind. It was like an electric shock. Instantly I was wide awake. I knew there would be no more sleep for me the rest of the night. So I lay there and prayed for the one who was trying hard to run away from God. When it is dark and the imagination runs wild, there are fears that only a mother can understand.

Suddenly the Lord said to me, "Quit studying the problems and start studying the promises." Now God has never spoken to me audibly, but there is no mistaking when He speaks.

So I turned on the light, got out my Bible, and the first verse that came to me was Philippians 4:6: "Be careful for nothing; but in every thing by prayer and supplication *with thanksgiving* let your requests be made known unto God." And verse 7: "And the peace of God, which passeth all understanding, shall keep your hearts and minds through Christ Jesus." Or, as the *Amplified Version* has it, "Do not fret or have any anxiety about anything, but in every circumstance and in everything by prayer and petition [definite requests] *with thanksgiving* continue to make your wants known to God" (emphasis added).

Suddenly I realized that the missing ingredient in my prayers had been "with thanksgiving." So I put down my Bible and spent time worshiping God for who He is and what He is. This covers more territory than any one mortal can comprehend. Even contemplating what little we do know dissolves doubts, reinforces faith, and restores joy. I began to thank God for giving me this one I loved so dearly in the first place. I even thanked Him for the difficult spots that taught me so much.

And do you know what happened? It was as if someone suddenly turned on the lights in my mind and heart, and the little fears and worries which, like mice and cockroaches, had been nibbling away in the darkness, suddenly scuttled for cover.

That was when I learned that worship and worry cannot live in the same heart: they are mutually exclusive.[2]

Pattie Harris

Overcoming Depression

Before joining the staff of Campus Crusade for Christ, Pattie Harris spent many years in the educational field. She served as an elementary music instructor, an early childhood education specialist, and an educational administrator in the United States and Africa.

As a Campus Crusade staff member with Christian Leadership Ministries, she ministers to college professors and administrators in Delaware and Southeastern Pennsylvania. Her campus ministry has included short-term projects in Kenya and South Africa. She is presently working toward a graduate degree in theology at Biblical Theological Seminary in order to integrate teaching of religion courses into her college campus ministry.

She continues to conduct workshops concerning many areas of the Christian life around the country and in the Carribbean.

Here Pattie shares her secret for overcoming depression and living joyfully and victoriously despite difficult circumstances in her life.

For most of my life I have battled a pervasive sense of sadness that I can only describe as a type of low-grade fever.

Knowing that I have a melancholy personality, for years I thought my despondency was normal. I believed that just as the universe needs to have both positive and negative forces to be in balance, so my personality was created to balance the optimists of the world. Once a friend asked me to imagine a scene of a young girl walking in the woods. True to character, I saw a dark and foreboding forest with danger lurking all around.

What I still find hard to understand is that I received some satisfaction in my feelings of dejection.

While it was true that my spirit was constantly downcast, my circumstances belied my negative outlook. I came from a loving family. Having only one child, my parents worked and sacrificed to provide every educational and cultural advantage for me. Because I had experienced so many positive times in my life, on the surface I would come across as a pleasant, cheerful person. Throughout this time, I managed to carry on a career as a teacher and educational administrator and as a staff member of a Christian organization, ministering to the spiritual needs of career and professional women. Ironically, I was trying to be a role model of the joyful Christian life.

By my thirties, the sadness had developed into a ghastly

sense of dread. In my forties, the feelings of dejection were full-blown depressions. Since I grew up believing that discussing your feelings was in bad taste, only a few people knew about my secret malady. I called upon my personal cheering squad night and day, and they faithfully listened to my moaning and groaning. Through their encouragement and prayers I would receive temporary emotional relief.

It took years for me to articulate why I was grieving. My thoughts had become stuck on the chapter of my life called "Disappointments and Unfulfilled Dreams." Here I was, approaching age fifty, still single and still suffering from an affliction of many single women—hope deferred. Time was moving on and leaving me behind to mourn myself into poor health.

The turning point came at my lowest moment. For several days, I had not been able to concentrate. Every time I looked at my work on the computer screen that I had been trying to write for weeks, I felt nauseated. Lately, my hours at work had been spent in an endless cycle of staring at the computer hoping for one clear idea, pacing my office floor, making inaudible screams, and heading back to the computer again.

Finally one day I said, "This is ridiculous," and went for professional help. I asked a counselor who was leasing an office in our suite, "What does it feel like to have a nervous breakdown?"

"One symptom," she said, "is the feeling of losing control."

I sighed. "That's what I'm feeling right now. What should I do?"

"Pattie, if you're really feeling that way, I think the best thing for you to do is to check yourself into a hospital."

I didn't expect that response. I wanted to hear something soothing and comforting. But hospitalization! I was both horrified and indignant. The whole world would now know that I was having a nervous breakdown. It's one thing to *feel* pitiful, but it's another for everybody else to regard you as pitiful.

I DETERMINED TO-SEEK JOY, CLAIM IT, SEIZE IT, TREASURE IT, AND DELIGHT IN-IT.

The next morning, as usual, I struggled to lift my head from the pillow. But this time I was enraged about my miserable state. "I'm *not* going to any hospital! I can't afford it. Plus, a lot of people are depending on me, so there's no time to be away."

My anger became the energy I needed to scream out to God in complete abandonment, "God, I need help, and I refuse to go to anyone but You! You will be my psychiatrist, my psychologist. I will seek Your face and claim Your promises."

God did meet my needs in a dramatic way. I never found it necessary to seek professional help again, though I don't criticize those who do.

I began to think about a verse that someone had shared with me many years ago about King David.

> David was greatly distressed, for the people spoke of stoning him, because the soul of all the people was grieved, every man for his sons and his daughters. But David strengthened [encouraged] himself in the Lord his God (1 Samuel 30:6).

David was in a no-win situation. For years he had cunningly escaped death at the hands of Saul and his army.

Now his own men blamed him for the kidnapping of their wives and children by a band of raiders and were planning to execute him. Who was there for David? No wife, no friends, no support group, no comforting book to read. No doubt David felt depressed.

Whatever happened between David and God resulted in renewed courage, confidence, and ultimately a victorious rescue operation. I asked God to show me how to encourage myself in Him as David had done. That day I began one of the greatest adventures in my Christian life.

Now, when the dark clouds begin to descend over my head and I start to focus on my hurts and disappointments, I put my self-encouragement formula into practice.

First, *be joyful*. I reason that if it is true that:

- in God's presence there is fullness of joy (Psalm 16:11)
- Jesus wants me to have His joy (John 15:11)
- it was joy that kept Christ on the cross (Hebrews 12:2)
- the joy of the Lord is my strength (Nehemiah 8:10)

then I must *always* have this joy. As an act of the will, I chose to be joyful. I determined to seek it, claim it, seize it, treasure it, and delight in it.

Second, *meditate on specific promises of God as they relate to my need*. In doing this I keep in mind what God has to say:

- about Himself
- about me
- about His love for me

As I read and meditate on the psalms, David's record of his times with the Lord, and affirm the truths recorded in them, explosions of joy take place in my heart. I actually feel the adrenalin surging in my body. I can bound out of bed and face my daily problems head on. Living by the spiritual principles I have observed in the life of David has taught me the greatest lesson of my life.

My life is radically different as a result. I tell people that I am happier and more content than I have ever been. I recognize that I may sound as though I am ignoring the hard times. So I follow up with, "I still have the same problems, the dark clouds descend, the pain remains, but now I know what to do about them. I have learned how to encourage myself in the Lord."

Jeanne Hendricks

"'Tis Death That Makes Life Live"

A native of Philadelphia, Pennsylvania, Jeanne grew up in a solid Christian home. Local church and youth activities were a vital part of her life. She attended Houghton College in New York and Wheaton College in Illinois and received her B.A. degree in journalism from Southern Methodist University in Dallas. She also has formal training in business and the Bible and has studied the American family and aging in America at Harvard University.

She has taken several study/ministry trips to Europe, Africa, the Middle East, and the Orient.

Married to Howard G. Hendricks, distinguished professor and chairman of the Center for Christian Leadership of Dallas Theological Seminary, she is the mother of four married children and has several grandchildren.

Professionally, Jeanne has been a pastor's wife and teacher, as well as a medical secretary and freelance writer. Presently *she is in great demand as a speaker for women's conferences and youth seminars, and she teams with her husband in teaching family life conferences.*

You will be inspired as Jeanne shares the lessons she learned while conquering her fear of death and discovering her real purpose in life.

Viewed from the heights of grandmotherhood, life tends to hide its shadows. When eyewitnesses are gone, older women tend to "forget" failures. And little-girl fantasies, wrinkled with age, can come alive to retouch family histories.

I am tempted to downplay my early tussle with the concept of death because for so long it held me by the throat. But I crave an ability to recall the way it really was because only then can I tell you what I learned about living and how I learned it from what Job called "the king of terrors."

For years I didn't even know I needed to learn a lesson about people. Like every newborn baby, I arrived into the world and people were there, talking and being who they were. I imitated them and didn't ask questions. But when suddenly some were not there any longer, that got my attention.

Robert Browning's words describe my experience:

You never know what life means till you die. Even throughout life, 'tis death that makes life live.

Death has made its statement in our world. It is the irreversible closure, the period—or exclamation point—or question mark, at the end of the human sentence. It is the most profound lights out, the end of the road, the final crush, the last ultimate humiliation of humanity. And it struck paralyzing fear into my six-year-old being when I met it head-on for the first time.

Aunt Carrie lived close by; she was my frequent baby-sitter, the mother of four favorite cousins, and it was at her home in suburban Philadelphia where our family ate nearly every Sunday dinner. Then came a stormy spring night when I sat on my daddy's lap in her darkened living room and saw her corpse.

Nobody could explain why to my satisfaction. My cousins seemed as confused as I was, and the adults in the family just didn't say much. At home Dad told me that she had too much fat around her heart; nevertheless, Aunt Carrie was gone and nothing was the same.

A decade passed, years in which uncertainty about life and death grew for me. During that time, I made a personal commitment of my life to Jesus Christ. I understood, at least in theory, the ultimate answer to death, but the churning torment of loss when a loved one was irretrievably gone had not been alleviated. I had no label for my inward terror, much less did I understand my real need. In no way was I prepared for another shattering loss.

This time I was alerted, but I plugged my ears. A childless couple who had become family friends when I was about eight years old began to invite me to spend time with them. Uncle Floyd and Aunt Grace enchanted me as they took me with them in their shiny car to visit their wonderful German relatives. One of his uncles owned a candy shop; another one had a small farm. All of them were marvelous storytellers and happy, friendly, and kind. My difficult early teen years were highlighted with these loving and high-spirited people who introduced me to having good clean fun. Then without warning, Uncle Floyd pulled me aside during a weekend retreat and told me he loved me and wanted to say goodbye; he was having heart surgery on his "leaky pump."

"No!" I protested. "You'll get better; I know you will!"

But he knew intuitively, and about a week later, the dreaded call came from Aunt Grace. I wanted to run away and scream, to somehow undo the personal knot that was choking me, to change it all. Instead I had to stand beside the casket and face the truth, but I could not bear to look at Uncle Floyd's face. I closed my eyes and tried to deny; I simply had no coping mechanism.

Every year we celebrated Christ's resurrection. I had memorized parts of 1 Corinthians 15. I had sung often, "O death, where is thy sting? O grave, where is thy victory?" But the monster kept pursuing me and moving in ever closer. As a young adult I tried to become a bit more philosophical. When three of my own babies died before they were born, I pretended that it hadn't really happened. But there was no escape; the day came when Mother told me that Dad was terminally ill with cancer.

No, not my daddy! He's too big and strong and warm and loving—God will make an exception. I believed it and I went home and sat with Mother in the living room and pleaded in prayer for Dad's miraculous recovery. But the disease persisted and took its deadly toll. Dad's ready wit and engaging personality faded. He whispered hoarsely and scanned me with serious and piercing eyes. I knew him well because we had often talked together, and he had many times given me advice that was filled with uncanny insight and common sense. Now it was his last opportunity, and

God allowed him to share with me the most important counsel he had ever given to this second daughter with whom a mutual trust had grown over the years. Dad held out his wasted arm to me and began to fill in my blanks.

"Honey, don't be sad. God gave me many years and that's what counts. Now, He's letting you and Howie and your youngsters carry on. So, you just use your life for the Lord. Just do what He tells you. And I'll be seeing you again…"

With months to prepare, I was still not ready for the icy words, "He's gone." Never had I wept with tears so bitter, so unable to be turned off. Never was there a colder, more bleak October day than that dreadful afternoon when Dad, my source of comfort and consolation since birth, sank into the sod.

Aunt Carrie had left a mysterious emptiness. Uncle Floyd had said he loved me, but I resented his absence. Dad had tried to prepare me, and finally I was beginning to understand. Death *is* bigger and stronger than I am, but I don't have to be its victim. I can learn from it.

Falling asleep has always been one of my best accomplishments. But after Dad died, I found myself lying awake in bed with a deep sense of loss and sadness. I often woke up in the middle of the night and cried bitter tears because he was no longer available to me—or was he? I began to think back over the words he had spoken.

First, there was the hope—"I'll see you again…" Of course, that is exactly what Jesus told His disciples when He was going to the cross. Death was not the end, not the real end.

Second, Dad was gone, but I was still here with my family. He had said that it was now my turn—he handed me the torch.

A new resolve began to set into my thinking. The little oft-repeated couplet surfaced: "Only one life, 'twill soon be past. Only what's done for Christ will last." Gradually I began to gain strength from remembering that parting scene by the bedside. Like a transfusion of spiritual vitamins, my goals crystallized. I began to see what Paul meant by the de-fanging of death and the grave.

Death is neutralized by life when that life continues in another warrior who "fights the good fight." The grave is a mere formality in the total scheme of God's grace.

When Mother died in my home, after twenty-three years of widowhood, I was sad, but also full of a deep joy that I had been privileged to come into the world as the product of her—and Dad's—love. The emptiness and void were there, but they were overshadowed by a sense of challenge: It's my turn now.

Jesus speaks to me with full force: "He who loves his life will lose it...Unless a grain of wheat falls into the ground and dies, it remains alone; but if it dies, it produces much grain" (John 12:24,25). And so with full speed ahead, I aim to pour myself into other lives so that Christ may say of me, "Well done, good and faithful servant."

Aunt Carrie's death left me with a fear, based on ignorance, of people. I simply did not know how important they were and I took them for granted. Uncle Floyd's passing left me with a fear based on unwillingness to allow people to come in (and go out) of my life. Dad helped me look my fear in the face, to break it and melt it by using death as a harsh, but very effective, teacher.

Aunt Carrie had cared for me; Uncle Floyd had reached out to a quiet little girl and shared with her the mainstream of his life. Dad dispelled for me the seeming impossibility of facing death's horror.

Possibly the most amazing fallout from these three significant deaths was the implant of love for people. I was known as a shy child, a painfully insecure, timid, and self-conscious teen. Always concerned with what people would think of me, constantly avoiding public visibility, I was slow to realize that my purpose in life was simply to relate to other people. Like the payload on a three-stage rocket, I found myself catapulted into a life of serving people, touching them with the love and confidence I received from Christ. Best of all, funerals were no longer the numbing horrors of my early years.

Whether human beings divert attention from funerals with political parades or try to drown them with laughter and liquor, we all cower in the presence of death. It is impossible not to. Jesus Christ sweat drops of blood and suffered incredible agony in contemplation of His death; He took it seriously and so should we. No one escapes its clutches, but we can escape its consequences. Salvation through Christ means victory over the grave. His words to John are my ultimate consolation:

> Do not be afraid. I am the First and the Last. I am the Living One; I was dead, and behold I am alive for ever and ever! And I hold the keys of death and Hades (Revelation 1:17,18).

Kay Coles James

I, TOO, HAVE A-DREAM

Kay Coles James has been active in the development, implementation, and analysis of American public policy for the past twenty years in senior positions in the public and private sectors. Among other positions, she has been dean of the School of Government at Regent University, senior vice-president of the Family Research Council, associate director for the White House Office of National Drug Control Policy, and assistant secretary for public affairs at the U.S. Department of Health and Human Services.

A native of Virginia, she received her B.S. degree from Hampton Institute. Long interested in family issues, she is one of the founders and a former president of Black Americans for Life. In addition, she and her husband, Charles E. James, founded the National Family Institute in 1985 to address the crisis within the American family.

Having had experience in varied businesses as a supervi-

sor, personnel manager, and administrator, she gained recognition as a volunteer for social causes including equal housing opportunities in Virginia. She also served as a member of the board of the Family and Children's Services and the Richmond, Virginia, Metropolitan Crisis Pregnancy Center. In 1988 she was appointed a member of the White House Commission on Children and the White House Task Force on the Black Family.

She also has been the director of public affairs of the National Right to Life Committee in Washington, D.C. Her experiences with legislative efforts have made her comfortable with the media, conducting national press conferences and numerous presentations before audiences in the U.S., England, and Ireland.

Mrs. James and her husband have three children and reside in Chesapeake, Virginia.

She balances beautifully a professional career and her strong commitment to biblical principles. In the following story she relates how the Christlike love of a young white girl and two white women touched her life and kept her from becoming a bitter, resentful, and angry woman over the racial injustices she has suffered since childhood.

As a woman I am constantly juggling many balls—some crystal, some rubber.

One of my crystal balls—our son, Robert—asked me to come to his elementary school and give a talk for Black History Month. The commitment was easy to make when it was weeks away, but by the time the day arrived the calendar was tight and I was called upon to do one of my best juggling acts.

I'll confess, I didn't view this as one of my more important speeches, and my preparation was minimal—just a few notes scribbled on a piece of paper. It could easily have been confused with one of Robert's homework assignments. When the children started filing in and I really began to focus on the importance of Black History Month, I suddenly became aware of the significance of this event and the tremendous opportunity to touch those young lives. I silently prayed and asked God's forgiveness for not having spent more time in preparation, and for not recognizing this as a truly crystal-ball opportunity. I asked for His help and guidance.

My assigned task was to share with the students what it was like growing up as a black child in the South during the Civil Rights struggle. I wanted to paint word pictures for the children so they could not only appreciate the facts, but perhaps even see themselves living my experience.

This is the story I told them:

> I want to tell you a true story. I know the story is true because it happened to me. There are two other main characters, and when I finish, I want you to tell me which one you want to be like.
>
> When I was in the sixth grade like some of you, my parents told me that the time had come to integrate the schools. Integrate means to mix. In those days, black children and white children could not go to school together. There were many white people who thought that because I was black, I should go to a separate school, that I should only live in certain neighborhoods, have certain jobs, and go to certain churches. Why? I still

don't completely understand. I suppose they were afraid of my family and me because we were different. We are African Americans. Our skin is darker, our cultural experience is different. Often people fear what they don't know and understand.

The first day of junior high school can be a frightening experience under the best of circumstances. But for me it was a nightmare. When I arrived, there were police cars, reporters, and angry parents. Some held on to their children and refused to let them come into the school; others walked cautiously past the crowd and entered the building. I was so confused. Why were those people saying those mean things to me? Why were they so angry with me? What had I done?

My parents walked me to the principal's office and told him that I was being left in his care in excellent condition and when they picked me up at three o'clock, they expected to find me in the same condition. I think he got the message. But the day did not get any better. The name-calling was bad, but constantly being stuck with pins as we changed classes was horrible. And although being stuck with pins hurt, being spat upon hurt even more.

Some of the teachers did their part to make us feel unwelcome. When my homeroom teacher read the menu for the next day, she said: "Tomorrow we will have vegetable soup, grilled cheese sandwiches, fruit cups, and brownies. Lord only knows why they're serving brownies, we have enough of *them* here already!"

The class laughed. I cried.

The harassment continued. The students kept up their pranks and the teachers tried to discourage the black kids by giving us bad grades no matter how good our work was. I wanted to give up and go back to my all-black school where the teachers cared about me and I had been president of the student government. Life was just fine in my segregated school.

Several months into the school year, things were not going any better. One day, as I was walking to class, a big white guy came up behind me and pushed me down the steps. As I tumbled down the stairs, I twisted my back and ended up in a heap at the foot of the steps. That was obviously not enough for him, so he kicked my books and scattered them in the corridor.

A crowd gathered. Some laughed, others cheered. Willard gloated as he continued kicking my books. A white girl stepped from the crowd and gathered up my books, then helped me stand as best I could. As she led me away toward the principal's office, the crowd turned on Ann.

"Nigger lover! Nigger lover!"

I was out of school for several weeks with a back injury, and when I returned I looked for Ann. I wanted to know if she had faced any trouble for trying to help me. She said that some kids were mean to her but they weren't nice kids anyway, so she really hadn't lost any friends. A friendship developed between Ann and I.

As I told my story, I explained to the children that even though it was more than twenty-five years ago, I still remembered Willard and Ann. Willard stands as a symbol of all the ugly, hateful experiences I had. Ann helped to shape the person I am today. I was well on my way to being a bitter, resentful, angry woman. She touched my life and helped shape my character for the better.

I then challenged my listeners to become "Anns" and

not "Willards."

I encouraged them to ask me questions. That's when I received my Black History Month blessing. A cute little white child raised his hand and asked, "Mrs. James, what's a nigger?" A few kids snickered, and he looked hurt. I asked him his age and he said he was ten. I wanted to hug him, his parents, and his teachers. They were obviously doing something right.

Unfortunately, the racism I experienced was not confined to junior high school. As I grew up I suffered institutional as well as individual racism. And while I am encouraged today by a young white child in Fairfax County, I know that racism is still a force to be reckoned with in our schools, in the work place, our communities, and our churches. Why, then, do I not live my life in anger and bitterness? It is because over the years the Lord continued to place "Anns" in my life, and I finally accepted as reality the biblical principles of forgiveness and the transcendent nature of God's love. And I always remember that faith itself is a mystery that demands trust.

> IN THEM I FOUND THE UTTERLY SELF-EMPTYING KIND OF CHRISTLIKE LOVE.

While in college, I met two women through InterVarsity Christian Fellowship. Joyce and Beth, both white, richly amplified the friendship I had experienced in junior high. In them I also found the utterly self-emptying kind of Christlike love. It was a love devoted not only to the content of my character, but to its Christian maturation as well.

They each had an emphasis in their witness to Christianity. Joyce represented the power of grace, Beth the presence of obedience to God's law. I was confident of the unconditional love that I received from both of them. Their effect on me is incalculable. It came as no surprise to anyone who knew me well that when my daughter was born she was named Elizabeth Joyce James.

As a part of my private Black History Month celebration, I reread Dr. Martin Luther King Jr.'s famous "I Have a Dream" speech. One of my favorite quotes became even more real to me:

> I have a dream my four little children will one day live in a nation where they will not be judged by the color of their skin but by the content of their character. I have a dream today!

What would my character be had Ann, Joyce, and Beth not entered my life? It frightens me to think of what I may have become. It is God's miracle that the Christian love of one white girl and two white women made Dr. King's words so important in my life.

In the mystery of God's wisdom, Dr. King's dream came true for me in the redemptive work of the Holy Spirit.

I, too, have a dream.

Margaret Jensen

THE LESSON OF THE HIGH BUTTON SHOES

When most people reach their late sixties they contemplate retirement. When Margaret Jensen reached her late sixties, she was just getting started in a personal ministry that has endeared her to hundreds of thousands of readers.

It began in 1983 with the release of First We Have Coffee, *Margaret's collection of warm-hearted personal stories centered around her godly Norwegian mother. The book generated so much interest that a major book club offered it as a main selection—and the rest, as they say, is history.* First We Have Coffee *became a national best-seller.*

In the years since, appreciative audiences across the United States and Canada have dubbed Margaret Jensen "America's favorite Christian storyteller." Margaret keeps a travel and speaking calendar that would exhaust a healthy twenty-one-year-old, and by popular demand she has authored several additional books.

The following story of high button shoes tells how Margaret learned a lesson that has had an impact on her life since childhood. Today, it is one of the most requested stories in her repertoire.

I had just exchanged a gift certificate for a pair of expensive shoes from an exclusive shoe store. I proudly clutched the gold-braided handle of the fancy box that held the navy blue pumps. Never had I owned such beautiful shoes—a perfect match for my navy blue suit! With hurried steps I headed toward the parking lot to turn my car homeward.

When I rounded the corner I found myself in front of a small shoe repair shop. I stopped! My gold-braided box fell limply to my side. In the window stood a pair of old-fashioned high button shoes. Hot tears clouded my vision. In a moment I was a ten-year-old child again, back in my home in Canada…

I needed shoes! I *always* needed shoes! Papa traveled throughout the province of Saskatchewan to minister to the needs of the Scandinavian immigrants, so our bank account was Philippians 4:19: "My God shall supply all your needs." He did—but not always my way!

The arrival of the "missionary barrel" was an annual event in our home. Every outdated relic from the past seemed to find its way into that barrel: moth-eaten coats, hats with plumes and feathers, corsets with the stays, threadbare silks and satins, shoes of all sizes and shapes.

Mama used the hand-me-downs from the missionary barrel to make clothes for her children. She wasted nothing. Buttons, silks, and furs were transformed into beautiful dresses and coats. The scraps were put together for pallets for the floor, or sewn into quilts. We never lacked quilts!

"Margaret," Papa called, "we have shoes!"

I started to run away. I had lived through enough missionary barrel debuts to know I probably wouldn't like the shoes Papa had found.

"I'm sure they won't fit," I replied as I kept running.

"Margaret!"

I stopped. I went to Papa and stared in horror when he held up the monstrosities: two pairs of high button shoes, a black pair and a brown pair. Oxfords were "in"; button shoes were "out"!

"Try them on." Papa left no room for discussion.

I complained that they were too big.

"*Ja*, that is good. We'll put cotton in the toes. They'll last a long time." No one argued with Papa.

Mama sensed my distress and tenderly said, "Margaret, we prayed for shoes, and now we have shoes. Wear your shoes with a thankful and humble heart. It is not so important what you have on the feet, but it is very important where the feet go. This could be one of life's valuable lessons." (No ten-year-old is interested in "valuable lessons.")

"OH GOD, KEEP YOUR MOUNTAINS, BUT MOVE MY SHOES. THANK YOU."

I knew better than to argue with God and Mama on this point, but I had a plan. Papa's sermons on faith told of Moses and the crossing of the Red Sea, and Daniel in the den of lions. "If you have faith, you can move mountains,"

Papa's voice echoed in my mind. I knew what to do.

I carefully placed the shoes (buttonhook included!) beside my bedroom door and prayed, "Oh God, keep Your mountains, but move my shoes. Thank You."

The next morning I fully expected the shoes to be gone. Was I in for a surprise. They were still there. Something went wrong! I had a strange suspicion that it might be related to Mama's "valuable lessons."

"Hurry, Margaret," Mama called. "It's time for Sunday school."

I buckled up my galoshes over those awful high button shoes and reluctantly trekked off in the snow to Sunday school. *If I can keep my galoshes on, no one will see my horrible shoes,* I thought to myself. *Tomorrow I'll think of something else.*

Upon arriving at church, I carefully wiped off my galoshes and started into class. A booming voice called out, "Margaret, no one goes into Sunday school class with galoshes on. You're dripping."

Slowly I unbuckled my galoshes, and there I stood, for all the world to see, in my embarrassing old high button shoes. My face grew hot as I felt my classmates' silent pity.

Then my friend Dorothy came in, and she was also carefully wiping off her galoshes. The same voice of authority boomed out, "Dorothy, take off your galoshes. You're dripping."

Slowly, Dorothy removed her galoshes…and stood before us in a pair of hand-knit socks. She had no shoes. There we were, two ten-year-old girls, learning life's "valuable lesson."

"Good morning, young ladies," came the crisp English accent of our beloved Sunday school teacher. Mr. Avery, a frail, elderly, blue-eyed gentleman with white hair and a goatee, quietly assessed the situation.

Each Sunday, as we formed a large circle in our class, Mr. Avery chose two children to sit beside him. It was almost like sitting next to God. This morning Mr. Avery announced, "Dorothy, you sit here on one side of me and Margaret, you sit here on the other."

The shoes and socks were forgotten. He had picked us! Mr. Avery had picked us! My old shoes and Dorothy's socks didn't matter to Mr. Avery. He had picked us anyway! I remember very little of what he said that morning—but I'll never forget what he did.

When it was time to leave, Dorothy and I pulled on our galoshes and walked out into the snow. Our heads were held high—Mr. Avery had picked us!

Mama was right. It is not so important what is on our feet, but where our feet go.

Alice McIntire

A WILLINGNESS TO BE USED

Alice McIntire loved entertaining as a monologist, but her life's passion was teaching the Bible. Throughout her life she taught different groups from youth and college age to the socialites of the San Diego area.

She and her husband, Eugene, a druggist, were active in San Diego area churches, including La Jolla Presbyterian Church and San Diego Presbyterian Church. They also helped to found a church in Rancho Santa Fe, an exclusive area of San Diego.

Although Alice went to be with the Lord in November 1998 at the age of 94, her impact on my life continues.

I met Alice when Bill and I traveled from Hollywood to La Jolla, California, with a group of students for ministry work. Although Alice is probably twenty years older than I, it was one of those relationships where we were mutually crazy about one another from the moment we met. She took great interest in me as a young bride in ministry. She encouraged me and prayed for me consistently. We talked on the phone regularly and became wonderful friends. She loved God in front of me, and we talked about Christ often. As I watched her walk with God, I thought, *I can do that.* Alice had a remarkable impact on my life because she believed in me, and believed in what God could do in and through me.

The following story reveals that, no matter what our circumstances, God uses us if we are willing.

Pink-clad angels frolicking on bookshelves and countertops matched the carpet, couches, and drapes of my Southern California home. The chatter of thirty to forty women and the clink of their tea cups quieted as I opened my Bible class in prayer.

Since childhood, I had dreamed of being, not a Bible teacher, but a monologist. Let me explain.

Being a monologist was exciting and challenging. You portrayed the actors in a story, not by describing them, but by taking their parts as they spoke to one another. Being a monologist was demanding. You assumed many different characters—parents, grandparents, children, aunts, uncles, and a whole list of eccentric people as they talked together and unfolded the plot. You conversed person-to-person by turning your head slightly to the left and to the right. As a monologist you were on stage without a single note or cue card to remind yourself of the next line.

Growing up in Los Angeles, I used to go to the theater to hear Ruth Draper and Helen Hayes, the chief monologists of their day. Their material ranged from serious drama to humor, all done from memory. The audience never missed having live actors on stage. The monologist's portrayal of the characters was so convincing that everyone sat in rapt attention throughout the program.

How could I get started in this exacting art? I found a book on monologues but the material was so outdated that it could be used for neither drama nor humor. The next best thing was to tackle writing it myself. This wasn't as hard as it sounded since I took excerpts from real life as I encountered them. In the beginning I practiced on school groups. They were usually friendly and most responsive.

The memory work, though extensive, was the least of my problems. The clear depiction of different conversations through voice changes was the most demanding aspect. As I continued to improve, I was rewarded with generous audience approval.

My agent, Gertrude Purple Gorham, arranged for all the Southern California Women's Clubs to meet together at the Ebell Theater in Los Angeles to hear a sample repertoire of several of her artist clients. As a result, I was booked for appearances by a number of clubs and had to have at least an hour's worth of memorized programs ready to go.

Soon I was also having wonderful opportunities before civic and church groups. One night, after a performance in Hollywood, I was offered a screen test at Fox Studios. I told them I appreciated the offer, but turned it down as I was content with what I was doing.

As it turned out, my life was about to change in other directions. My husband, Gene, was transferred to La Jolla, just north of San Diego. In order to continue my work in Los Angeles, I asked my agent to book my performances there three days in a row. I would stay over and then return home to San Diego, where requests were also coming in. Soon after that our son Mike came along. My new responsibilities curtailed my out-of-town trips and I took on more local appearances.

For special occasions such as Christmas and Easter, I turned to the Bible for inspirational material and discovered my audiences welcomed it. I began to see the need in people for spiritual help, so I introduced little bits of Scripture at first, then added more and more. I found that the drama plots from the Bible proved to be exciting material for the women's groups I addressed.

Finally I wove together many favorite passages from the Pauline epistles and memorized them. When I presented these as a personal letter to each listener from the apostle Paul, I was overwhelmed with the emotional response. Soon other groups were asking for a repeat performance. To my amazement, some 400 women gathered together to put on a surprise luncheon for me at which time they "demanded" that I make a recording of "A Letter from Paul." The explosive reaction to this record was like starving people grasping for food. Christian Education specialist Dr. Henrietta C. Mears said, "This is a record that can be heard over and over again with increasing interest because the Word of God lives. I wish that this record could make its way around the world, and that it might be in every home."

After learning about Dr. Mears' Bible classes in Los Angeles, I realized people were just as eager for something like that where I lived. So I held a tea in my home and asked the women three questions:

- Would they be willing to open their homes for a Bible class?

- Would they be willing to teach a Bible class?
- Would they be willing to attend a Bible class?

Some answered "Yes" to all three questions, and everyone wanted to be in a class. As a result, Bible classes sprang up around San Diego County where the women learned to memorize Scripture and to honor God in their lives.

I had accepted Christ as my Savior when I was eight years old and, over the years, taught the church Sunday school curriculum to various age groups. But it is one thing to teach in that setting and another thing to launch out with your own material in a Bible class of women from various backgrounds. It was a new adventure which prompted me to study the Bible as never before. Whereas many people go to seminary to learn how to teach the Bible, I had to study on my own night and day to keep ahead of my students. As women's lives were changed through the Living Word, God showed me this was all the applause I needed. My monologue programs faded in importance as I gradually gave them up. Movies and television have replaced this ancient art in today's society, but nothing can replace the Word of God.

The Bible classes kept in close touch with one another so when a special event was planned we could spread the message quickly. In 1964, two weeks before Billy Graham was scheduled to be in San Diego, we decided to organize a luncheon as part of the preparation for the crusade. We were told it couldn't be done in such a short time. The announcement went out to our network of classes, and the largest crowd they had ever accommodated came to the Crown Room of the Hotel Del Coronado to hear Eleanor Searle Whitney, New York philanthropist, speak of God's grace in her life.

One Christmas we put on a party at the old El Cortez Hotel. The police had to be called to handle the traffic jam as over a thousand women came from the Bible classes. We continued these holiday luncheons with well-known speakers like Dr. Lane Adams and Dr. John McArthur for several years. We found this was an excellent time to invite new friends to the classes. Those get-togethers with dynamic speakers were so successful that at least one church in San Diego began a similar program on a monthly basis that is still continuing.

After several years of public life with exciting results, my activities were suddenly curtailed due to a severe accident. Bruised and battered, I found myself bedridden in my own home. This drastic change was very hard to accept. My room was turned into a hospital unit, with around-the-clock nurses brought in to care for me. I thought that, because of my physical limitations, my work for the Lord was over. However, I soon began sharing God's vast mercy and love again—this time with the nursing staff who cared for me day and night. These nurses became real friends to me. As they opened their hearts, I listened to their struggles. But I was not only a sympathetic listener. It was just natural for me to apply biblical principles to their problems. To my delight, some of these women trusted the Lord Jesus for salvation and began to grow spiritually.

One day my long-time friend Mary Stuard said to me, "Alice, you thought your work for the Lord was finished, but it's no such thing. You are still teaching the Bible, but in a different setting."

The truth of her statement flashed through my mind with a sudden burst of happiness. *I was still being used by the Lord.* God showed me that regardless of our circumstances, He still uses us if we are willing to be used. My advice is this: Be sure you don't give up too soon. Somewhere, sometime, there may be someone who is hurting, who needs your help and encouragement with biblical words. If necessary, use your bed as a pulpit and share the needed Scripture that will heal the wounded.

After thirty years I am still teaching. The Lord sent Betty Tafflinger, a Bible teacher, to assist me. Rather than using a lecture style, we developed a conversational method of teaching, with Betty and me discussing a selected passage of Scripture. Each week a group of women come to my home to memorize verses and learn how to pray in public. In the past I was speaking in schools, churches, and beautiful clubs for women. Now I am teaching in my home and enjoying every minute of it.

The greatest lesson I have ever learned was that you don't need to stand in front of large audiences to be used. God can use you in whatever circumstances He has placed you —even if you have to use your bed as a pulpit.

Yes, the applause of the world is sweet, but brief. The promises of God are *joyous* and *everlasting!*

Editor's note: Although Alice died after this story was written, she was used by God until He took her home.

Eleanor Page

GOD ANSWERS IN-WAYS BEYOND OUR IMAGINATION

Tangy, buoyant, and feminine, Eleanor Page emanates a zest for life wherever she speaks. The primary aim of her life involves helping to meet the needs of women who "have it all" and still find something lacking in their lives.

Eleanor has shared God's love around the world. She's delightful at luncheons, motivating at seminars, encouraging at retreats—everyone is refreshed with a visit from Eleanor Page.

In 1972 she arrived in Washington, D.C., as a staff member of Campus Crusade for Christ to work at the Christian Embassy. She began to teach, train, and challenge congressional and senatorial wives and secretaries to be God's maximum women. She taught Bible classes in the White House and to members of the State Department during the

Nixon, Ford, and Reagan administrations.

She turned down a promising singing career to marry George Penzold Page of Norfolk, Virginia. After their marriage, much of Eleanor's life revolved around politics and the military. During World War II, her husband fought on the Normandy beachhead. Tragedy struck years later when George died of cancer.

Eleanor's tenacious spirit held on, however. After asking the question, "I must have a purpose. What could it be?" she discovered how to have an overflowing life with more spice and added dimension than she ever dreamed possible.

She is a beautiful woman whose energy exceeds that of most women even half her eighty years. She has been described as having the strength of Golda Meir, the grace of Amy Vanderbilt, and the courage of the biblical Queen Esther. I deeply appreciate her friendship and ministry.

In reading her story, you will find her radiance exciting and her faith refreshing as she tells about the beginnings of her fruitful ministry and how God miraculously answered her prayers.

During my years of Christian service, I have learned to rely on a simple formula for receiving answers to prayer: pray, believe, and go to God's Word for direction. By following this pattern, I have discovered how God can use our willingness to serve Him in ways beyond our imagination.

One of my most meaningful times in ministry has been among government and military leaders in Washington, D.C. Let me share how this opportunity came about in answer to prayer.

As the widow of a military man and trained in discipleship and evangelism by Campus Crusade for Christ, I was a natural candidate for ministry in the center of our nation's political and military life.

To say that I was frightened when I learned of the opportunity would put it mildly. I knew no one in Washington, had no place to stay, and didn't know how to get started. But I wanted to win souls for Christ and so accepted the challenge.

I have never thought small; by nature I always strive for the best. Not knowing what my mission field would entail, I asked God for the White House and everything else under its wing. I was willing and daring enough to believe that a miracle-working God could use me to minister among government wives and secretaries and congressional and military officials from the White House to the Pentagon.

In accepting this challenge I was faced with some immediate needs, one of which was God's direction in what I would do when I arrived in Washington.

I began to apply my formula for seeking His answer.

I read God's Word systematically, always picking up today where I left off yesterday. I keep a notebook and sometimes write down my impressions. Later, I go back to see how these ideas fit into my circumstances as I live day by day.

In seeking God's leading about my Washington ministry, I found myself in the second chapter of Paul's epistle to Titus:

> As for you, speak up for the right living that goes along with true Christianity. Teach the older women to

be quiet and respectful in everything they do…These older women must train the younger women to live quietly, to love their husbands and their children, and to be sensible and clean minded, spending their time in their own homes, being kind and obedient to their husbands, so that the Christian faith can't be spoken against by those who know them (Titus 2:1,3–5).

I began to see God's direction. I was a woman, a widow. I wasn't a spring chicken, and with my experiences of the past, I was primed for this mission. It was my calling to reach women wherever I could find them—in this case, Washington, D.C.—and share God's love and forgiveness, teaching them to be disciples for Christ.

I knew my calling. Now the next need: How do I find my mission fields?

The Bible tells us to let our requests be known to God. In bringing answers, He often uses people. I was asked to speak at a women's luncheon one day, and after I finished my talk an elderly woman came up to me. During our conversation, I told her I was leaving the area for Washington, D.C.

"Oh, I have a daughter in the Washington area who would love to hear you teach!" she exclaimed excitedly, then asked, "Do you have a place to stay?"

"No," I replied. "I'm going there tomorrow to find a real estate agent. I'm hoping he'll find me a place in 'Old Town' Alexandria."

She beamed. "My daughter lives in Alexandria."

"Is she a real estate agent?" I asked.

"No. She's a senator's wife. Virginia Spong."

Oh, my! My contact! I thought.

Not long after I arrived in Washington, God provided me with a comfortable apartment. After I settled in, Virginia invited me to her prayer group which met weekly in her home.

Word spreads fast in Washington, and by the time I had my telephone installed, I received a call from a general's widow inviting me to church.

"I understand you can teach the Bible," she said. "Will you come to my home and teach some of the military wives?"

I was amazed at how fast my ministry was falling into place. But I felt impatient to have all my requests for ministry fulfilled. "What about the White House?" I asked the Lord.

The way He arranged this for me was exciting. I had met a congressman at a seminar in Florida before moving to Washington. He had invited me to call his wife when I arrived in Washington to let them know where I was living. By the time I got in touch with her, she had heard that I was teaching a group of Senate wives.

"If I invited a group of congressional wives to my home for a Bible study, would you come and teach them?" she asked.

Would I!

I began the studies by teaching them God's plan for a wife as recorded in Titus 2. They seemed fascinated that God had a plan for women that they could follow.

These Bible studies began to generate much interest among the wives of our political and military leaders. One day several women who worked at the White House visited my new friend, the congressman's wife, and asked about our meetings.

"Do you suppose Eleanor Page would consider teaching

at the White House?" one inquired.

The call from the White House came to me a few days later, and my joy knew no bounds. God had answered every one of my prayers. Before the month was out, invitations to speak to the women in the Departments of Commerce, Transportation, and Health and Welfare filled my schedule.

One day after speaking to women at the Pentagon, a woman invited me to teach military wives in her and her husband's quarters at Fort Myer. She gathered a group of women, prepared tea, and introduced me as a military widow. She told them that I would teach them "God's Blueprint for Women." That study continued until she and her husband were transferred to another base. Then the commanding general's wife of Fort Myer invited the group to their quarters. Soon the women in this study began to reach others in their own spheres of influence.

Then the wife of the Chairman of the Joint Chiefs of Staff approached me to teach a group of wives of the admirals and generals in their quarters. These Bible studies lasted until he retired.

Can we pray and receive answers? You bet!

Through these experiences, I've learned how God operates. He says, "If you abide in Me, and My words abide in you, ask whatever you wish, and it shall be done for you" (John 15:7).

Do I believe it? With all my heart.

Dede Robertson

NO ROOM
FOR SELF-PITY

The wife of "Pat" Robertson, founder and chief executive officer of the Christian Broadcasting Network, Dede Robertson was appointed in 1982 by Secretary of State George Schultz as the principal U.S. delegate to the Inter-American Commission of Women. She represented the U.S. at all official IACW meetings and traveled in that capacity to Central and South America.

With a master's degree from Yale University School of Nursing, she is on the board of trustees of Regent University and serves as a board member and vice president of the Tidewater Area Birthright Organization. She also has been secretary and member of the board of directors for CBN since its founding in 1960.

She has traveled extensively in Asia, the Middle East, and Central and South America. Selected Christian Woman of the Year for 1986, she is an author, gifted interior design-

er, and antique expert.

Despite the many credits and successes in her life, Dede has struggled with bouts of self-pity. In her story she shares how she was restored to a life of peace and joy and gives insights to help us achieve better self-esteem.

Once upon a time there was a young girl who was her "daddy's little girl." She dreamed of a great knight on a white charger who would sweep her off her feet and marry her in a grandiose fashion. Then they would live happily ever after.

This little girl met her great knight. He swept her off her feet and, not under the best of circumstances, they eloped. Did they live happily ever after? Not for awhile.

Their lives were stormy. Time was always a problem. Not enough togetherness to satisfy her dreams. Then he found Jesus Christ as his Savior and decided to live on "faith." She didn't understand. She didn't believe that you could know Jesus. She became harsh and critical. She was anything but understanding. How the fur did fly on occasion!

Then she, too, discovered the wonder of knowing Jesus. She and her "knight" began to pray together, read the Word together, listen to the Lord together. They struggled and began a ministry together. They shared the hard times, but the good times in their lives made those hard times dim by comparison.

They had three children and a fourth one was expected. She had to curtail some of her activities outside the home,

and he began working twenty-hour days. She could do nothing right—at least it appeared that way to her. Self-pity set in. Her dream world was becoming a nightmare.

Once self-pity took over, everything seemed to center around it, feeding it, making it bigger. Reality became unreality. Everything was seen and interpreted according to self-pity. Pity parties became a must.

The reality: The great knight was extremely shorthanded on staff. He was doing eight-hour shifts in two places, plus the day-to-day business of running a ministry. Funding was short, so in addition to balancing the books he had to appease the creditors.

Meanwhile, his wife was in the hospital to have a baby, and two of the three children were sick with measles, one dangerously ill. He was trying to keep house, cook three meals a day, take care of the sick children—all this on top of the demands of his ministry. No baby-sitter could be found except for a few hours a day.

The way she viewed it: He was gone all the time. He even had to pick up the mail and read it on the way to the hospital. (She asked the Lord to let her have the baby in the car to punish him!) She had several leisurely hours to wait in the hospital before the baby was born. Where were the flowers and praise? Where were those tender moments to share as you gaze at the precious life God entrusted to you both?

Postpartum depression set in with a bang. When all the children were well, the mother and mother-in-law visits were over, and she was physically recovered, it was still there—the awful loneliness, aching, self-pity, depression!

That little girl was me, Dede Robertson; the great knight was Pat Robertson. And I wasn't a little girl anymore! I was in my middle thirties. I had duties and responsibilities, yet I couldn't seem to get anything done but the bare essentials. I felt rejected, worthless, unhappy. I couldn't enjoy my friends. I couldn't play with my children, and I was so consumed with myself that I was unaware of how my attitude was affecting them. I couldn't read or study the Bible. I found it hard to pray except for "Please, Lord, get me out of this mess."

I couldn't share this with my husband; he seemed too busy. I couldn't share it with a friend; I had none that close. When the invitation to visit my parents over the Fourth of July came, I grabbed it. I just wanted to get away, even if it meant packing up all the children, spending a night on the train, and putting them in an environment different from that to which they were accustomed.

As we left, my husband told me of a church I might enjoy. I'm not one to go up to strangers and introduce myself, but suddenly going to this church became the most important thing for me to do.

It was a lovely church; the service was Bible centered. I met the pastor and his wife at the door and introduced myself. They remembered Pat and asked where I was staying. It turned out that they lived just two blocks away from my parents. In fact, they lived in the same house in which one of my high school friends had lived in.

Perhaps sensing my need, they graciously opened their home to me for visits, prayer, Bible study, and fellowship. I was over there at every possible opportunity. I sensed the same great love, peace, and joy in their home that I had known as a new Christian—that I had lost when I let self-pity take over my life.

Slowly, with their love and counsel, that peace, love, and

joy became a part of me once more. I can remember one prayer meeting where I just put my head back and began drinking in the Holy Spirit who was all around me. The Word of God came alive again, and oh! how I hungered for more of it.

Along with drinking in that love, peace, and joy, I became aware of how much God loved me. I knew He was responsible for all of this. I realized that He really cared about me. He was meeting my needs. He did not want me to be discouraged or depressed. He did not want me to feel unworthy or worthless. He loved me. If I was loved by the King of kings and Lord of lords, I had to be worth something. I was His and He was mine. That, I concluded, made me special in His sight. If I was good enough for Him, I was good enough for anyone. Not because of who I am, but because of who He is.

> IF I WAS LOVED BY-THE KING OF KINGS, I HAD TO-BE WORTH SOMETHING.

I began to see that my children, not my duties, were my joy and hope. Shortly afterward the flowers came—a dozen red roses—followed by my great knight

in his white station wagon. We all piled in and returned to our home in Portsmouth, Virginia, with eager anticipation of whatever the Lord would do next in our lives.

He has never let me down. He has never disappointed me. He knows my needs before I do. He even gives me the desires of my heart.

There's no room now in my life for self-pity. It distorts reality and can lead to endless trouble and doubts. Neither do I have room for dreams and fantasies, which can turn to nightmares. I have room only for Jesus. He fills my life completely. My will is His will. He is my happiness, my everything.

I was the product of the popular notion, "Get married and live happily ever after." When this didn't happen, I didn't know where to turn. But through this experience, the Holy Spirit showed me that I could always turn to Jesus. I can always count on Him. He will supply all my needs by His riches in glory—even my heart's desires. In doing so, God sometimes works through my husband, but often He chooses other ways. No matter what my need, He never fails. He's always there to forgive, to heal, to love—just as His Word promises: "My God shall supply all your need according to His riches in glory by Christ Jesus" (Philippians 4:19).

Dale Evans Rogers

LEARNING HUMILITY: PAINFUL BUT PRECIOUS

The wife of the late Roy Rogers, Dale Evans is one of America's most beloved personalities.

Actress, author, humanitarian, mother of nine, grand-mother, and great-grandmother, she has been the recipient of many awards and honors. With Roy she is the holder of nine all-time box office records, and today she hosts her own tele-vision show on the Trinity Broadcasting Network.

She and Roy endeared themselves to my husband and me in many ways. Throughout their careers, Roy and Dale have represented honesty, decency, and faith in God and coun-try. Experiencing the tragic loss of three children with all of their varied experiences gave them a message that the world desired to hear, and wherever they appeared, America's heart was with them.

Dale's Christian testimony is known around the world. One of the most dynamic statements I have ever heard was when Dale was speaking to a congressional wives' breakfast in Washington, D.C. She began her remarks with, "Ladies, God is real; I know, I have experienced Him." This was just a few weeks after the tragic loss of a second daughter, Debbie, in a church bus accident. Everyone knew her faith was real as she shared her victory through heartbreak.

At a luncheon where Dale was to speak later that day, there was "standing room only" as so many wanted to hear more and called friends to come. This same faith sustained Dale after the death of her beloved Roy in 1998. God has given her a ministry by first giving her a message—painful to learn, but precious to know and real to share. Here she shares a lesson on humility learned through the life and loss of her precious daughter Robin.

For forty-two years, God has been teaching me to be humble—to realize that of myself, my own ego, I am absolutely nowhere.

As you can imagine, this has been a difficult process for one who has been an extrovert since she was a small girl.

Often throughout my childhood I heard comments that helped to give me self-confidence: "Frances [my given name] is pretty; Frances is smart; Frances is talented; Frances will make her mark in the world." Consequently, the idea formed in my mind that I must live up to what was expected of me.

When I was eleven, I suffered a nervous breakdown and

spent the entire summer vacation in bed. I had skipped three grades in school and, thinking I was grown, had little to do with children my own age. I had a compulsion to be in everything, had to excel. You would think that that illness would have taught me a lesson, but I dreamed of being an actress, a ballerina, a singer, a writer—you name it.

At the age of ten, I accepted Jesus Christ as my Savior, but not as Lord of my life. Nothing ever quite satisfied me. Psalm 37:4 says, "Delight thyself also in the Lord; and he shall give thee the desires of thine heart." I knew nothing about delighting myself in Him. My own desires were paramount; never mind what the Lord wanted for me.

Not surprisingly, there was no peace in my heart. Somehow I felt everything depended upon me. Today I realize that everything—and I mean *everything*—depends on God.

At age thirty-seven, something happened that I could not control. God sent an "angel unaware" into my life in the person of Robin Elizabeth Rogers, the only child born to Roy and me. She was a pretty little blue-eyed blond Down's syndrome baby with a defective heart.

We had absolutely no place to go for help, except to God. I was devastated and heartbroken, for I had desperately wanted a little girl. I took refuge in God's Word, "Come unto me, all ye that labor and are heavy laden, and I will give you rest. Take my yoke upon you, and learn of me; for I am meek and lowly in heart: and ye shall find rest unto your souls. For my yoke is easy, and my burden is light" (Matthew 11:28–30).

Here I was, with a grown son, my Tom, three stepchildren, and a husband who was Number 1 in western box office with a huge following. It is quite clear that God was teaching me a valuable lesson.

I had asked Him at age thirty-five, shortly after my marriage to Roy, to take over my life completely, in every area. I wanted Him to use my life for His glory, not mine. In my heart, I believe our little Robin was the rod of correction He used to stop me dead in my tracks, to force me to take a hard look at where I had been and where I was going.

There is no scythe quite so sharp for scaling down pride like bringing a mentally and physically defective child into the world. It gets right to the root of the tree of pride.

As I went to Him in complete submission and humility, He began bestowing wonderful blessings in the midst of my anguish—peace in knowing that He would handle it, for I had given myself and my burden totally to Him. Deep within my heart, I knew that Jesus would chart and direct my path.

After Robin died, God enabled me to write *Angel Unaware*. People have asked me, "What has been the highest point of your life?" Without hesitation I reply, "The day Fleming H. Revell Company sent me a contract for publishing *Angel Unaware*, not for my glory, but for the glory of God."

To learn humility is painful, but precious. I have learned to humble myself in joyful recognition of the awesome power of God.

At the time of Robin's birth, no one admitted to having a Down's syndrome (mongoloid) child. Those little children were hidden from public view. The media mostly knew of our Robin's condition but in mercy and kindness never leaked it to the public. We lived then on a small ranch in Encino, California. We were highly publicized and to keep strangers out, we erected an electric gate. Even so, bus loads of curious sightseers would stop in front of our house, hoping to see us and our children.

When movie magazines sent reporters and photographers to our home, they kindly allowed us to edit any pictures taken of little Robin.

In vain we tried to find medical help for our baby, but we were told by a top pediatrician in the Mayo Clinic that it was useless to run here and there to specialists, for Down's syndrome could not be treated. We had the means to afford the best in the medical field, but nothing we could do would help. It was indeed a humbling situation.

HUMILITY AND DEPENDENCE ON GOD ARE NOT BESTOWED. THEY ARE LEARNED.

Had we not been committed Christians, this tragedy probably would have broken our marriage or our health. Gradually, the peace of the Lord took over and we knew that He would teach us what we needed to learn.

Humility and dependence on Him, you probably have discovered, are not bestowed. They are learned. The apostle Paul said, "I know both how to be abased, and I know how to abound: everywhere and in all things I am *instructed* both to be full and to be hungry, both to abound and to suffer need" (Philippians 4:12).

Someone asked me recently my definition of humility. I replied, "To be teachable." God is shaping us for eternity. He is knocking off our rough edges. I believe He wanted to make me teachable. When I "let go" of myself and asked Him to move into my life, I was on my way to learning obedience and humility.

I have had a hard schooling, but He has been faithful to

His promise to be with me in the process.

Some think humility is best pictured as a cowering, hand-wringing Uriah Heep. I believe humility is recognizing that "God so loved the world that He gave His only Son that whoever believes in Him will not perish but have everlasting life." Without Jesus, I do not believe there is any real abiding peace or joy in this life. Lucifer, the most beautiful of God's created heavenly beings, fell through pride. In his beauty, he wanted to be equal to or even greater than his Creator. One would think that he should have been grateful and happy to obey his Creator, thankful that God's plan for him was flawless.

How I wished I had understood this when I accepted Jesus as my Savior, but not my Lord.

My main regret in life is that I waited so long, made so many mistakes before "heeling to the Master."

Since my commitment to Christ in the spring of 1948, there have been tall, forbidding mountains to climb. But my Lord has been faithfully equipping me through prayers, study of His Word, and strength for the task. How He has tested me! I thank Him with all of my heart for teaching me the golden lesson of humility.

Joyce Rogers

SONLIGHT AT MIDNIGHT

Joyce Rogers has pioneered in the area of women's ministry. She has led in planning and has chaired nationwide women's conferences with thousands in attendance. She serves on the advisory board of Concerned Women for America as well as the Council of Biblical Womanhood, and has participated in the White House Meeting of Christian Women Leaders. She has also been elected president of the Southern Baptist Convention Ministers' Wives Conference for the year 2000. She is the author of The Wise Woman, The Secret of a Woman's Influence, *and* The Bible's Seven Secrets for Healthy Eating.

Her husband, three-time president of the Southern Baptist Convention, now pastors the historic Bellevue Baptist Church in Memphis, Tennessee, one of the world's largest churches. Joyce is first of all a homemaker—this is her greatest joy—yet she also enjoys a life as a leader of women, an

author, speaker, singer, and world traveler.

She and her husband have led many trips to the Holy Land, and she sang the lead in the video production "From Israel With Love," which was filmed in Israel and hosted by Adrian.

Joyce is the mother of two sons and two daughters, and she has six grandchildren.

One of the greatest lessons I have learned from Joyce is not to ask God "Why?" but to ask Him "How?" As she shares her "greatest lesson," Joyce was obviously in the midst of one of the most difficult trials of her life. She doesn't have to share specific details to be helpful in relating tried-and-true principles that are meeting her present need—principles that will also help you meet your need.

God has enrolled me in an advanced course in His school of Christian living. The name of this difficult subject is "Waiting on God in Times of Darkness."

I showed up for the beginning class, "Times of Darkness 101," thirty-two years ago when our precious baby, Philip, was snatched into the arms of Jesus by sudden crib death. It was a lovely Mother's Day afternoon, and I was going to take a nap. Before lying down, I decided to check on the baby in the crib.

Philip looked blue. Frightened, I called for my husband. "Adrian! Come quick!"

Horror stricken, I asked, "Is he dead?"

Adrian quickly picked him up and said, "You stay here."

Our two other children, ages four and two years, were taking their naps. Adrian placed Philip's little body inside his coat and drove as fast as he could to the hospital. While he was gone, I quoted aloud those familiar words from the 23rd Psalm that I had learned as a child.

> The Lord is my shepherd, I shall not want…Yea, though I walk through the valley of the shadow of death, I will fear no evil: for thou art with me. Thy rod and thy staff they comfort me…

It seemed like an eternity before Adrian returned. I knew from the look on his face as he came up the sidewalk that Philip was gone. We had never lost a loved one. It felt dark, oh so dark, as we embraced each other. We had comforted others. We desperately needed comfort now.

Adrian and I made a few calls to family and friends. Soon they began to arrive, offering their love and sympathy.

Philip's funeral was held in our hometown sixty miles away. As we were leaving our house, the windows of our church next door were open, and we could hear the people singing, "No, never alone; no, never alone. He promised never to leave me. Never to leave me alone."

Although the darkness was never deeper, God's presence was never so real. What had until now been an easily sung song became a promise and a reality that I clung to with all my might: *"He promised never to leave me. Never to leave me alone."*

Even so, torrents of grief would repeatedly engulf me. Sometimes I literally held my hands up to God and said, "Lord, here, take my broken heart—it's too much for me to bear."

In time, I began learning to lean on the Lord. Someone

I didn't know sent me the following poem. In the ensuing years I have given many copies away. I memorized the words in those days. I treasure the message still.

Lean Hard

Child of My love, lean hard,
And let Me feel the pressure of thy care;
I know thy burden, child, I shaped it;
Poised it in Mine own hand, made no proportion
In its weight to thine unaided strength;

For even as I laid it on, I said,
I shall be near, and while he leans on Me,
This burden shall be Mine, not his;
So shall I keep My child within the circling arms
    of My own love.

Here lay it down, nor fear
To impose it on a shoulder which upholds
The government of worlds. Yet closer come;
Thou art not near enough; I would embrace thy care
So I might feel My child reposing on My breast.

Thou lovest Me? I knew it. Doubt not then
But loving Me, lean hard.

When we found Philip, there was no time to pray—no time to plead with God. He was gone.

The waiting on God came afterwards. This involved learning to lean hard on Him.

The waiting and leaning involved giving up my right to understand why. Through the strength of God's Holy Spirit and with the help of a Spirit-filled song by Ira Stanphill entitled "We'll Talk It Over," I handed my "right to understand why" over to God and was content to "wait for reasons 'til afterwhile."

The greatest lesson I learned in this "course" was praising the Lord at *all* times—even when it was dark. Not that this dark time was good—but I praised the God who was able to take even the bad things and work them together for good.

I discovered Psalm 63:3, which became my life's verse: "Because Your lovingkindness is better than life, my lips shall praise You." Then I was blessed by Psalm 34:1, "I will bless the Lord at all times; His praise shall continually be in my mouth." The Lord brought to mind Job 1:21, "The Lord gave, and the Lord has taken away; blessed be the name of the Lord."

I didn't feel like praising God, and I didn't want to fake my praise to God. That would produce no more than a sick grin. God showed me that He wanted me to *faith* my praise to Him. How I thank Him that it works. He also taught me just to *glance* at my circumstances but gaze upon Jesus. During this period of learning and waiting, He became my focus. I came to know Him in a way I never had before. In the words of Roy Hession, I learned that "it is enough to see Jesus and to go on seeing Him."

Then in a very practical lesson, God taught me to do what lay at hand—fold the diaper, sweep the floor, visit the sick, cook the meals, sing a song, study God's Word. Day by day He took me by the hand and led me out of darkness into His marvelous light.

But I told you that God had enrolled me in an *advanced* course in His school of Christian living—"Waiting on God in Times of Darkness." At this writing, I'm in a very difficult class, "Times of Darkness 401." In fact, it's the most difficult class in Christian living that I've ever experienced.

I don't want to fail. I need all the help I can get.

Because the situation is still being worked out, I do not have freedom to give the details. I would not want to cause any further grief or embarrassment to those involved, for they are precious to my husband and me. But I can testify that the experience, humanly speaking, is like the blackness of midnight!

When my baby died, I knew that I could either cast myself completely on God or turn away from Him. At that time I found Him to be more than sufficient for my need. My present hour of darkness has been worse than death. I've asked a thousand "whys," trying to figure it all out. But I come exhausted to the end of many a day knowing that only God holds the answer to the question why.

I'm grateful for the lessons I learned in "Times of Darkness 101." They have helped me to endure the present struggle. I've cast myself on my God over and over again. I know what it is to "lean hard" on Him, but I still struggle with giving up my "right to understand." Somehow it was so much easier to do when Philip died.

Oh, I've praised Him; and when I do, He brings such peace! I cannot describe the peace He brings in the midst of the storm—the joy with which He floods my soul when my eyes are filled with tears.

I find great comfort, too, in this poem by Janice Rogers Brock:

Joy Through My Teardrops

Joy through my teardrops, and gains through my losses
Beauty for ashes, and crowns for my crosses;
He binds my wounds, and He dries all my tears
Calms every storm and He conquers my fears.

He gives me hinds' feet to walk on high places
He floods my soul with His heavenly graces;
When I am weak then His strength makes me strong
I know I can trust Him, He's never been wrong.

Trials may come and temptations assail me
Though I may falter, He never will fail me;
So Satan, I bind you in His holy name
For at the cross Jesus' blood overcame!

When the doubt comes, when I'm lonely,
When my heart is sad;
I'll lift up mine eyes to my Savior above
And Jesus will make me glad.

When in my heart there is sadness and sorrow
Jesus has promised a brighter tomorrow;
Victory is mine; yes, it's already won.
I've only to claim it by faith in God's Son.

All of my cares I will cast down before Him
Even in trials my heart will adore Him;
He bears my burdens; He comforts my soul;
Oh, why should I worry when He's in control?

Lord, in the time of deep grief and emotion
I will yet serve You with constant devotion;
You have not failed me one step of the way,
That is the reason I'll trust You and say:

I will praise You! I will praise You!
Jesus Christ my King;
For You fill my heart with a song in the night.
Yes, You make my heart to sing!

I feel so helpless—so powerless! If there were only something I could do in my present situation. But I have had to find contentment in waiting on God.

Why does God take longer than we want Him to? He wants us to look to Him, to get to know Him better, to desire the Giver more than the gift. He also desires for us patience, endurance. I've discovered how very impatient I am. I want an answer *now*.

Andrew Murray once said, "If anyone is inclined to lose hope, because he does not have such patience, be encouraged. It is in the process of our weak and very imperfect waiting that God Himself by His hidden power strengthens us and works out in us the patience of the saints, the patience of Christ Himself. And if you sometimes feel as if patience is not your gift, then remember, it is God's gift."[1]

> "IF YOU SOMETIMES FEEL AS IF PATIENCE IS NOT YOUR GIFT, THEN REMEMBER, IT IS GOD'S GIFT."

"In waiting on God it is important that we submit not because we are forced to, but because we lovingly and joyfully consent to be in the hands of our blessed Father. Patience then becomes our highest blessing and our highest grace. It honors God and gives Him time to have His way with us. It is the highest expression of our faith in His goodness and faithfulness. True patience is the losing of our self-will in His perfect will."[2]

In recent months my attention has been drawn to how many times we are called upon to wait. I've waited at the red light and the stop sign. I've waited at the doctor's office and in the hospital. There is even a room in some places called the "waiting room." I wait for my husband to come home for dinner, for my grown children to come for the holidays. I wait for the clerk in the department store. I wait in line at the bank. In fact, much of my life is spent waiting.

I've also learned that if I wait on others very long I get impatient. What will I do while I'm waiting? I've never even thought about it before now, but over the years I've developed a plan—things to keep me occupied and fill my waiting moments.

When I'm home there are a multitude of things to do—fold socks, write letters, make phone calls. The hardest time to wait is when I'm ready to go somewhere and I wonder if we'll be late.

One of the most effective things I've learned to do during those waiting times is to sit at my piano and play and sing praises to God. Sometimes I carry Scripture cards with me in the car. The seconds seem to fly as I memorize a phrase of God's Word while waiting at red lights. I almost always take my Bible to the doctor's office or to the beauty parlor.

Other times I'll take a book to read or some paper to write a letter. Recently I spent about twelve hours in the hospital, waiting for a grandbaby to be born. During that time I talked, read, wrote a letter, toured the gift shop several times, and prayed. I've written three books—much of them on airplanes, in hotel rooms, and under the dryer at the beauty parlor. This strategy helps me focus on God rather than my circumstances or difficulties.

Recently God revealed to me that the thing I did the least while I was waiting on others was *pray*. This was vividly brought to my attention when I found myself in one of the examining rooms at the doctor's office. I had forgotten to bring my Bible or a book. There was not even a magazine to read, or paper to write a letter. I thought to myself, *What a predicament, what a waste of precious time!*

Then came the inward rebuke: "You can always pray! You don't need pen or paper. You don't need a book or even the Bible to make contact with Me. Isolated from everyone, sitting on this examining table, you can have fellowship with Me—the source of all your needs. I am at the red light, under the dryer in the beauty parlor, in the waiting room at the hospital—yes, in the doctor's examining room. It doesn't have to be a waste of time as you are waiting on circumstances or waiting on others. If you could only recognize these times as opportunities to 'wait on Me,' it would revolutionize your life."

It is in times of waiting, whether planned or unplanned, that we come to recognize who He is—the One we are waiting for. He is a good God, filled with mercy and judgment. He has all power and wisdom. He is the source of our love and joy and peace. We must be still and wait to know His presence.

Andrew Murray said, "Seek not only the help or the gift, seek Him; wait for Him. Give God the glory by resting in Him, by trusting Him fully, by waiting patiently for Him. This patience honors Him greatly; it leaves Him as God on the throne to do His work; it yields self wholly into His hands. It lets God be God."[3]

I'm just beginning to remember this truth—waiting on others can remind us to wait on Him. Instead of becoming impatient, I find myself looking forward to those times. But I am so forgetful. I have a long way to go.

Surely one of the chief things God wants us to do while we wait on Him is to diligently search His Word. What delight I find in His truth. Psalm 18 is my favorite chapter in all of the Bible. I've gone back to it time and time again.

It is the story of how David waited on God in times of

darkness. He recounts those circumstances:

> The sorrows of death compassed me, and
>   The floods of ungodly men made me afraid.

> The sorrows of hell compassed me about:
>   The snares of death prevented me.

> The earth shook and trembled.

> The Lord also thundered in the heavens, and
>   The Highest gave his voice;
>   hail stones and coals of fire.

> The channels of waters were seen, and
>   The foundations of the world were
>   discovered at thy rebuke. (vv. 4,5,7,13,15)

The surroundings in David's life were extremely dark. There seemed to be no possible escape. But even before David tells of these dark days, he makes a declaration of love to God upon whom he was waiting and expecting deliverance:

> I will love thee, O Lord, my strength.

> The Lord is my rock, and my fortress, and my deliverer; my God, my strength, in whom I will trust; my buckler, and the horn of my salvation, and my high tower.

> I will call upon the Lord, who is worthy to be praised: so shall I be saved from mine enemies. (vv. 1–3)

David's love and trust never wavered. No matter what happened, he knew God's presence was with him. His faith was personal and intimate.

Then he recounted all the *distress* surrounding him. There were the threats of death, ungodly men, earthquake, and flood. It seemed as though not only men but God Himself opposed him. But in his distress he cried out to his God:

> In my distress I called upon the Lord, and cried unto my God: he heard my voice out of his temple, and my cry came before him, even into his ears. (v. 6)

David knew God heard. But deliverance didn't come. There was a *delay*. Then more distress. In fact, darkness set in. But in the midst of the darkness we see someone flying on a cherub on the wings of the wind (v. 10). Can it be? Yes. It is God Himself! He was there in the darkness. He was in control. In fact, "darkness was under His feet" (v. 9).

Then things got worse. God thundered in the heavens; He sent out His arrows; He shot out lightnings—the floods broke loose. All seemed lost and then—oh then, *deliverance* finally came.

> He sent from above,
> He took me,
> He drew me out of many waters.
>
> He delivered me…
> He brought me forth also into a large place;
> He delivered me, because he delighted in me.
> (vv. 16,17,19)

And then:

> The Lord rewarded me according to my righteousness; according to the cleanness of my hands hath he recompensed me. (v. 20)

The darkness lifted!

> For thou wilt light my candle: the Lord my God will enlighten my darkness. (v. 28)

It seemed as if a whole army had marched against David and he was up against a brick wall. He declared:

> For by thee I have run through a troop; and by my God have I leaped over a wall. (v. 29)

I believe I can hear David singing, "Hallelujah, Hallelujah!" Oh, I can't understand why God delayed His deliverance, but "His way is perfect" (v. 30). Oh, the praise and thanksgiving that followed!

> For who is God save the Lord? Or who is a rock save our God? It is God that girdeth me with strength, and maketh my way perfect. He maketh my feet like hinds' feet, and setteth me upon my high places. (v. 31–33)

And besides all that:

> Thou hast also given me the shield of thy salvation: and thy right hand hath holden me up, and thy gentleness hath made me great. (v. 35)

And more!

> Thou hast enlarged my steps under me, that my feet did not slip. (v. 36)

Deliverance hasn't come for me yet:

But my God
    I will love You

You are my strength
    My rock
    My fortress

You are my high tower.

Oh my God
    I run into You to hide.

Oh God, it is so dark
    I cannot see.

Please hold my hand
    and lead me through
    this darkness.

Take my hand.
    We can run through the troop
    and leap over this wall.

Hallelujah! Hallelujah!

There's nothing I can do, Lord. I wait on You. Thank You for *Sonlight at midnight!*

Edith Schaeffer

STAYING IN GOD'S FOGS WHILE TRUSTING HIM

Edith Schaeffer, with her late husband, Dr. Francis Schaeffer, co-founded the well-known Christian community in Switzerland, L'Abri Fellowship. The work of L'Abri began in the midst of their own young family in 1955 in the village of Huemoz, Switzerland. Today L'Abri has six branches around the world—one each in Switzerland, England, Holland, Sweden, and Korea, and two in the United States.

Born in China of missionary parents, who were serving with the China Inland Mission under Hudson Taylor, Edith is the author of numerous books on a variety of topics. A resident of Rochester, Minnesota, she has four children, and many grandchildren and great-grandchildren. She is active with L'Abri in Rochester, and is a speaker and counselor in the United States and abroad.

The account of Edith's lesson of trust cannot help but encourage faith that God can meet our every need and that He may choose to meet our need "just in the nick of time."

Perhaps you have discovered, as I have, that memory needs to be sharpened if we are going to learn valuable lessons in life.

As I walk through my memories, I realize that it was always during "impossible" moments—when the brick wall ahead of me was without a "door" in sight—that I learned my most important lessons.

I am in my eighties now, but still very sensitive to the fact that I am *far* from being a "finished product" and that I have much to learn—and that even the *same* lessons need to be learned over and over again.

No doubt you have discovered, as have I, that we do make progress in our learning. But there is never any room for smugness or pride!

Back in 1955 (you can read the whole story in the book *L'Abri*), my husband, Francis, and I were in one of our most "impossible" positions. We had two-year-old Franky, with polio, and thirteen-year-old Susan, with rheumatic fever. Floods and avalanches had filled our downstairs with mud, which had taken us a week to fight with shovels and sandbags. In addition, we were being evicted from our home.

Although we had lived in the Swiss village of Champery for more than five years, on February 14 we received two sheets of paper from the village gendarmery (police) notifying us that we had six weeks to get out because "You have

had a religious influence on the village of Champery."

In the midst of our prayer about what to do next, as a family with four children and no money, we were told that the only way to appeal the edict was to find another house, in another village, in another canton, and to make arrangements to live in it. The sheaf of papers to be filled out for the appeal had spaces to put the address of a house and the signature of someone who would declare that we indeed had made arrangements to buy or rent it. We were given only five days to make such an arrangement.

We had been looking in villages that we could reach by train, when a Czechoslovakian couple we knew stopped us in distress, and I was pressed into accompanying them to a hospital miles away because of an imminent, premature birth. Having given up the search, Fran had gone back to our own chalet to pack. We had planned to leave Switzerland if we could not find a house in another village.

I spent a sleepless night in the Lausanne hospital, then called my husband in the morning. "Oh, Fran, I'm going to go on looking. If I find a chalet today, will you come tomorrow to look at it with me and fill out the papers?"

"Yes, if you do…though I doubt that you will," he replied.

This fired me with determination to find something. I prayed, but with spiritual pride that *I* had not given up and *I* had faith enough to keep on.

That day I felt like a lost child gazing wistfully at other children safe in their homes and was close to tears as I tramped through the snow in Villars. Suddenly I saw a "for rent" sign on a weather-beaten, rustic chalet. I inquired into the whereabouts of the owner, and walked on, another mile and a half, to a school in Arveyes where the owner was headmistress. I planned to inspire her to compassion by a story so appealing that she could not resist renting the chalet to us at a very reasonable price. I was shown into her parlor.

This dignified lady quoted the rent, then went on to mention a grand piano, antiques, Persian rugs, and the many other features of the chalet. But the rental price blurred the rest out, and I burst into tears. The price for *one month* was what we had paid for a *year* in Chalet Bijou.

I dabbed my eyes with my handkerchief. "Oh, excuse me, I don't usually break down like this. But I had no sleep last night, assisting at the birth of a baby. Now I have to find a chalet within an hour, or we'll have to leave Switzerland."

She looked at me pityingly, and I read in her eyes, "This person is a little off her head; better ease her out of here." And before I knew it, I had been gently propelled to the front door, and I was outside!

Feeling I had made an utter fool of myself, I walked slowly down her path into deeper snow. I was filled with a sudden realization of how God saw me and began to pray, "Oh, heavenly Father, forgive me for insisting on my own will today. I really do want to want Your will. Please help me to be sincere in this. Forgive me for closing the door on the possibility of Your having a totally different plan for the next step of our lives. Oh God, I am willing to live in city slums, if it is Your will."

I felt a surge of trust in the God of Elijah, Daniel, and Joseph and continued, "But God, if You want us to stay in Switzerland, in these mountains, I know *You* are able to find a house, and lead me to it in the *next half hour*. Nothing is impossible to You."

I reached the main street of Villars just as a chattering, laughing crowd was returning from skiing and crowding into the tearooms. I kept my eyes on the snowy pavement, not wanting to see anyone, as my eyes were red with weeping.

Suddenly I heard my name. *"Madame Schaeffer, avez-vous trouve quelque chose?"*

I looked up to see Monsieur Gabuz, a real estate dealer to whom we had talked days before. He had not shown us even one chalet, because he said everything he had was "deluxe" and far above our price range. I was surprised that he remembered my name.

I answered, *"Non, Monsieur Gabuz…rien."*

"Hop in," he said. "I think I have something that might interest you. Would you mind living in Huemoz?"

"Huemoz, where's that?" I asked.

We drove on down the mountainside, fog blotting out the view, and weariness dampening my enthusiasm. The car stopped beside a postal bus stop sign and a mail box. Climbing out, we went up a pair of log steps buried in the snow, opened a gate, and crunched our way to the front of the chalet. It was tightly shuttered with full-length balconies. We walked into a musty dark room, and Monsieur Gabuz opened shutters while explaining that it had not been lived in for a long time. There I was, in a chalet within the half hour, not because I had had wisdom or cleverness to find it, but because God had answered my prayer. This I believed to be the *only* explanation.

I arranged to meet Monsieur Gabuz the next morning with Fran. Then I remembered something.

"Oh, Monsieur Gabuz, I forgot to ask…how much is the rent?"

"Oh, it's not for rent," he called out of the car, "it's for sale." Then he shot up the road.

"For sale," I repeated to myself dully. "For sale! We have no money, and even if we were millionaires, *who* would buy a house in a country without a permit to live there?"

This seemed the last straw to me. I was feeling sick with exhaustion from sleeplessness and the emotional struggle. As I rode down on the bus, and up on the train to Champery, I began to review the last days and hours. It seemed that the markers of answered prayer definitely indicated that God *had* been leading up to this point. Before I arrived at Chalet Bijou in Champery, I was convinced that God had given me a clear sign and that we must go back the next day.

When I arrived, Fran gave me the most recent news. "Berne has given us an extension. We may stay in Switzerland until the matter has been studied, but Sion will give *no* extension of time, and we have to be out of this chalet and this village and this canton by midnight March 31. Franky's doctor even telephoned to tell them that the children should not be moved at this time for health reasons. But Sion would give no extension unless we and the children would sign a paper saying that we would not talk about religious matters to people in or outside of our chalet!"

That night I prayed again. One can't put an hour of talking to God in a paragraph, but it is important to say that it *was* an hour, not a sentence. As I asked for God's guidance about the chalet, which had seemed such an exciting answer to prayer that afternoon and now seemed so impossible, I determined to ask the owner to change his mind and rent it. But suddenly I felt flooded with assurance that nothing is impossible to God. My prayer changed, startling me as I asked, "Oh, please show us Your will about this house tomorrow, and if we are to *buy* it, send us a sign that will be

410

clear enough to convince Fran as well as me; send us $1,000 before ten o'clock tomorrow morning."

The following morning, the postman—on skis—handed us three letters. We opened these on the train. One was from Paris, one from Belgium, and the third was from a man and his wife in Ohio. They had been following our work with interest and prayer for quite some time. However, they had never given financial help to our work, nor were they wealthy. Mrs. Salisbury wrote:

> I have a story that will interest you. Three months ago Art received an unexpected sum of money. His company had decided to pay insurance premiums for all their employees, retroactive for those who had worked there a number of years. Our thought was to invest in a little house, which we would rent. As we looked over a very likely house, I suddenly saw signs of termites in the beams. "Look, Art, doesn't that remind you of the verse in Matthew, 'Lay not up for yourselves treasures upon earth, where moth and rust corrupt, and where thieves break through and steal: but lay up for yourselves treasures in heaven, where neither moth nor rust corrupt, and where thieves do not break through nor steal'? Art, would you be willing to take this money and invest it literally in heaven? Would you be willing to give it to the Lord's work somewhere?" He replied, "Yes, Helen, I would."
>
> For months, we have been asking God to show us what He would have us do with this money. Tonight we have come to a definite decision; both of us feel certain that we are meant to send you this money…to buy a house somewhere that will always be open to young people.

The amount of money was exactly $1,000!

I poured out the story of my prayer and the fact that the house was for *sale*. As the train arrived at Ollon, Fran and I were convinced that God was leading us to *buy* Chalet les Melezes. The perfect timing of the arrival of the letter and of my certainty at the moment I had prayed for that money were amazing. Mrs. Salisbury's statement that the money was for buying a house "that will always be open to young people" was a prophecy of our future work that neither she nor we could have known at the time.

A short time later we stepped off the bus at the bus stop that was to become familiar to a variety of people in coming years. That morning it was deserted, with an empty house above it, and another enormous empty house at one side. We were soon looking through the chalet to see what God had chosen for us, with the feeling that we were not making a choice at all.

"Yes, we'll take it" was easy to say that morning with our excitement and assurance over the unmistakable sign from God. When the agent told us that we needed a $10,000 mortgage and would need $7,000 cash, we didn't bat an eyelash...not then. We were in a hurry to fill in the sheets of paper and send off our appeal.

We went immediately to Lausanne to see a lawyer, the police, and a notary. The Chief helped us to fill in the papers properly. We learned that we had found the chalet just in time; another day would have been too late!

Arrangements were made to make the promissory payment the following day, and binding papers were signed. We had paid 8,000 francs (about $2,000), which had come in surprisingly small amounts, and said we would pay another $5,000 by May 31 or forfeit all that had been paid, plus a lot more! This rigid and binding agreement was frightening to sign. The clarity of guidance was followed by impossibility. In other words, a brick wall with *no* door seemed to be where the choice led, but signposts behind us gave fresh assurance!

The greatest lesson I was learning then is one that I am *still* learning. We never become a finished product. Isaiah wrote:

> Who among you fears the Lord and obeys the word of his servant? Let him who walks in the dark, who has no light, trust in the name of the Lord and rely on his God. But now, all you who light fires and provide your-selves with flaming torches, go, walk in the light of your fires and of the torches you have set ablaze. This is what you shall receive from my hand: You will lie down in torment [or sorrow] (Isaiah 50:10,11).

Throughout life, we must discover time after time *when* we have crossed the fine line between trusting and relying upon God and lighting our own fires (forcing our own plans).

I learned to be alert and sensitive to my own danger of stepping *out of the fog* to ignite my own sparks. Fires so often seem more secure than staying in God's fogs and trusting Him.[1]

Joni Eareckson Tada

IT'S CALLED "UNITY"

In 1967 Joni Eareckson broke her neck in a diving accident that left her paralyzed from the shoulders down. Learning to draw with a pencil held between her teeth during her two years of rehabilitation, she is now an internationally known mouth artist.

She is recognized by her first name in many countries, largely as a result of her twenty-six best-selling books, including her autobiography Joni. A full-length feature film of her life, in which she played herself, has been seen all over the world, and her inspirational radio program is heard daily over more than eight hundred broadcast outlets by millions of listeners.

Joni has served on the National Council on Disability to which she was appointed by President Reagan in 1987. She has been chairman of the Christian Council on Persons with Disabilities, a national consortium of Christian ministries serving disabled persons, and has served on several advisory groups and boards, including the Lausanne Committee for World Evangelization.

She is the founder and president of Joni and Friends, which provides an information and referral program, workshops, audio-visual materials, and the Christian Fund for the Disabled, a financial assistance program.

Residing in California with her husband, Ken Tada, a high school social studies teacher, Joni travels extensively on speaking tours throughout the United States and many foreign countries. She holds an honorary Doctor of Humanities degree from Gordon College and an honorary doctorate from Columbia University, and has been chosen to serve as honorary chairman of the Sino-American Higher Education Center for Special Education in Jiangxi, China. She is the recipient of the American Academy of Achievement's Golden Plate Award and the Courage Award of the Courage Rehabilitation Center. She was named "Churchwoman of the Year" in 1993 by the Religious Heritage Foundation and "Layperson of the Year" by the National Association of Evangelicals.

Joni's radiant smile, happy spirit, and sensitivity to the needs of others are a great encouragement to Bill and me and all who have opportunity to meet her. The following account reveals this sensitivity and her special insight into other people.

It's not often that you see a parable lived out before your eyes. But it happened to me on the spring morning I went with my husband, Ken, to the Los Angeles Special Olympics.

Band music, colorful banners, and flags were everywhere. Scattered across the infield were teams of mentally handicapped young people with their friends and families. Everyone was on tiptoe with excitement, waiting for the games to begin.

I positioned my wheelchair near the grandstand so I could get a good view of Ken who was serving as track and field coordinator. I spotted him at the far end of the track in his red warm-ups and visor, with whistle and clipboard. He was helping to pin numbers on the back of each contestant.

After a few minutes, it was time for the fifty-yard dash to begin. Ken blew his whistle to signal for the contestants to line up at their starting blocks. A Down's syndrome girl with thick glasses and a big smile jumped up and down clapping her hands. A short, stocky, mentally handicapped boy in baggy gray shorts kept kicking the dirt. A tall, gangly young man waved to his family in the stands. These kids could barely contain their excitement.

Ken quieted the runners. There was a moment of stillness and then a "bang" from the starting gun. Off they sprinted—six contestants bobbing and weaving down the track to the wild cheers of the crowd. Some skipped, a few stumbled, but each one raced, as best he could, toward the other end of the track.

Suddenly, one of the runners—a Down's syndrome boy in a blue T-shirt—skipped the curb of the track and began running toward his friends in the infield. Ken blew his whistle, waved and called to the boy, trying to direct him back to the track. It was no use—this was one contestant determined to race away from the finish line.

At that point one of the other runners, the girl with thick glasses, noticed the boy's detour. She stopped a few yards from the finish line while the other contestants raced past her. She called to her fellow runner in the infield and shouted, "Hey, come this way!"

When the boy in the blue T-shirt heard his friend's voice, he stopped and turned around. The girl with glasses waved and called again, "This is the right way...come back!"

He stood there and looked around, somewhat confused. Exasperated, but with a smile on her face, she ran toward him and gave him a big hug when she caught up with him. They linked elbows and together got back on the track, finishing the race arm-in-arm. The last to cross the finish line, the two contestants were hugged by their friends who had finished long before them.

The entire crowd was standing at that point, enraptured by the poignancy of the scene. Some clapped, many cheered, but most, like me, sat in wonder, trying hard to hold back the tears. We knew we had witnessed something special.

That night, Ken and I sat at our kitchen table talking about the day's events. He shook his head and smiled as he sipped his hot chocolate. "I've been track and field coordinator there for many years," he sighed, set down his mug, and then continued, "but nothing has touched me like that little girl today. She set aside her goal in order to help a confused friend reach the finish line."

We had seen a parable lived out before our eyes that day. And it didn't take much to find a verse from Scripture to match the meaning behind that unique race.

Ken flipped to Romans 15 and found the exact words:

> We who are strong ought to bear with the failings of the weak and not to please ourselves. Each of us should please his neighbor for his good, to build him up... May the God who gives endurance and encouragement give you a spirit of unity among yourselves as you follow Christ Jesus (Romans 15:1,2,5).

We closed the Bible and sat there a long moment. "Each of us should please his neighbor for his good, to build him up..." I thought of all the times I failed to set aside my goals long enough to help a weaker friend in need. I thought of all the times I had watched a fellow believer get off the right track, get lost and spiritually confused, and yet I kept right on going. I recalled times when the Lord told me to forget my carefully outlined agenda in order to help someone else, some friend unsure of where to go. Sadly, I often neglected to do so for fear of not "winning," of not crossing my personal "finish line."

And I'm not the only one. Unfortunately, there are few who, when they become Christians, automatically begin "looking out for the interests of others," as Scripture puts it. That's why it's no surprise that the Bible also says we need to be "trained in godliness." And as we "press on toward the prize of the high calling of knowing Christ Jesus," we must remember that there are others running the race with us, even in the lanes next to us.

WINNING ISN'T IMPORTANT, BUT HOW WE RUN THE RACE IS.

The Lord Jesus doesn't seem as preoccupied as we do with "winning." In fact, as Ken reminded me, the object behind Special Olympics games is simply to encourage everyone to finish the race. It matters little if a contestant comes in first, second, third, or even last. Every runner is surrounded by a grandstand of witnesses, cheering and applauding the efforts of all. Winning isn't important, but how we run the race is. And we are to run it "bearing with the failings of the weak."

Since that spring morning, I've seen many parables come

to life before my eyes, but none so poignant and powerful as watching those two handicapped runners cross the finish line arm-in-arm. If I want the Lord Jesus to be glorified in my life, I must run the race not to please myself, but to please the Lord—and that will often mean taking time to stop and put my arm around a weaker friend. Romans 15 has a word for it. And if you asked the handicapped girl and her friend, they might even say it.

It's called "unity."

Vonette Zachary Bright

IN SEARCH OF IDENTITY

As the publisher and I were talking about this project, I thought he was going to let me off the hook. But no, he wanted a story from me as well. So I went back into my memories, and this particular lesson is one I felt led to share. Whenever I have shared these principles, women have told me it meant a lot to them.

I am a very practical-minded person. I look for reasons, answers, and applications. This is why I am so excited about this book. So many times we forget that the Bible is God's textbook to mankind. It contains truths and principles to help us solve or cope with every problem we can face, though we are prone to first look everywhere else for answers. It is in the Bible that God tells us how to relate to Him, to each other, to our spouse, and to our children.

Fortunately for me there were women I admired who directed me to the Bible for answers when dishes, diapers, dust, and drudgery tempted me to escape to what seemed so much more glamorous.

Here's how I found my identity which put life and priorities in focus for me.

With Campus Crusade for Christ staff in more than 180 countries, my husband and I do a great deal of traveling. Our ministry responsibilities usually require us to visit each continent every year, where we meet with staff, other Christian leaders, and government officials.

Around the globe, I have encountered the poor and the rich, the illiterate and the highly educated, the discouraged and the greatly motivated. I have met people of all ages in many different cultures and stations in life. I have observed their lifestyles and the way they express themselves and relate to each other. All this has taught me that people around the world are much alike, separated only by language and culture.

Modern travel and communication have shown us that, though our cultures are different, there is a thread of commonality in all of us: We have similar needs for fulfillment; we have unanswered questions in our quest for identity.

In my lifetime I have seen major changes in our value system that have had a dramatic effect on what people believe will provide maximum fulfillment. As a college student in the late 1940s, when family was still important, I was encouraged to prepare for a career—in case I needed it, and for the pleasure of culture, knowledge, and understanding.

At that time, women in large numbers had experienced

the liberty of working outside the home in defense plants to aid the war effort. As the post-war years rolled by, they were taught that fulfillment came in achievement and that their maximum potential was to be found in the marketplace where they would have visible leadership and identity. As a result, even more women sought careers, only to discover frustration and disillusionment.

In recent years I have seen the mood of women in the United States come full circle from an era when the family was most important, through the disillusionment of the '60s and '70s, then through the '80s when marriage and family once again became of greater value, though coupled with the woman's career. The mother of the '90s, according to the December 4, 1989, issue of *TIME* Magazine, is returning home to care for her family if it is at all economically possible.

Often, in the very moment of achievement, there is no satisfaction. Have you ever felt empty or unfulfilled at the point of accomplishment as though something inside were saying, "So what? Big deal"? The rewards of achievement and visible leadership are rarely enough.

The road to achievement often is a struggle for power—all the power you can get. But the Word of God—and even secular psychologists—tell us that there is much greater fulfillment in giving than receiving. Thus the steps we often take toward achievement are leading us in the opposite direction of fulfillment.

In many countries and cultures, today's woman is trying to stretch herself into a number of roles at one time. Perhaps for economic necessity or personal achievement, she may have her own career; she must be a perfect lover and companion, a good mother, devoted to social causes with perfect calmness and composure, and she must *achieve* in each area. The result, doctors tell us, is that more women are suffering from heart attacks and stress-related illnesses than ever before.

I have learned that lasting happiness is found in relationships, not achievements. What happens if the function or circumstances in which a woman places her identity changes? If identity is in *career* and that fails, where is her identity? If identity is in *marriage* and that fails, then what? If identity is in *children*, where is her identity when they leave home? We need to place our identity in that which will not change.

The great French physicist and philosopher, Blaise Pascal, is well known for having said, "There is a God-shaped vacuum in the heart of every person which cannot be satisfied by any created thing, but only by God, the Creator, made known through Jesus Christ." People think they can find identity in things of this world, but these can all change. I believe a rewarding, sustaining lifestyle is that which is found in a personal faith and trust in Jesus Christ and in being obedient to whatever He desires us to do. We must place our identity in the One who will not change.

WE MUST PLACE OUR IDENTITY IN THE ONE WHO WILL NOT CHANGE.

Identity in Jesus Christ is the glue that has held my life together. Although I grew up in the church and appreciate my religious background, God was not a reality in my life. Life was routine and happiness depended upon circumstances. Into my confusion walked Bill Bright—handsome, moral, and successful. We had a whirlwind romance but waited three years to be married.

During that time, Bill was growing in his faith. I was getting farther away from mine. I decided he had become a religious fanatic, and he detected that I was not a Christian. Since we were idealistic enough to seek agreement on every major issue, we questioned our coming marriage.

To make a long story short, I was very much impressed with Bill's friends at Hollywood Presbyterian Church. He introduced me to Dr. Henrietta Mears, director of Christian education, who compared the reality of knowing God personally to performing a chemistry lab experiment. Since I minored in chemistry in college, it made sense to me to add the person of Jesus Christ to the ingredients of faith I already knew. I received Jesus Christ as my personal Savior. As a result, God has become a vital reality in my life giving me identity and direction.

Early in our marriage, Bill and I committed ourselves totally to Christ as a couple. God blessed us with achievement.

My teaching career was successful, and a course of study written for my master's project was selected to be taught in the Los Angeles public schools and syndicated throughout the United States. God gave Bill the idea for a Christian movement that would help reach the world for Christ and help bring our nation back to the fundamentals on which it was established.

I chose to work with him so we could build and achieve God's purpose for our lives together.

I used my experience in teaching to help write our staff training manuals. Together we have influenced two human beings—our sons Zac and Brad—to become accountable, responsible, godly young men who are both now in Christian ministry. Through them and our thousands of full-time and associate Campus Crusade staff, we are touching tens of millions of lives around the world with the life-changing message of Christ's love and forgiveness.

There were times of adjustments, hard work, great concern, and many joys that have given me a message to share and enable me to minister to the lives of others today.

In examining my life and analyzing my identity, I realize that God has given me role models in women whom I have admired and sought to emulate. Some of these are mentioned in Scripture. My favorite among Bible women is Esther, the queen of the Persian Empire who risked her life to save her people, the Jews.

Another model is Catherine Booth, wife of Salvation Army founder William Booth. She was the mother of eight children, yet maintained a vital personal ministry. No doubt some said, "Catherine, your children are going to go astray while you maintain such an active ministry." But she lived a godly life and was obedient to what God called her to do, and all eight children entered some phase of Christian ministry. Catherine's story exemplifies that a mother can indeed have a ministry while keeping her home life a very high priority.

What about some more recent models? Mother Teresa, the Albanian nun who received worldwide recognition (including the Nobel Prize) for her mission to the poor and dying in Calcutta, is an inspiring model to many. When asked by someone how she dealt with so much failure, her reply was, "God has not called me to be successful. He has called me to be faithful."

Henrietta Mears, a single woman who invested her life in Christian education, is another. She influenced many in her lifetime, including Bill and me and more than four hundred young men who entered the ministry as pastors of many different denominations.

Let me tell you of a couple of "ordinary women" who, in addition to my mother, served as role models to me.

Mrs. Louis H. Evans, Sr., the wife of one of America's most outstanding Presbyterian pastors, was the mother of four children. She totally devoted herself as a wife and mother to her family who are making their mark on the world.

The other woman was a beautiful and gifted school teacher who married a rancher. At age sixteen she had committed her life totally to Christ, telling Him that for the rest of her life she wanted to do only what would glorify God the most.

Her life on the 5,000-acre ranch in rural Oklahoma was hard. She gave birth to eight children, one of whom died shortly after birth. Her home was the rural entertainment center for the community, and at meal times she was never sure how many people she would be serving in addition to her family.

Her children recall how she spent time reading her Bible each morning and evening and sang hymns as she went about her work. The most Christlike person in the community anyone could recall, she lived thirty-five years with a non-Christian husband, then lived another thirty-five years with him after he received Christ.

She was extremely ill most of the nine months that she carried her seventh child. There was little hope from the doctor that she would live to give birth to the child. She prayed earnestly, promising the Lord that she would commit this child to Him and His service, if He would let her live to give birth.

This woman was truly a Proverbs 31 woman whose 109

members of her family, including children, grandchildren, great-grandchildren, and great-great grandchildren, made their way to her bedside to express their love and appreciation before her death at age ninety-three. All of them have risen up to call her "blessed." This woman continues to have a great influence, perhaps even in your life, for she was my husband's mother, Mary Lee Bright.

All of these women had one thing in common—their identity in Christ. Inspired by the models in my life, I decided to follow Christ. I learned to apply the Scriptures to daily living, not content to declare one thing and live another, or to export that which didn't work at home.

Each of us is a special person with unique skills, gifts, and capabilities. Each of us has a unique sphere of influence. Whoever we are and wherever we go, we are going to be a role model for someone. The question is, what kind?

The greatest lesson I have learned is that my significance, fulfillment, maximum potential, and identity come not from achievement, recognition, or position. They come from a relationship with a Person—the most remarkable Person of all time, One whose life literally changed the course of history: our Lord Jesus Christ. I desire to have others know that lasting identity, too.

Bringing It All Together

There you have it—twenty-three women who are living lives of significance, making a personal contribution in their sphere of influence. Some are more visible in their influence than others, but that does not matter. What does matter is that they are taking advantage of the opportunities they have to help make the world a better place in which to live. There is a thread in each experience that is common to all. They each have found peace and direction in their heart that enables them to reach out to touch the lives of others.

Pondering the content of this book, I have asked myself, "What is missing?" I am reminded of a woman in Oklahoma City who came to me after I had spoken to a women's luncheon. "Thank you," she said, "I now know why my friend has been bringing me to these luncheons month after month. I decided if there were not some specific directions given to me today, I would not attend again. We have heard women tell inspiring experiences of how their lives have been changed, but none has been explicit as to how I might experience the reality of God in my life. Today, you have given me the answer—and I believe I have begun the adventure I've been hearing about."

This woman's statement is typical of what has been

repeated many times to me around the world. It was true in my own experience. I had gone to church all of my life. I am so grateful for my church background; it helped me stand strong when some of my friends were disintegrating morally around me. I had endeavored to live as much as I could (in my own strength) according to the teachings of the Bible. I am grateful for pastors, Sunday school teachers, and godly individuals who invested their lives in mine. Yet, God was not a reality in my life.

I once discussed this with my pastor, the late Dr. Louis Evans, at that time minister-at-large for the Presbyterian Church USA. He explained that it does not make any difference *when* a person receives Christ—as a child, a young adult, or a senior adult—but it is important that he *has* received Christ and that he knows for sure that he is rightly related to God. He went on to explain that it is impossible to grow in your personal faith until you have the assurance that Jesus Christ is in control of your life.

But how can you be sure you are rightly related to God? I know no better way to share with you than what was made clear to me and what the woman heard in Oklahoma City.

Because I searched so long for a definite understanding, I have determined never to speak without an attempt to make clear how an individual can know God personally. The same is true of this book. Every one of these women would want to share with you in personal conversation, if possible, how the dimension of personal faith in Jesus Christ has allowed them to find true peace and fulfillment.

Are you looking for answers? Would you like to know God personally? If you are still searching, let me share four principles[1] that, if applied, will enable you to know the reality of God in your life.

1 GOD LOVES YOU, AND CREATED YOU TO KNOW HIM PERSONALLY.

While the Bible is filled with assurances of God's love, perhaps the most telling verse is John 3:16:

> For God so loved the world, that He gave His only begotten Son, that whoever believes in Him should not perish, but have eternal life.

God not only loves each of us enough to give His only Son for us; He desires that we come to know Him personally:

> Now this is eternal life; that they may know you, the only true God, and Jesus Christ, whom you have sent (John 17:3, NIV).

What, then, prevents us from knowing God personally?

2 MEN AND WOMEN ARE SINFUL AND SEPARATED FROM GOD, SO WE CANNOT KNOW HIM PERSONALLY OR EXPERIENCE HIS LOVE.

We were all created to have fellowship with God; but, because of mankind's stubborn self-will, we chose to go our own independent way and fellowship with God was broken. This self-will, characterized by an attitude of active rebellion or passive indifference, is evidence of what the Bible calls sin.

> All have sinned and fall short of the glory of God (Romans 3:23).

The Bible also tells us that "the wages of sin is death" (Romans 6:23), or spiritual separation from God. When we are in this state, a great gulf separates us from God, because He cannot tolerate sin. People often try to bridge the gulf by doing good works or devoting themselves to religious practices, but the Bible clearly teaches that there is only one way to bridge this gulf...

3 JESUS CHRIST IS GOD'S ONLY PROVISION FOR OUR SIN. THROUGH HIM ALONE WE CAN KNOW GOD PERSONALLY AND EXPERIENCE HIS LOVE.

God's Word records three important facts to verify this principle: 1) Jesus Christ died in our place; 2) He rose from the dead; and 3) He is our only way to God:

> God demonstrates His own love toward us, in that while we were yet sinners, Christ died for us (Romans 5:8).

> Christ died for our sins...He was buried...He was raised on the third day, according to the Scriptures... He appeared to Peter, then to the twelve. After that He appeared to more than five hundred... (1 Corinthians 15:3–6).

> Jesus said to him, "I am the way, and the truth, and the life; no one comes to the Father, but through Me" (John 14:6).

Thus, God has taken the loving initiative to bridge the gulf that separates us from Him by sending His Son, Jesus

Christ, to die on the cross in our place to pay the penalty for our sin. But it is not enough just to know these truths...

4 WE MUST INDIVIDUALLY RECEIVE JESUS CHRIST AS SAVIOR AND LORD; THEN WE CAN KNOW GOD PERSONALLY AND EXPERIENCE HIS LOVE.

John 1:12 records:

As many as received Him, to them He gave the right to become children of God, even to those who believe in His name.

What does it mean to "receive Christ"? The Scriptures tell us that we receive Christ through faith—not through "good works" or religious endeavors:

By grace you have been saved through faith; and that not of yourselves, it is the gift of God; not as a result of works, that no one should boast (Ephesians 2:8,9).

We're also told that receiving Christ means to personally invite Him into our lives:

[Christ is speaking] Behold, I stand at the door and knock; if anyone hears My voice and opens the door, I will come in to him (Revelation 3:20).

Thus, receiving Christ involves turning to God from self ...and trusting Christ to come into our lives to forgive our sins and to make us the kind of people He wants us to be.

If you are not sure whether you have ever committed your life to Jesus Christ, I encourage you to do so—today! Here is a suggested prayer that has helped millions of men and women around the world express faith in Him and invite Him into their lives:

> Lord Jesus, I want to know You personally. Thank You for dying on the cross for my sins. I open the door of my life and receive You as my Savior and Lord. Thank You for forgiving my sins and giving me eternal life. Take control of the throne of my life. Make me the kind of person You want me to be.

If this prayer expresses the desire of your heart, why not pray it now? If you mean it sincerely, Jesus Christ will come into your life, just as He promised in Revelation 3:20. He keeps His promises! And there is another key promise I suggest you write indelibly in your mind:

> The witness is this, that God has given us eternal life, and this life is in His Son. He who has the Son has the life; he who does not have the Son of God does not have the life. These things I have written to you who believe in the name of the Son of God, in order that you may *know* that you have eternal life (1 John 5:11–13).

That's right—the man or woman who personally receives Christ as Savior and Lord is assured of everlasting life with Him in heaven. So, in summary, when you received Christ by faith, as an act of your will, many wonderful things happened including the following:

1. Christ came into your life (Revelation 3:20 and Colossians 1:27).
2. Your sins were forgiven (Colossians 1:14).
3. You became a child of God (John 1:12).
4. You received eternal life (John 5:24).
5. You began the great adventure for which God created you (John 10:10; 1 Thessalonians 5:18).

If you would like free literature to help you grow in your new walk with God, please write to me:

Vonette Bright
Campus Crusade for Christ International
100 Lake Hart Drive, Dept. 2100
Orlando, FL 32832-0100

I would be delighted to send you home study material that will help you understand your new relationship with God; understand His Word, the Bible; and enable you to start in your new life with Him.

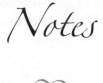

Notes

Ney Bailey

1. Portions of this chapter were adapted from *Faith Is Not a Feeling* by Ney Bailey (San Bernardino, CA: Here's Life Publishers, 1978). Used by permission.

Jill Briscoe

1. Portions of this chapter were adapted from *Thank You For Being a Friend* by Jill Briscoe (Grand Rapids, MI: Zondervan, 1980), pp. 180–192. Used by permission.

Sally Christon Conway

1. Portions of this chapter were adapted from *Your Husband's Mid-Life Crisis* by Sally Conway (Elgin, IL: David C. Cook Publishing Co., 1987), pp. 13,14 and *What God Gives When Life Takes* by Becki Conway Sanders and Jim and Sally Conway (Downers Grove, IL: InterVarsity Press, 1988), p. 36. Both used by permission.

Ruth Bell Graham

1. Titus 2:3–5.
2. Portions of this chapter were adapted from *It's My Turn* by Ruth Bell Graham (Old Tappan, NJ: Fleming H. Revell, 1982), pp. 131,136,137. Used by permission.

Joyce Rogers

1. Andrew Murray, *The Believer's Secret of Waiting on God* (Minneapolis: Bethany House Publishers, 1986), pp. 68,69.
2. Murray, *The Believer's Secret*, pp. 67,68.
3. Murray, *The Believer's Secret*, p. 57.

Edith Schaeffer

1. Portions of this chapter are adapted from *L'Abri* by Edith Schaeffer (Wheaton, IL: Tyndale House Publishers, 1969). Used by permission.

Bringing It All Together

1. The four principles are adapted from *Would You Like to Know God Personally?* (*NewLife* Publications, 1995). Used by permission.

Resources

Resources by Vonette Bright

The Joy of Hospitality: Fun Ideas for Evangelistic Entertaining. Co-written with Barbara Ball, this practical book tells how to share your faith through hosting barbecues, coffees, holiday parties, and other events in your home.

The Joy of Hospitality Cookbook. Filled with uplifting Scriptures and quotations, this cookbook contains hundreds of delicious recipes, hospitality tips, sample menus, and family traditions that are sure to make your entertaining a memorable and eternal success. Co-written with Barbara Ball.

Beginning Your Journey of Joy. This adaptation of the *Four Spiritual Laws* speaks in the language of today's women and offers a slightly feminine approach to sharing God's love with your neighbors, friends, and family members.

Resources for Evangelism

Witnessing Without Fear. This best-selling, Gold Medallion book offers simple hands-on, step-by-step coaching on how to share your faith with confidence. The chapters give specific answers to questions people most often encounter in witnessing and provide a proven method for sharing your faith.

Reaching Your World Through Witnessing Without Fear.
This six-session video provides the resources needed to sensitively share the gospel effectively. Each session begins with a captivating dramatic vignette to help viewers apply the training. Available in individual study and group packages.

Have You Heard of the Four Spiritual Laws? This booklet is one of the most effective evangelistic tools ever developed. It presents a clear explanation of the gospel of Jesus Christ, which helps you open a conversation easily and share your faith with confidence.

Would You Like to Know God Personally? Based on the *Four Spiritual Laws*, this booklet uses a friendly, conversational format to present four principles for establishing a personal relationship with God.

Jesus and the Intellectual. Drawing from the works of notable scholars who affirm their faith in Jesus Christ, this booklet shows that Christianity is based on irrefutable historical facts. Good for sharing with unbelievers and new Christians.

A Great Adventure. Written as from one friend to another, this booklet explains how to know God personally and experience peace, joy, meaning, and fulfillment in life.

Sharing Christ Using the Four Spiritual Laws (audio cassette). Imagine being personally trained by Bill Bright to use the remarkable *Four Spiritual Laws* booklet. Through a five-part teaching series on WorldChangers Radio, this cassette will increase your confidence level and desire to share the good news with those you know.

Would You Like to Belong to God's Family? Designed for elementary-age young people, this booklet gives the simple message of salvation and includes the first steps for starting their new life in Christ. (Based on the *Four Spiritual Laws*.)

"Living in Christ" Resources

Living Supernaturally in Christ by Bill Bright (ISBN 1-56399-145-4). A refreshing cascade of hope, power, and renewal, *Living Supernaturally in Christ* vividly illustrates the many benefits of knowing Jesus Christ personally. With rare clarity, it reveals how your relationship with Christ will help you live in harmony with God's plan. It will introduce you to scriptural passages and principles that convey the incomparable blessing we share in Christ, and help you open the door to victorious Christian living.

Why Do Christians Suffer? by Bill Bright (ISBN 1-56399-149-7). Why do Christians suffer? It's a valid question that many believers—even some nonbelievers—wrestle with from time to time. As a stand-alone booklet or a companion piece to Dr. Bright's book *Living Supernaturally in Christ*, this informative purse or pocket guide will direct you to the Bible's illuminating answers. By remembering the acrostic TRIUMPH, you can experience God's peace even in the midst of adversity, pain, and heartache. Ideal for personal reference or to share with friends in need.

Are You Prepared for Battle? by Bill Bright (ISBN 1-56399-148-9). For Christians, battling the awesome powers of darkness is inevitable. But victory is attainable—in fact, assured—for those who are properly prepared. This conveniently sized booklet explores the secrets of standing firm against the devil's schemes, defusing the power of his attacks and sending him fleeing in retreat. Learn to dress for spiritual success by wearing God's protective armor. *Are You Prepared for Battle?* is an ideal companion booklet to *Living Supernaturally in Christ*, *Why Do Christians Suffer?* and *The Supernatural You*.

The Supernatural You by Bill Bright (ISBN 1-56399-147-0). Written in a convenient, take-along format, this booklet helps you discover and live according to your new, supernatural identity in Christ. The booklet outlines five essential steps to living supernaturally in Christ, made easily memorable by the acrostic CROSS. Apply these biblical truths to discover a life of incomparable power, liberating freedom, triumph over adversity, everlasting peace, and infinite joy. *The Supernatural You* is an ideal companion booklet to *Living Supernaturally in Christ*, *Why Do Christians Suffer?* and *Are You Prepared for Battle?*

A Child of the King by Bill Bright with Marion Wells (ISBN 1-56399-150-0). *A Child of the King* is a fictional tale based on the truths of Dr. Bright's book *Living Supernaturally in Christ*. Written in the tradition of C. S. Lewis's *Chronicles of Narnia* and J. R. R. Tolkien's *The Lord of the Rings*, this thrilling allegory will teach adults and teens the invaluable truths of supernatural living, even in the midst of spiritual darkness and warfare. Follow the adventures of Jotham and others in the Kingdom of Withershins...and realize your own high calling as a child of the King.

"Discover God" Resources

GOD: Discover His Character. Everything about our lives is influenced by our view of God. Through these pages Dr. Bright will equip you with the biblical truths that will energize your walk with God. So when you're confused, you can experience His truth. When you're frightened, you can know His peace. When you're sad, you can live in His joy.

GOD: Discover His Character Video Series. In these 13 sessions, Dr. Bright's clear teaching is illustrated by fascinating dramas that bring home the truth of God's attributes in everyday life. This video series, with the accompanying leader's guide, is ideal for youth, college, and adult Sunday school classes or study groups.

Our Great Creator (Vol. I). Dr. Bright explores God as all-powerful, ever-present, all-knowing, and sovereign, and how those attributes can give you hope and courage.

Our Perfect Judge (Vol. II). God your perfect Judge, is holy, true, righteous, and just, and Dr. Bright explains how those characteristics help you to live a righteous life.

Our Gracious Savior (Vol. III). Dr. Bright introduces you to the God who is loving, merciful, faithful, and unchangeable, and shows how you can experience those awesome attributes every day.

GOD: Discover His Character Audio Edition. Based on the *GOD: Discover His Character* video series, Dr. Bright's insights into God's wondrous character are certain to attract many non-Christians to faith, and to energize the walk of many believers. In each of 15 dynamic messages, Bill Freeman, familiar voice of Campus Crusade's WorldChangers Radio, enhances the learning experience with practical life application questions.

GOD: Knowing Him by His Names. *El-Elyon, Adonai, Jehovah-Sabaoth.* To most Christians, the Hebrew names of God are unknown and unpronounceable. In this compact overview of the meaning and significance of God's names, you will not only learn more about our heavenly Father, but also become more worshipful of His nature. The booklet includes 16 character-revealing names of God, as well as the names of Christ.

GOD: Seeking Him Wholeheartedly. Based on the Great Commandment, recorded in Matthew 22:36,37 ("Love the Lord your God with all your heart…"), this booklet explains seven steps for seeking God with a whole heart. Bill Bright deals with the sincerity of our love for God, the priority of our relationship with Him, and the evidence of our wholehearted devotion—obedience. His insights enable any follower of Christ to grow closer to our heavenly Father and enjoy the fullness of His blessings.

GOD: 13 Steps to Discovering His Attributes. In this abbreviated guide to discovering God's attributes, Dr. Bill Bright shares the fruit of his lifelong study of God. These wonderful truths are certain to enrich your life and energize your walk with God. Keep this handy booklet in your pocket or purse to read during quiet moments, or to share with friends or loved ones.

GOD: Discover the Benefits of His Attributes. As an individual resource, or as a companion to *GOD: Discover His Character* or *GOD: 13 Steps to Discovering His Attributes*, this sturdy, four-color laminated card will energize your Christian life as you're frequently reminded of God's amazing character. Just 3" × 5", it makes a great bookmark, slips easily into purse or pocket, and is conveniently sized to share with friends.